MY
DELIGHTFULLY DYSFUNCTIONAL FAMILY

(And Me)

LORAINE C. HARTLEY

 FriesenPress

Suite 300 - 990 Fort St
Victoria, BC, V8V 3K2
Canada

www.friesenpress.com

Copyright © 2020 by Loraine C. Hartley
First Edition — 2020

I attribute Chapter 7 of this book to my mother, Dale E. Geils, as she is actually the author of it. She tells the story of when she was lost in the wilderness of Yoho National Park, overnight, with her son-in-law, and three young grandsons.

My sister, Louise deserves huge gratitude for her patience in trying to guide me through my technology dificiencies. I appreciate your efforts - Thank-you Louise.

ISBN
978-1-5255-7825-0 (Hardcover)
978-1-5255-7826-7 (Paperback)
978-1-5255-7827-4 (eBook)

1. BISAC code 001

Distributed to the trade by The Ingram Book Company

TABLE OF CONTENTS

PROLOGUE

My family is one of many dysfunctional institutions of the 21st century. I am going into my seventh decade right now, having just turned 64. I find it interesting how the structure of the family has changed in the last 60 years. What structure? There is no structure anymore! These changes all started in the 1960s when women decided that they needed to be liberated. They wanted more out life than the drudgery of day to day living, with gardening, preserving food, cooking, cleaning, and having and raising children. Some of them even had to put up with demanding, ignorant, and inconsiderate husbands! Life wasn't that much fun. It was time for a change. Women were ready and capable, and decided to prove it to themselves and others.

When women actually went out to do something else, such as work outside of the home, or go travelling on their own, or partake in other, more daring ventures, they enjoyed their new-found freedom, and independence. Well, my mother was one such woman and here is the beginning of my story.

My mother was born in Edinburgh, Scotland on August 27, 1927. Her mother was of Scottish heritage and her father was Irish. She was the youngest of four children, two older brothers, Alex and Walter, and one older sister, Betty. Her father died when she was five years old, so her mother struggled as a single mother during the 1930s. She had uterine cancer and my mother was pulled out of school to look after her. One of my mom's most vivid memories was hearing her mom calling, "Ethel, help me please! I am in so much pain!" My mom said she felt useless because there was nothing she could do. During the bombing blitz of Sheffield, England, when the whole family was taking refuge in the bomb shelter, my grandmother almost bled to death. Once the bombing ceased, an ambulance came, and they took her to a small hospital in Brixton, where she took her last breaths.

When my mother was 21, she wanted to leave England, and come to Canada. An uncle who lived in Williams Lake, B.C. was willing to sponsor her. She arrived in Halifax in 1948 by ship, and made her way across Canada to Vancouver to settle there. She soon met my dad, Steve, and did like most young women in those days: she married him. She wanted a home of her own, and a family.

My dad was a big strong Ukrainian fellow, who changed his name because of the racial prejudice that made it difficult to get employment if you had an Eastern European name. His family history was unhappy and insecure. He was born on February 6, 1926, in Kruenberg, Manitoba, re-named Fraserwood. He said, "They didn't have hospitals in those days, so my dad delivered us all." He was big, handsome, and rather crude. His mother became a single mother, struggling to raise several children during the Great Depression. My dad was never sure how many siblings he had. He knew his father briefly, but apparently he spent a lot of his life in labour camps and died when Dad was twenty.

When he was 11, dad was sent to reform school, because he had been caught stealing from a store. When his mom came to see him she said, "I don't want him." Dad was farmed out as a child labourer to a local farm, slept under the steps, and was forced to work very hard. He said, "I stuck it out there until the spring of 1941, then I took off like a scared rabbit. I was lucky I found a job in a tie camp, making railway ties. We got one cent a tie for peeling them with a draw knife, plus room and board, and sometimes we even got paid." He laughed.

"After that, I wandered around until I ended up in Winnipeg in 1942. I was then 16 years old. I heard that the Army paid $1.30 per day, and they paid you every 2 weeks. It was the first good job I had." He fought over in Europe during the Second World War, and talked about when the Canadian Forces liberated Holland, and how beautiful, those Dutch girls were. Before he died, he'd wander around town on Remembrance Day, displaying the medals that he won for so-called bravery, hoping that someone would ask how he got them. His response was always the same. "War is nothing but the working class people in one country, fighting the working class people in another country, so the rich can get richer. I wasn't a hero," he'd state adamantly. "I just joined the Army so I could get three squares a day and a roof over my head!"

He never said much more about the war, or his family. He had told us that his mother died, but when I was 17 I found out that she was, in fact, still alive. I was told that she was some kind of Gypsy, from a tribe that wandered around the Carpathian Mountains in the Ukraine, or Austria, or Russia. The country's boundaries kept changing.

Both my mother's and my father's childhoods were all very vague. People didn't talk as much about family, what they went through, or what they did as children, as they do today. Their stories now are lost forever with the death of the characters of that generation.

My parents divorced in 1967 when I was 15, my sister Louise 17, and my little brother David, only 8. When the divorce was finalized, my mother left us with my dad and moved to Vancouver where she went to college, took a bookkeeping course, and began her life as a single woman at the age of 38.

That's when everything went all to hell. Believe me, it's a lousy time for parents to divorce when they have two teenage girls. It was very hard for my sister and I, having our lives turned upside down like that. It was also very odd that my dad had custody of us, and not my mom, as was usually the case. Well, Dad had no clue how to guide teenaged girls into the adult world, so we both had to find our own way. Louise wanted to go to university. She had studied and studied in high school and was a prime candidate for a scholarship for anything that she wanted to pursue. My dad was either unable or unwilling to guide Louise into the university world. No one else stepped up to the plate, so she was left on her own to figure it out. Sadly, Louise gave up her dream and ran off with a charming young man with no ambition, with whom she thought she was in love. It did not turn out so well.

I couldn't have cared less about school. I just wanted to get married and have babies. I ran away, took the bus to Vancouver, and lived with my mom. She didn't really want me because she was too busy going back to school and getting her own education. However, she agreed to accommodate me, and enrolled me in King George Secondary School in the west end of Vancouver. I was just happy to be with my mom at the time.

Mom struggled to get an education so she could support herself. She studied, and worked part-time, being very frugal, but she did it! After two years, she finished her courses, found herself employment, and began to enjoy her life.

My dad was having a great time as a single man. He had time, all the women he wanted, and all the money he wanted. He dated and partied until the cows came home—his morals had always been a bit slippery anyway. But after four years, Dad's wild behaviour abruptly stopped. He met Victoria through relatives, fell head over heels in love with her, and married her.

CHAPTER 1

IT WAS EARLY SPRING , 1972, and I was tired of living in Vancouver. The previous November and December, it had rained for 62 days straight. I had always wanted to live somewhere in the bush farther north, where there was actual snow and ice, and one could be guaranteed of a white Christmas, every year. When I met David, who had previously walked along through the mountains from Kitimat to D'Arcy, with nothing but a map and a compass, I was greatly impressed! As he explored the coastal mountains of British Columbia, he'd seen abundant wildlife, crossed dangerous rivers, and climbed cliffs. I was mesmerized! A member of the then-popular Greenpeace movement, he was one of the chosen few, fortunate enough to be to be part of the crew of the *Phyllis Cormack*. Greenpeace sailed the *Phyllis Cormack* up to the Aleutian Islands, to protest the Americans' plan to test their nuclear bombs' effectiveness. He had this ingenious idea to move to Smithers, build a geodesic dome in the middle of the Telkwa Pass, and live off the land. He was confident he could do it, and I was extremely enthusiastic about the whole idea. It was during the Hippie Era, and many young people were doing that very thing. Some succeeded and some did not. He suggested that I buy a motorcycle and drive it up to Smithers to meet him there. I emptied my savings account, bought a 175 Honda, quit my job, bought some jeans and a jean jacket, packed my few belongings and left Vancouver, following my heart and Highway 1 to Hope and on to Smithers.

When we met in Endako, I was soaked to the skin as it had been pouring rain all day,. The Endako Hotel felt warm and welcoming. He told me then he had to go to work elsewhere, and that he'd made arrangements for me to stay with a friend of his in Smithers. We kept in contact via phone, but there were still no definite plans for us to begin our life together.

Louise and he also kept in touch, using the house where I was staying as a mail drop. I never thought anything about it, but one day my curiosity got the better of me and I opened one of the letters. I was stunned! She was in love with my fiancé, and he was in love with her. Then I remembered back to one visit, where they were both there. I remembered the way he touched her, and I had, had, a fleeting thought that they were closer than I was aware of, but I'd pushed it out of my mind. My fragile little ego was shattered by their betrayal and I was sorely disappointed that I wouldn't have the life in the bush that I'd dreamed of. I stayed at his friend's house until I organized a room and board situation for myself.

NOT LONG AFTER MOVING, I went down to Vancouver to visit my dad and mom. When I arrived in Vancouver, I stayed with my mom, and phoned my dad. Vicky's daughter Melody answered the phone. "Hi, Loraine. How are you?"

"Pretty good," I said, "but can I speak to my dad?"

"Actually, he's not here. He's in town, making arrangements."

"For what?"

"They're getting married."

"What? When?"

"Tomorrow," Melody said.

I was so shocked, I couldn't remember any of the details she told me. Dad never even told me he was getting married! This was a big thing, and it was going to change my whole life! He should've at least warned me or given me a hint, but there had been nothing.

I needed some time to absorb all of this. Mom was out, so I could at least sit alone and think about it. I'd met Vicky a couple of times, but I didn't really know her. She seemed nice enough, but having her as a step mother was something else. We had all heard of "The wicked

Step-mother" as children. I didn't know what to do. I wondered what it would be like to have Melody as an actual sister.

I'm really not even invited to the wedding. Maybe Dad doesn't even want me there. Melody's going, and my brother David will be there. What should I do? I have to talk to Dad.

He phoned me about 2 hours later. Yes, I was invited. Yes, he wanted me to come. He said he never told me because he knew I was coming down anyway and wanted to surprise me. Some surprise!

The wedding was a simple affair with mostly Vicky's relatives, of which she had many. I stayed another day or two, then headed home to my own life. I was 20 years old and supposed to be leading my own life. Really, perhaps it was none of my business whether my dad and Vicky got married. Dad referred to Vicky and her daughter Melody as his "new family," as if his old family was defunct. He'd always brag about Melody, about how she worked all day in the hospital laundry in the heat, trying to save money for nursing school. He told me of her plans to go to Israel and bragged about how brave she was to undertake such a trip on her own. He made Melody sound like an interesting and important person.

I'd been living on unemployment insurance that summer. Always up for a bit of excitement and adventure, I dipped into the rest of my savings and decided to hike the Chilkoot Trail. I caught the CN passenger train at the Smithers station and headed to Prince Rupert, and settled in a window seat. The scenery between Smithers and Prince Rupert is unbeatable, the mountains rise up to the sky, the waterfalls, rivers, and creeks run every which way, and there is bush, more bush, and wildlife.

I camped overnight in Prince Rupert, then bought a ticket to Skagway, with an overnight stop in Juneau. I had to stay one night on the boat, but to save money, I did like many others, pulled up a piece of floor and put my sleeping bag down on it. We arrived in Juneau fairly early the next morning and it was amazingly beautiful! The sun was shining, and it was clear and fresh. I bought a few supplies, and caught a cab to Mendenhall Glacier where I found a place to set up camp and did a bit of exploring. The lake was in front of the glacier, and large pieces of ice regularly broke off and fell into the water, causing huge waves. I sat there throughout the evening and watched, mesmerized, until I was so tired I had to sleep.

The next day, a Juneau local I'd met on the ferry took me for a hike. We found an old trapper's cabin and were sitting inside having a rest, when all of a sudden it started to shake. The tools, frying pans, and kitchen utensils that were hanging about on various hooks and strings began to swing back and forth.

"What is that?" I hollered. "Is it one of those Alaskan earthquakes? Let's get out of here!"

Outside it wasn't much better. It was like I was drunk. I couldn't walk straight. The ground was weaving and waving up and down. It was downright scary. I didn't know where to run to or what to do, neither did the local who, was with me. Thankfully it didn't last very long, so as soon as we could stand straight, we started walking out. I found out later that the earthquake was 7.9 on the Richter scale.

Back at my campsite, I said good bye to my companion, collected my camping equipment, and caught the ferry to Skagway. I met a chatty fellow from Skagway who tended to follow me about the boat. Most of the information that I'd been able to find about the Chilkoot Trail was rather vague, so I was interested in what he had to say, as he knew a fair amount about it.

"It's very remote," he said, "and you're on your own so there's no help available. The trail itself is rather grown over in places, so the chances of you getting lost are quite large. There are grizzly bears, black bears, and moose up there, and wolves. What if you fall and injure yourself? No one will be there to help. No one will look for you, so listen … … … …

"I've been on the trail before. Why don't you let me come with you?" he pleaded.

Who is this guy? I don't even know him, and I'm not about to launch into the wilderness of Alaska with some complete stranger, no matter how nice he seems to be. Besides, I was 20, and he must have been 30 or even older.

"No," I said.

"Well, I don't think you should go by yourself," he said. "It's absolute foolishness! If you want to see the country, why don't you take the White Pass & Yukon Railway to Whitehorse? You'll still see the scenery and will be much safer. If you want me to, I'll take you to Dyea. We can look for antique bottles from the Gold Rush, and I'll show you the trail. I know some good places we can go. You can stay at my house and you can catch the train tomorrow. I have lots of room at my place and you can have your own room," he offered eagerly.

"Well," I said, "okay, but don't try any funny business. I'm not that kind of girl."

"I won't, I promise I won't," he said with relief. I think he was actually concerned for my safety, and I did kind of trust him, so I agreed to stay with him for the night and catch the train the following day.

The night was uneventful, thank God. The next morning, he took me to Dyea, where we hunted for old bottles. I was amazed at the ones we found because they were purple and green glass. I still have them today.

Later, he took me to the train station, where I boarded the White Pass & Yukon Railway to Whitehorse. It was a breathtaking trip. There were several places I saw remnants of the Gold Rush—old stoves, rusty prospecting equipment, even bits of what looked like old boats and wagons. The scenery was awe-inspiring!

I met Heartha, another single woman traveler, on the train. As we admired the view together, she told me she was from a Quaker family in Pennsylvania.

"I want to go up to Inuvik way up in the Northwest Territories, it is up inside the Arctic Circle," she informed me confidently. It sounded really exciting, and so remote. I was a bit envious. I was planning just to hitch-hike back to Smithers, from Whitehorse.

"Why don't you come with me. It would be fun!" she exclaimed.

"Well, I really don't have the money to do that, but I wish I did. Then I would."

"Well, that's too bad. It would be nice to have the company."

Silence followed, as we enjoyed the scenery, each of us lost in our own thoughts.

When we arrived, we went to the Whitehorse Hotel.

"I'm sorry. We're full up," said the attendant at the front desk. "Well, almost. We have one room left with twin beds that you could have if you want."

Heartha looked at me and I looked at her. We both said, "Why not?" We got the room, and she continued to try to convince me to come with her to Inuvik. I was trying to figure out how I could get the money, and I had previously mentioned my motorcycle.

"Sell your motorcycle," she suggested.

"How can I? It's there and I'm here."

"Well, ask your friend if he can sell it for you." she offered.

"Well, I guess I can try," I said. I phoned the friend that I had been staying with, and he asked me to give him a day or two and he'd see what he could do. We stayed in Whitehorse another night. He called that evening and told me he'd been able to sell it. We left the next day.

The flight was most interesting. There was Heartha, myself, and four men. One was named Bob, and he was the supervisor of L.I. Adam Contractors. I told him how much I loved the bush, and how my dream was to get a job cooking in a camp, way up North in the middle of nowhere. As it turned out, he hired the cooks for his camp crew. He had this unusual idea that if he hired an attractive young lady to cook, the fellows would be better behaved, and the crudeness would be minimized. Would I be interested? Of course I was, but I figured it was just a pick up line. I gave him my phone number, though, just in case, and he said that he would call me in November.

Inuvik was unique, and unforgettable. I don't remember everything, but Heartha and I slept in our sleeping bags in the igloo-shaped Catholic Church. I vaguely remember waking up at 1:00 a.m. and looking out the window. The sun was shining in. I was in "the land of the midnight sun." We went to a local dance, and there was this old Inuit lady with no teeth who was having a great time. She danced all night. I remember the children, as many of them appeared to have no skin on their hands and forearms. It looked peeled off. I asked one of the locals about it and they said that when the parents of the children were drunk and partying, they would often throw the children outside in the cold and lock the house door. The peeling skin was a result of freezing. The locals also regaled me with stories about burying people. Because of the permafrost sometimes, in the spring, bodies would appear on top of the grave rather than in it, and would have to be re-buried. After a couple of days, Heartha and I flew back to Whitehorse. She returned to Pennsylvania, and I hitchhiked back to Smithers, where I was able to get a job at the Royal Bank. My life settled down somewhat—except for that one, awkward moment at the Royal Bank when –THEY – showed up.

My sister and my ex-fiancé showed up one day while I was working. I tried to escape to the bathroom. No luck. My manager saw me and directed me back to my station because I had customers standing in line! He had no idea who the customers were. I hadn't even seen her since I'd discovered their deception. I tried to direct her to the next teller, but she was having none of it. I didn't want to talk to her because I was too busy nursing a grudge, which was quite difficult because it went totally against my character. Cornered! I had no choice. I forced a smile, made an attempt to put on a pleasant demeanor, and gave her the money that she withdrew from her account. It crossed my mind that I deserved a tip, so I considered withholding ten percent, but I knew it'd go over like a lead balloon with my boss. As she walked out, I thought, *Does she look sad, unhappy–or is that just my wishful thinking?*

CHAPTER 2

IN NOVEMBER, BOB CALLED me at work. "Are you still interested in cooking at the camp?"

"Sure, I'd love to."

"Can you leave tomorrow? L.I. Adam will arrange and pay for your flight up North."

I was shocked. He was for real. It wasn't a pickup line after all.

"No, I can't go tomorrow. I have a job. I have to give notice. I need to get organized."

"How much time do you need?"

"A week, I guess. I could do it in a week."

"Okay, well, let me call you back," he said.

I figured it just wouldn't work out, so put the thought of it on the back burner. *It'd be fun, though. I'd really like to do it.*

He called me back the next day and said it would be okay if I came in a week.

I was somewhat stunned, but I went to my boss and gave him a week's notice and resigned. It was scary and exciting at the same time. I worked for another week, got everything organized, and soon I was up in Inuvik again, waiting to be flown into camp.

THE PLANE SEEMED ARCHAIC—LIKE a relic out of World War II. I could not believe that this was happening to me. I was nervous–not sure what I was getting myself into. We flew into the seismic camp base where they had a proper runway. The camp was a series of trailers spread around a cleared area. There was power, water–even showers—and a huge kitchen. The cook was a warm and happy gentleman who seemed to love his job. The food was amazing—everything that you might want to eat. He fed me and told me that I would be going to the smaller seismic camp, and where I'd be cooking for between six and eleven men.

Later that day, when the helicopter landed to take me to the smaller camp, I was told that I could call up the big camp if I needed it to fly back there for any reason–like a shower or something. I loved the idea, and felt like a queen. I got in and we flew low. It was so clear we could see forever. I saw a pack of wolves that the pilot pointed out and a big bull moose. The pilot was a Vietnam deserter. He'd flown a helicopter in the war that we'd protested so much, as teenagers. I was reminded of the "Peace and Love – not War," signs that we had frequently marched the streets of Vancouver with. I was sure he'd have some interesting stories, and hoped to hear them at some point.

Bob met me at the smaller camp and took me to my own little trailer, which had a full kitchen with a little bedroom at the back with a single bunk. This would be my accommodation until Christmas, when we would all fly out.

I settled into my new role and began to cook right away. I didn't have any experience as a cook, but I enjoyed it and knew how to make a few good dishes. I cooked three meals a day, so sometimes the days were quite long. I enjoyed the relaxed atmosphere, even though I was busy. We would frequently hook the trailers up and move farther south. The small seismic camp broke trail for the bigger seismic camp that would do the actual drilling for the oil.

We made our way, south, through the Ogilvie Mountains, toward a First Nations settlement called "Old Crow." It was very cold, often as cold as 50 degrees below zero. At night, the northern lights were bright reds, purples, and sometimes greens—always visible and always mesmerizing. I loved it! The wolves would sometimes howl at night, and the stars seemed so close you could almost touch them.

It was a fun time, with lots of laughter and jokes. When you are as isolated as we all were, it seemed everything was funny. I think that might be what they call "bushed."

One morning, as we were on the move, I was puttering around in my little trailer and I heard a sound like an explosion followed by a huge crash. I thought the stove had exploded! I panicked and ran outside in my nightgown and bare feet, then got onto the skids the trailer was being pulled on.

I remember looking down and thinking, *Thank God it's only 20 degrees below zero. Boy, if I fell off and landed underneath, they'd keep on driving and wouldn't even miss me. I'd freeze to death!* I was very careful as I made my way around to the front of the trailer. When I got there, I hollered and hollered at Roy.

He was oblivious, didn't hear me.

I hollered again, and then stuck my fingers in my mouth and gave an ear-piercing whistle.

He turned around sharply, saw me frantically waving, and slammed on the brakes. He got down off the CAT and came toward me. "What's up?"

"The stove blew up." I didn't think about what a sight I must have been in my nightgown and bare feet. It must have been most unnerving for him.

He went into my trailer, looked, and came out grinning like a Cheshire cat.

"What?" I asked, wondering what the heck was going on.

"The coffee pot fell over." He laughed. "You sure have a heck of a mess to clean up."

I went into the trailer myself, not really believing him. There it was—the mess. I was embarrassed. The guys had a good laugh about that for a while and I bore the brunt of their jokes.

AFTER A FEW WEEKS, the novelty of being surrounded by men wore off. I had a very strong desire for some female company. Ivan, the foreman, kindly arranged my transportation to a nearby camp where a woman was cooking there with her husband. I remember almost crying when I saw her. She reached out and gave me a big hug. "How old are you, dear?"

"Twenty," I said.

"You look so young! I thought you were no more than a teenager." She was sweet, and motherly, just what I needed. I think perhaps she had the same desire as me for female company. We talked and talked until I had to leave, but I did feel much better.

I LOVED THE CONSTANT moving. I got to see so much country, and it was all beautiful and so pristine! We drove up and down mountains, through tundra and trees, and even over rivers and swamps. It was amazing how much wildlife lived so far up North. We saw moose and wolves, foxes, pine martens, rabbits, and even some owls, and, of course, crows—crows were everywhere. I was in heaven! It was like my dream come true, and I didn't mind the cold. I liked it. Sometimes there were blizzards, and we had to stay put, but they'd always clear up after a few days, and we'd just dig ourselves out and continue on our way.

Christmas was just around the corner. We were all getting quite excited about getting out and seeing friends and family again. The weather closed in on us, clouding up and starting to snow. Then the wind came up. How long would it last? Would we actually be able to get out for Christmas? We were going to be picked up by a crazy bush pilot. John had a reputation for being very experienced, but he tended to take chances. Hopefully he'd be able to get in to pick us up and take us to the main camp, where we'd be flown out by the archaic DC-3.

The snow increased and the wind began to howl. A full blown blizzard was coming in. There was no way anyone could go anywhere. The guys were cussing and I was praying. I didn't realize how much I wanted to get out. "Please, Lord, even a little break in the storm would allow John to get in here."

The blizzard continued the next day and the next. On the third day, it lessened somewhat, and we were told to get our stuff packed and ready to go. I was walking around outside and thought I heard a plane. I went back into the kitchen trailer where the guys were all sitting around drinking coffee. "I think I heard a plane," I said. "Did you guys hear anything?" They jumped up and ran outside looking up.

"Shhht," Stan, one of the workmen said. We stood quietly listening. There it was again, only closer this time. It was still snowing a bit, but the wind had died down, and the clouds were higher. There was a round hole in the clouds above us.

Ivan said, "Watch that hole! That's where he'll come in." Ivan had been around a long time, so he knew John and knew what he would do. We watched the hole, and as the sound got louder we saw the plane come down.

"Yeahhh!" we all cheered in unison.

"He's here. Let's get out of here! Whitehorse Hotel, here we come!!" yelled the guys. John landed without incident, but we didn't have much time, so we grabbed all of our things and quickly climbed in. He flew six of us over to the main camp just in time for lunch, where we waited for the DC-3. At least we were at the main camp, and if we were stuck there for Christmas, it'd be better than out where we'd been.

It seemed clearer there. They had a proper air strip, so we had faith that the bigger DC-3 would make it in that afternoon and that we'd be in Inuvik by the evening. A small crew would stay behind for the Christmas holidays, just to maintain the camp. I was glad I wasn't one of them. The DC-3 landed early, and we got to Inuvik, then to Whitehorse that same night.

We went down to the bar and danced and drank. We were all in party mode. Stan followed me around, asking me to dance, and telling me how he felt about me. He loved me, and asked me if I'd consider marrying him. I liked him. He was a very nice, gentlemanly fellow, and he owned a farm—there was my farmer. I couldn't do it, though. I wasn't in love with him.

It was a fun night, and I got to know the guys that I had been locked in the bush with for the past six weeks. As the evening went on and we talked, drank, and danced, I counted my blessings that I had been able to go up North and live my dream. I retired to my hotel room early because I was tired and wanted to be alone.

We were flying into Grande Prairie the next day, and Bob had told me that I wouldn't be back after Christmas. The crew were going up to the Arctic Ocean where there were no accommodations for a woman. He also told me that L.I. Adam would only pay my fare to Grande Prairie, and if I wanted to go to Smithers, I had to pay for that myself. I needed to figure out what I was going to do. I didn't have time. I was asleep almost as soon as my head hit the pillow.

We flew to Grande Prairie the next day, December 24, 1972. I got myself a hotel room until I could figure out what to do. Bob, in his kindness, invited me to his house for Christmas the next day. There, I met his wife, Bonnie, who turned out to be a lovely lady, and I enjoyed the visit, the dinner, and the company. Bob suggested that I stay in Grande Prairie as he knew they needed people to work at Canadian Bechtel, the firm that was building the Proctor and Gamble pulp mill. Grande Prairie was booming and he felt that I wouldn't have any problem finding employment. I went back to my hotel room at the end of the evening and pondered. I really had nothing to go back to at Smithers—no job, no sister, not really any friends. I decided to stay.

I had to find a place to live, and a job, before my money ran out. Bob and Bonnie helped as much as they could, but he didn't have much time because he had to go back to camp. I looked in the local newspaper and found a board and room situation I could move into the next day. A couple of days after the New Year I went to Canadian Bechtel to apply for work. They hired me immediately. I felt that Grande Prairie was where I was supposed to be.

CHAPTER 3

I STARTED WORK THE next week, doing office-related chores, found the staff very friendly, and I liked the atmosphere of the place. Everyone was happy, and social. There were a lot of good-looking young men around, who seemed to like to check me out. It was a promising place to work. I had my eye on one, particular young fellow, who I thought was very handsome, and charming, although I wasn't sure whether he was interested in me or not.

Dave worked in a different department—I was in the administration corner. I was never really sure where he worked or what he did. He would come over and talk to me once in a while. His story was that I always was following him to the Xerox machine—that may have been true. He was funny and interesting, and had curly hair and a big beard. He was tall and dark, and handsome, and walked with a bit of a limp. I assumed that he had injured himself. He talked about his family (his mom, dad, sister, and brother), but most often he spoke of his grandparents. He and his siblings went over to his grandma's place almost every Sunday for dinner, and so did all his cousins. I'd always wanted grandparents and never had them.

I loved the concept of family, and I'd come from such a dysfunctional background that this sounded exactly what I needed. They were a farm family—perfect! Well, almost. He still lived with his mom and dad, and they lived in town, but his grandma and grandpa lived on a farm way out at Bezanson. Finally, one Sunday he invited me, and I met his mom Evelyn, dad Bruce, brother Eddie, sister Connie, and several of his cousins and friends. They were all welcoming and friendly, and I felt quite at home. Everyone was laughing and talking, telling family stories and jokes. It was great! The long, wintery ride out there didn't seem so bad. Everyone kept talking about Joanne and said that I simply must meet her. She was Dave's favourite cousin, and she sounded like quite the character.

At that time (1973), Grande Prairie had a population of about 10 000. The roads were mostly gravel, and downtown consisted of one road with board sidewalks. Most of the residents of the area were farmers and ranchers, or they worked in the oilfield. It reminded me of a frontier town in the cowboy movies I had seen. The pulp mill that Procter and Gamble was building would change the area's demographics significantly.

Dave and I spent lots of time together, mostly with his family, visiting and getting to know each other, or going out in the bush to sight see or do a bit of ice fishing. After three weeks, we talked about marriage. I don't really remember a specific proposal, but I think it was something that we just decided to do. His family was ecstatic! They loved the idea and the planning was immediately underway. We decided March 31 would be a good day. My new friend Gerlinde and Dave's sister Connie, would be my attendants. Dave's best man would be his brother Eddie, and his second best man would be Helmut, Gerlinde's husband.

I phoned my mom at 11:00 p.m. "Guess what, Mom? I'm getting married!"

"Don't phone me at this time of the night and tell me such nonsense." She slammed down the phone in my ear.

I was hurt, but thought, *Oh, she's just mad because I woke her up. I'll phone her again tomorrow.*

My dad's response was a bit better.

"When?" he asked, "and where? Of course we will come up to the wedding. Why wouldn't we?" He sounded quite excited at the prospect of a good old party.

It was a good time! We were married at St. Paul's United Church on Main Street, and the reception and dance were held out at the Bezanson Hall. March was a muddy month, so muddy we weren't even sure that all the vehicles could get in to the hall. When we drove out to check it out,

Dave's Chevy got stuck in mud up to the running boards. The hall was dirty and dusty and smelly, as it hadn't been used since the previous fall. I wasn't sure how it was all going to work out, but we cleaned it up the best we could, and proceeded with the plans.

The hall was full to bursting with over 200 people there. My dad came, and my mom came. Vicky didn't come because she felt my mother should be the one to attend. Even my childhood friend Laurie came. We had a great old country band, and the dancing was constant–the two-step, the chartreuse (a traditional Scottish dance), the butterfly, and the waltz. Liquor flowed freely and food was plentiful.

My dad laughed. "Yeah! I went outside for a smoke and looked to my right and two guys were punching the shit out of each other! I looked to my left and there was Bruce and his nephew having a go at it! I come back into the hall and the dust is so high that you can't see anyone–just dust. So, you can go outside and freeze to death, or come into the hall and choke to death! Yeah! It's a great time! I haven't been at a dance like that since I was a kid in Manitoba." My dad still talked about it before he died.

I'D WANTED A BABY since Dave and I had married. In early December, I said to him, "I want to have a baby, and it isn't happening." Our friends, Rod and Debbie had told us they were expecting and I was feeling down and depressed. I thought, *What if I never get pregnant? I don't think I could bear it.* I couldn't imagine seeing Rod and Debbie's baby and not having one of my own. "Please God help me get pregnant," I prayed.

A couple of weeks later, while sitting in the tub, I looked down at my breasts and thought, *They look kind of different. What is different about them?* I looked closer; they were a bit puffy-looking. *Maybe I'm pregnant.* I looked again. *"No, it's just my wishful thinking."*

A couple of weeks after that, when I still had no period and tender breasts, I decided to go to the doctor. I still figured I wasn't pregnant because it would have been too good to be true, but I went anyway. He checked me, called me back a week after that, and told me my pregnancy test was positive.

I was pregnant! I really was! I took off right away to where Dave worked, and told him. We were both so happy, and I remember Dave picked me up and swung me around. I was due the following September, and Rod and Debbie's baby was due the following August. That would be great! Our kids could grow up together.

ABOUT TWO OR THREE months later, I was depressed again. *I'm not pregnant. The doctor made a mistake. I should be showing and I am not. Debbie is so fat, and I'm still a little skinny thing. I should be fatter.*

I started bawling my eyes out and I drove over to Dave's mom's place. "I'm not pregnant," I told her. "I'm sure the doctor made a mistake."

"Lay down on the floor," Evelyn commanded.

I lay down and showed her my flat belly.

She put her hand on it. "The little bugger is there! Look! Put your hand here, and you can feel the bump."

"Really? I guess you're right!" I exclaimed, much happier then. Evelyn was like a mom to me. She taught me so many things, and I loved her dearly. She still holds a special place in my heart.

* * *

ONE WEEKEND IN EARLY May, when Dave couldn't wait any longer to get up to the lake, we decided to go for a couple of days even though we knew the ice wouldn't totally be off the lake. Grandpa was up there with his boat, and Grandma and Grandpa had their camper. Dave and I were going to sleep in their camper with them, as it was a bit early for tenting. Evelyn and Connie were up there with Evelyn's camper, and Eddie was planning on coming. It would be a wonderful, long-awaited family get-together. Andy and Marion, Dave's aunt and uncle were planning on arriving the following day, and we were all hoping that Joanne and Norman, and their two kids would be able to make it.

Dave decided to go out in the canoe and fish. Ice patches were still on the lake, but he figured that he could go between the ice patches and catch lots of fish, since they would be pretty hungry after the winter. Grandpa was working on his boat at the dock, and I was walking around on the shore, just looking around and watching everyone. All of a sudden, Dave's canoe tipped over and he was in the water! I hollered at Grandpa and he looked, fear crossing his face. He pulled the cord to try to start his motor. It wouldn't start.

Dave began to struggle, his heavy winter clothing was pulling him down. He sank, then came up. I wanted to rip my clothes off and go in after him, but I was going on 5 months pregnant. He wasn't that far from the shore, maybe 50 or 75 feet, but I was truly afraid of losing my baby. Down he went again.

I looked at Grandpa–he was frantically trying to get his boat started. *What are we going to do? My husband is drowning! I'm a good swimmer, but ...*

Poor Grandpa looked desperate! This time when tried his motor, it started. He roared out to where Dave was going down for the third time. Eighty-plus-year-old Grandpa reached down under the water, grabbed 190 pound Dave, by the collar of his coat, and hauled him up over the edge of the boat.

He sped back to the dock. Dave was staggering as Grandpa practically dragged him out of the boat. He was shaking so violently, he could hardly control his movements.

Grandma had gone into the camper and turned the stove on full blast. When Dave got to the camper, she stripped off his clothes, and wrapped him in a warm wool blanket. Grandpa came in and poured him a huge shot of whisky. "I am buying a new boat and motor," he announced. "Can't trust this stupid old thing."

Dave was crying. "I was going down for the third time, when I could feel myself being grabbed and pulled up. I thought I was a dead man! I couldn't swim—I couldn't move my arms or legs. It was like they were frozen and heavy, and the water was so cold!"

When Joanne and Norman and their children arrived, they were anxious about how Dave was doing and wanted to hear all about his adventure. All Dave wanted to do was stay in bed and keep warm.

I WAS WORKING AT Borstad Welding, and Dave was driving truck for Canadian Linen. Proctor and Gamble's mill was complete, and Canadian Bechtel had closed down and gone somewhere else. Spring passed into summer, and with a baby on the way, Dave didn't want to spend another winter in the clapboard house we'd been living in since soon after we were married. We bought a brand new trailer and parked it at the trailer court just at the edge of town. It was nice, and a good compromise, since Dave preferred to live in town, whereas I always wanted to live out of town. With some help, Dave built a boot room onto it.

My baby was due in September, and because Dave knew that I wanted to stay home, he applied, yet again, to Proctor and Gamble. He had applied before, but had been declined because of his limp, due to polio when he was about 2 years old. This time they hired him. He'd make more money, and I'd be able to be a stay at home mother.

Mid-September came along. No baby. I was induced without success. Two weeks later, I was induced again. Still no success. I was admitted to the hospital a third time for induction, but late that afternoon, I started to have labour pains. I didn't realize how much it would hurt. I felt like my back was going to break.

Joanne came and rubbed my back. Evelyn and Connie both came and sat with me. Dave came and went. I think it was as hard on him as it was on me, but he wanted to be present when the baby was born. Jeffrey Allan was born at 1:06 a.m. on October 7, 1974. He had a big head of curly blonde hair and was very cute! He was my pride and joy, and all I wanted to do was look at him, hold him, and show him off.

I phoned my dad, and told him he had a grandson. He and Vicky were so excited that they offered to fly me down to Vancouver so I could visit them in Squamish, where they still lived. My mom still lived in Vancouver, so it would give her an opportunity to see Jeff as well. It was my parents' first grandchild. It was a good visit. I began to get to know

Vicky, who I liked a lot, and starting thinking of myself as having three parents. I also started to think of Melody as my stepsister. I liked her and I began to embrace them both as part of my family, my delightfully dysfunctional family.

* * *

GRANDE PRAIRIE WAS VERY cold in the winter, but I insisted that Jeff get some fresh air. Cross-country skiing was just beginning to make an impression in Grande Prairie. Some enthusiasts organized some trails in the Wapiti River valley, not far from where we lived. I always loved skiing, and had done some downhill skiing when I lived in Squamish, but never cross-country. Grande Prairie was basically prairie, with the only hills being within the Wapiti River valley. There was a small, downhill skiing area, but it was too expensive for me, and I was used to downhill skiing on actual mountains. Cross-Country sounded like a great alternative.

Not wanting to let a baby stop my outdoor activity in the winter, I put Jeff in his car seat, packed my snuggly, and I went to find the trails.

It was relatively warm—only about twenty below zero. Jeff was bundled up, and I put him in his snuggly on my back, put on my skis, and started down one of the trails. I did not know where they went, or how difficult they were. It was beautiful! There was hoarfrost on the trees, and the sun was shining and reflecting off the ice crystals. I felt like I was in heaven. I seemed to take pretty good to the skiing, but I always seemed to be successful at every sport I tried.

We skied along. Jeff was a bit more than two months old, but he was able to look around and see the scenery, until he fell asleep. I was sweating so I figured my body heat would be enough to keep us both warm, and wasn't concerned at all about him.

I was going along just fine when, all of a sudden—bang! I fell and started rolling down the hill. Jeff went flying and I didn't know where he was. I couldn't hear anything. No crying, nothing. Was he dead? Had he hit a tree and got knocked out? Where was my baby?

I got up and took my skis off. I was on a steep side hill that had trees everywhere. The snow was up to my thighs and it was hard to get around. I just wanted to find my baby. I started calling him. "Jeffy, Jeffy, where are you?" *How stupid is that? He's only two months old. As if he's going to answer.* I stopped and listened for a cry. Nothing. I made my way down the hill a bit, then up again, trying to figure out what direction he had flown.

Finally, I heard a loud wail straight in front of me. I made my way toward it, and soon I saw the snuggly. Jeff was still in it. His hat had fallen off and he was lying on his back, howling as loud as he could. My first thought was, *His head! His head! Babies loose heat from their head. I need to cover his head up.* I took my toque off, put it on him, picked him up, and hugged him close. He was still crying, but not howling. Thank God he seemed unhurt.

I made my way back, picked up my skis and poles and proceeded to climb up the hill. With a baby in my arms, 3 feet of snow, and packing skis and poles and wearing ski boots, it was not an easy task. I made my way up to the trail, put Jeff on my back again, put my skis on, and skied back to my vehicle. I was glad to get home and get warm again. I gave Jeff a feed and tucked him into his crib. He fell asleep right away. I realized what a dumb thing it was to do, and I was ever so thankful that no harm had come to either of us.

CHRISTMAS ARRIVED. CHRISTMAS EVE, the whole family drove out to Grandma's. All of Dave's cousins, aunts, uncles, friends, and even friends of friends would come. It was always fun. This year, it would be even more exciting, because Norman, Joanne's husband would be out there with the family band, playing music.

Where would we fit them all, I thought. *Grandma's house isn't very big and it doesn't even have an indoor toilet.* I needn't have worried. Grandma and Grandpa moved all of the furniture to the side to make room for everyone. There were chairs everywhere! Norman had all of his instruments out and his band members were plucking away and tuning their guitars. He even had a bass player and a drummer with full equipment. I could tell we were in for one heck of a party. Once everyone arrived, we started to feast. Every family brought something so Grandma didn't have to do it all. There was plenty of food to go around, and even booze available for the drinkers. After we had all eaten, and relaxed for a bit and visited, the instruments and music began.

There were waltzes and two steps and even the old chartreuse and butterfly dance. Everybody was dancing, even the children. We were all partied out by about 1:00 a.m. I was glad that we only had Jeff. He was too young to be up early in the morning to open his gifts. Dave and I could sleep in.

CHAPTER 4

I WANTED TO MOVE out of town again. "There is a new subdivision opening up out at Riverview Pines," I told Dave. "We could buy five acres. We could haul the trailer out there, and I could even have a garden. Can we please just go and check it out?"

It was around March and the roads were muddy, and sometimes impassable, but once they dried out a bit, we drove out there and had a look. The acreages were 5-acre parcels, and several of them had been sold, and some houses started already. It was a scenic area, close to the Wapiti River. Pine trees were everywhere, and the ground was sandy and gravelly.

"What about water?" Dave asked, "what about sewer? It all costs money to build. I don't think we can afford it." We left. It was really me that wanted to move out there, not Dave, so I put the idea on the back burner for a while.

A couple of weeks later, it was a nice sunny day, so I decided to put Jeff in the truck and go out to Riverview Pines again. I thought that I might be able to find someone out there working, and I could ask them a few questions. I was in luck! Someone was out there building a house. I asked them about water and sewer. They were putting it in themselves. Apparently you could build a cribbing out of two by fours, four feet by four feet, and as you dug down, the cribbing would fall as you removed the dirt under it. It was expected that you would hit water at about 40 – 50 feet. As for the sewer, outhouses were a temporary solution for that, until you put in your own.

I was immediately encouraged. They were doing it so why couldn't we? They were a young couple with a child, just like Dave and I. I went home and approached Dave with the idea, when he came home from work. We discussed it, and he had second thoughts.

"Maybe I'll talk to Reg and Donnie and see what they think. Maybe they can help us," he offered. He knew how badly I wanted to move out to the acreage.

"Oh sure," both Reg and Donnie agreed. "Give us a phone call and buy us a beer and we would be glad to come out and help." Dave talked to his dad, and his brother Eddie, and they too offered to help. So, we bought the acreage and planned to move the trailer out there when the roads dried up enough. It felt good. It was something to look forward to, and we would truly have our own place.

April came and went, and when May arrived we got the trailer hauled out to the acreage and set up house. It was lots of work. We had to organize an outhouse, put the skirting and insulation around the bottom of the trailer, get power in, and start working on where to dig the well. Dave was working, so he was only available in the evenings and on weekends, but we were both strong and healthy and had lots of energy.

Our first priority was the well. Hauling water from town was only a temporary solution. Dave would bring some home every day when he came home from work. We found a likely spot and began to dig the well. It was easy at first. We used a shovel and a 5-gallon bucket. It seemed to be working until it got about 5 feet deep. Then Dave hooked up a pulley on the back of his truck. One of us would fill up the bucket, place it on the hook, signal to the other, pull the bucket out, empty it, and send it back down the hole. If we were alone, we would have to climb up out of the hole, start up the truck, pull the bucket, dump it, and then go back down.

When we got below the bottom of the cribbing, we would dig under it, all around the four-foot square, causing the cribbing to drop. The key was to do it evenly, so it would drop in a straight line all the way down. It was long and tedious work. I would do it on my own when Dave was at work, and he would continue when he came home. The soil was heavy clay mud and difficult to dig. We built a little corner ladder on the cribbing so we could climb in and out.

One day I had a good day of digging, and when I was finished, I went to climb out and the ladder rung was too far for me to reach. "Ohhhh shit!" I said. I looked at my watch, it was about 3:00 p.m. Jeff was about to wake up from his afternoon nap, and Dave wouldn't be home until 6:00 that evening. What was I going to do? I was a pretty good climber, I knew that, and I knew I was fairly strong. I had to be after all of that physical labour I had been doing, forever, it seemed.

The bottom rung was about two feet above my up-stretched arm. Could I jump? I tried. I couldn't get quite high enough. Could I stand on the upturned bucket? I tried, and still couldn't reach it. I would have to dig under the cribbing, and try to get it to fall down a bit. It was above my head. What if it fell on my head? We usually didn't dig this far down before we knocked the cribbing down. It was a bit iffy but I felt I had no choice. I had to get out of there. Jeff was probably up and crying in his crib and he would need a change and a feed. It was too high above my head to dig under the cribbing. I couldn't get any pressure with the shovel. I sat on the upturned bucket, trying to solve this dilemma.

I knew I had to get out of it myself. There was no one around, as it was a work day and everyone was gone. My only option was to dig little holes in the wall up to the cribbing and try to climb up far enough to reach the bottom of the ladder. It wasn't easy. I dug three foot holes and two hand holes, hoping that the third hand hole could be the bottom rung. Then my plan was to pull myself up to the second rung and climb out. "Please help me Lord," I prayed.

I started to climb, clinging to the dirt wall with my fingers. Up I went, placing my left foot in one hole and my right foot in the other hole, and grasping hard into the hand holes. I brought my left foot up and put it in the third hole, and realized I would have to hang on with only one hand, while I tried to grasp the bottom rung with my other hand. "Please help me, Lord," I prayed again. "Give me the strength."

I managed to catch the bottom rung with my left hand, and hang on by one arm. Man, it was tough. I had to get my other hand on the rung and then try to grasp the second rung. I had never been very good with chin ups, but if I dropped down, I didn't think I would have the energy to try again. Both hands grasping the bottom rung, I used my feet to climb up the mud wall, and managed to grab the second rung. It was easier, but I still wasn't out of the woods. I got my second hand on the second rung, and reached for the third rung. This time it was easier, because I was sticking my feet into the hand holes. Finally I got my knee up to the bottom rung, organized myself and started to climb out. I was exhausted!

"Thank you, Lord," I said. I was covered in mud, and wet and cold. I went into the trailer, and checked on Jeff. Thank God he was still asleep. I changed my clothes and sat down to a cup of tea. I was done for the day.

DAVE AND I BOTH worked on digging the well on the weekends. Our friends who said they would help somehow found other things to do when we asked them. It was always, "Yeah! I'd love to help but I can't today." Or if they did come out, all they would do is drink beer.

Dave and I both realized that we were on our own. Anyway, the well was getting finished, but the going was slow. We were at about 38 feet that weekend, and Dave was down the well digging, and I was hauling the clay out of the well with the pulley that Dave rigged up. It had been going pretty good that day. Jeff was in his play pen, I was above the ground, and Dave was below the ground.

I was hauling up a full bucket, and all of a sudden the chain snapped – the full bucket fell back down the hole. I hollered at Dave! I heard the bucket thump down onto the bottom. It was only a 4-foot-square hole and Dave was down there. There was complete silence. I thought I must have killed him. I slowly walked over to the well–scared shitless. I never even prayed I was so stunned. I looked down the hole, yelled to Dave, and then saw his form, slowly climbing out of an apparent hole in the side of the well. "Whew!," I breathed a sigh of relief. He was okay! I hadn't killed him!

He came up the ladder and sat beside me. "I was just noticing that some water was spurting out of the corner there while I was digging, so dug into it to see if I could get more water. There was just enough room that when you yelled, I was able to squeeze myself into the hole. The bucket grazed me on the shoulder, though—look," he said, as he pulled his shirt down. There was a big red scrape there. I was just glad that he was alive.

We had hit water, and it was coming in with quite a bit of force, and the well was filling up. We were done, at least for then. We sat there and had a couple of beer to celebrate our success. Dave had dug another 4 feet. That was our 42-foot well dug with a bucket and a shovel. Great! Our well was rather unproductive though, so we were always running out of water. One bath, or one load of laundry was all we could do at a time. Then we had to wait for the well to fill up again.

DAVE WORKED SO MANY long hours, and we were so broke I had to save up for three months to buy him a winter coat. We had enough to eat, barely, but we would have been lost if it wasn't for Grandma's garden, and Dave's success at moose hunting. He went moose hunting every year and was always successful. That, and fish—usually jackfish or pike—is what sustained us during those early years. The winter of 1975 was particularly brutal. I was pregnant with my second child, due in the beginning of June 1976. Our pipes froze, and the trailer was freezing cold because it wasn't very well insulated. Our power bills were high, and it was a long way from town, so we used lots of gas. For water, when everything was frozen, I would bundle Jeff up, put him on the sleigh, hike to the Wapiti River, cut a hole in the ice with an axe, and fill two big garbage cans full of water. I would haul the water home, on the sled, and put Jeff on my back. It was an all-morning, or all-afternoon venture. Other people lived on the subdivision, but I did not know them very well, so couldn't go and ask them for help. We stayed there for a year, and gave up. We sold our place and planned to live in a rental house until we could afford to get a new house built.

I had always thought it would be neat to have a baby on my birthday, May 29, so we planned that with our second child. Mitchell was due on June 2, 1976. Because I wanted him on my birthday, the morning of May 29 I took 4 ounces of castor oil and went for a 6-mile walk. A friend of ours was supposed to be getting married that day, so we had a wedding to go to at 4:00 p.m. When I got back from the walk, I started having pains, but just ignored them. They started to get worse, so I lay down for a while.

Our friends Rod and Debbie were also going to the wedding, so they came over. Debbie watched me for a bit and said, "If you're having that much pain, you're probably in labour." I didn't believe her. I wanted to go to the wedding so got up and got myself washed and dressed.

Connie came over to babysit Jeff, and looked at me questioningly as well. "Are you sure you aren't in labour. Loraine?" she asked.

"No." I continued getting ready, and was standing at the sink brushing my teeth when *swoosh*, there was water all over the floor. Dave helped me in the car, and we drove up to the hospital. By this time, the pains were quite intense. We got to the train tracks, and a long freight train was crossing the road. We had to wait and wait, and my pains were getting pretty bad. Dave was concerned that he would have to deliver this baby in the car. The train finally came to an end, so Dave drove as fast as he could up to the hospital.

When they saw me in admitting, a nurse came immediately and put me in a wheelchair and brought me up to the delivery area. "You are 6 cm," she said as she examined me. "I'll bring you some Demerol." She gave me the shot and left me there on the delivery table. Dave was there, staying with me.

"I think I have to push!" I did have to push, so I did, and out came the baby. He was blue/black. My first thought was, *Maybe he's dead?* There was no movement—no crying. Dave had run out, calling for the doctor. The doctors and nurses came rushing in and began to resuscitate the baby. It was another boy.

Soon, I could hear a plaintive wail, and the nurse came over to me and said, "I think he will be alright." I was relieved, and pretty soon he began to holler. I cuddled him and fed him. As it turned out, he was fine, but no, we did not make the wedding. At least I didn't. Dave went and had a great time. After all, he had two events to celebrate.

CHAPTER 5

WE LIVED IN THE rental house for the following year, while our house was being built on the south side of Grande Prairie in a new subdivision. I was excited because I was able to pick out the colours of my walls, floors, and even appliances. I was really looking forward to moving in. It was to be our final home. Both of us were tired of moving around so much and wanted to settle down. It was a good neighbourhood, with most of the people being about our age, with children the same age as Jeffrey and Mitchell. It was at the edge of town, so it was quiet, and there were still birds, deer, and a few bears that showed themselves on occasion. I thought it was a perfect compromise because, as I said before, Dave always wanted to live in town and I always wanted to live out of town.

IT WAS THE SUMMER of 1977, and we had moved into our new house earlier in the year. Jeff would be turning three in October, and Mitch was a little over a year old. The building of the subdivision was still in progress, so there was unfinished infrastructure everywhere. Jeff had made friends with Ryan and Travis, two other little boys who lived in the neighbourhood, and they all had little tricycles that they peddled all over the place. There were lots of things for them to see and do. It was total heaven for them, and they were happy to play outside all day, even in the rain.

There were deep holes full of water and uncovered pipes everywhere, just big enough for a three year old to climb into. There were piles of dirt and gravel to climb up and play in, and there were non-descript fences, and non-fences constructed to try to discourage the exploratory efforts of the children. The fences did nothing to deter them.

One dull but not so rainy day, Jeff wanted to go outside. He had run out of things to do in the house, so I relented and was hoping he would go over to Ryan's. I guess he did, and convinced Ryan's mom to let him out as well. It was nearing supper time, and Jeff had not come home yet.

I went out and called him—no answer. I had a whistle and blew it, in hopes of attracting his attention. I was met with silence. Dave wasn't home, so I didn't want to leave Mitch alone in the house to go look for Jeff. I phoned Ryan's mom, and asked if Jeff was there.

"No," she said, "I thought he was at your house."

Oh! Oh! Some alarms went off in my head. I was thinking of the open pipes that I knew Jeff could crawl into. I thought about the pits full of water. I needed to go out and look for him. I called my neighbour, Marion. Travis was in the house, and fortunately her husband Danny was home, so she offered to come over and keep an eye on Mitchell while I went to look for Jeff. I went outside and met Ryan's mom. Both of us walked the streets, calling our children, and calling them again.

"If we don't find them soon," I said, "we'll have to call the RCMP."

"Let's look a bit longer," Ryan's mom suggested.

"Okay." So we looked. I went to all of the open pipes and called Jeff's name from the entrance. I was too big to crawl into the pipes, but Jeff wasn't, and I was afraid that is just what he had done. Perhaps he was lost back in there—took a wrong turn or something. What a horrible way for a little guy to die.

"We have to call the police," I said. I was getting really worried.

"Okay," Ryan's mom said. "I'll go in and call them, and you keep looking."

"Good idea," I said. I was always a doer, and could not sit still, so I kept walking and looking into every water-filled pit that I knew of. I called and called, to no avail. I heard the police siren, and soon after that, the police car came around the corner.

"I can't find my son and his friend," I wailed.

The policeman looked around. "Where have you looked?"

"Everywhere," I replied.

"Well, we have some others coming to help. Let's just wait until they arrive, and we can do a proper organized search."

I could hear another siren, but could not stop. I was frantic! I thought my baby was dead or injured or even worse. Maybe someone had kidnapped him.

I ran up to the top of a sand pile. There was a hole on the other side, and it was full of water. I could see two little figures crouched on a tiny sand island barely large enough for the two of them. There was water all around them. How could they have gotten in there? I ran down the side of the sand pile and into the water. I sunk up to my knees in the mud, and the water was up to my chest. I freed my feet and swam toward the boys. I yelled at the police officer and told him I had found them.

When I got closer to Jeff and Ryan, I asked, "Are you okay?"

"Yes," they said, but I could see that they had been crying.

I put them on my back, one at a time and swam them over to the shore, which was nothing but a steep mud bank. The policeman had come over and was helping them up the bank. They were cold and wet, but alive and un-injured.

I breathed a sigh of relief. I returned Ryan to his very happy mom and took Jeff home. Dave had just gotten home, so I told him what had happened and sent Marion back to her family.

We lived in that neighbourhood for about two years, and that was where we were living when my third son Cordell was born. The neighbours were lovely, and there were lots of children for Jeff and Mitch to play with. Why did we decide to sell and move? I don't remember, but I do know that the house had only one door, and that really bugged me.

There was another new subdivision being developed on the northwest side of town, called Crystal Ridge. Grande Prairie had been developing mightily since the opening of the Procter and Gamble pulp mill. We decided to buy a lot there and get another new house built. There was a lake behind the lot that we had purchased. Perhaps I could skate on it in the winter. The long-term plan was to develop a park-like setting in the area around the lake. Our friends Rod and Debbie were building a house just down the road from us. I would walk down to Debbie's and have tea. She would light up a cigarette, hand one to me, and we would sit there drinking tea and smoking, and indulge in deeply philosophical conversations. Those times were precious to me.

* * *

MY DAD AND VICKY continued with their wonderful full life. Dad was always proud of the fact that he and Vicky were in the top three percent of the "retired wealthy." Melody had graduated from nursing school and had accepted her first job at Bella Bella, on the central coast of British Columbia. She soon transferred to Bella Coola, a larger hospital nearby, and fell in love with a handsome, romantic forester there named Wayne.

Melody told me, "Wayne and some other foresters always seemed to be finding excuses to come to the Nurses Residence." In 1979, they were married in a beautiful ceremony at the Unitarian Church in Vancouver. Melody and her new husband purchased a piece of property in Bella Coola that was an old homestead with a small orchard and great garden potential. Melody had an affinity for gardening and eating natural, organic foods. It sounded lovely, but they sold it before I was able to see it.

Louise had moved on with her life. She and her partner had separated, and shortly after he was killed in a motor vehicle accident on the highway between Smithers and Telkwa. Louise was obviously devastated, but she picked up the pieces of her life and continued living in Telkwa. Her passion was community work, trying to get funding for and organizing projects such as a co-op, which would allow residents to buy and sell local garden produce. She also renewed her interest in politics and kept herself busy with meetings and fundraising for different events.

She soon met Jim, and they became partners in some of those ventures. Jim was a lawyer, working for Legal Aid, an organization that assured that people who needed legal assistance were given it, even when they had no funds of their own to pay for it. They enjoyed doing hiking and canoeing, and other outdoor activities together. They soon moved in together and in 1980 they had a son named Franklin. She was with Jim for a number of years.

LIVING IN GRANDE PRAIRIE was a long way from the Lower Mainland where my parents lived. I had always wanted a grandmother when I was a child, so I made an effort to take my children down to Vancouver every summer to see and get to know their own grandparents. It was always an ordeal because I would drive with my three very young sons and it would take me two or three days to get there as well as back. I would plan on going down there for about two weeks.

My dad always phoned me about two days before I was planning on leaving. "Do you have enough money get down here, and then get home again?"

"Yep," I would answer.

"Good, because I will give you three squares a day and a roof over your head, but I am not giving you anything else!"

I actually knew that, because he was a little bit tight-fisted with his money when it came to me and my sister. I would pack my children, my tent, sleeping bags, and other camping equipment, and head out. We went through Jasper, my favourite way, because we could explore and camp in some of the most beautiful country in the world.

Our favourite campsite was Honeymoon Lake. There were always other children for my kids to play with, and I was always busy because the equipment I had was very rudimentary. I cooked everything over a fire, and cleaned up by warming water over the fire, and then, of course, there was always wood that needed chopping. My dad and Vicky still lived in Squamish, and my mom was in Vancouver.

Even though I was married and had three children, I felt extremely alone and lonely. Dave was always working, and generally had no interest in coming on holidays with us. When he wasn't working, he would sit and watch television. He didn't do much with the boys, which was a great disappointment to me, because when I was a child I remember my dad always playing with us. He would take us on hikes every Sunday and let my mother sleep in. Somehow he often found nickels and dimes under rocks, but Louise or I could never find them. He would take us fishing, and we would roast the fish on a campfire. They tasted so good! He would take us exploring, and teach us the names of different kinds of rocks, as he was a prospector at heart, and had lots of knowledge in that area. I expected the same thing from Dave, and was disappointed when he didn't deliver.

I tried to make up for the loss by attempting to be both the mom and dad. I also shouldered the responsibility of the house, so I was the one who did all the painting, gardening, and fixing of our home. I was busy, as there was always a lot to do. It seemed like he did his thing and I did mine, but we really did very little together. The boys and I would go off on our own while Dave was at work. Dave was fine with this. He pretty much let me do what I wanted to do. I had Debbie, for a friend, and I would visit Evelyn and Grandma, but I soon discovered that I was much different from most of the people I knew, except maybe Gerlinde.

Gerlinde had divorced Helmut, and was quite involved in downhill skiing. She would occasionally go on hikes with me, but she was busy with her job and her life. We both had an adventurous spirit, and always wanted to do things. I wanted to hike in the summer, and ski in the winter. She did more than I did, especially with skiing. However, she did not have any children, and I had three of them. I liked rivers, mountains, lakes, and hills. No one else I hung around with was interested in those things. I was born and raised in British Columbia, where the people were different. Everyone I grew up with was like me. I pined for the mountains, and the oceans, to the point where at times I felt ill.

I thought often about the rock climbing my friend Laurie and I did. I would have enjoyed pursuing that as a sport. Laurie had discovered Outward Bound, an organization that taught young people how to survive in the wilderness. I was intensely envious of her because she was learning how to run a river in a kayak and professionally rock climb. She took part in all sorts of adventures.

Someone, I can't remember who, told me about the Red Willow River. It was a river that was relatively small, not too far from home, and had a wonderful, scenic waterfall that fell into a pool below. It was a pristine turquoise blue, reminding me of the rivers in British Columbia, and was an inviting location to either swim, or fish for walleye. It became my retreat, and I took the boys there often.

CHAPTER 6

IT WAS SEPTEMBER 1980, and Jeff was going into grade 1. Melody, my stepsister, had delivered a baby boy the previous July, and she and her husband, Wayne, were in Georgia so Wayne could go to university there to study chiropractic arts. My dad had bought a house for them to live in while Wayne was studying, and Melody would support the family by going to work doing nursing. It all sounded rather wonderful to me. Louise was, involved in different things, and going on canoe trips and other outdoor adventures, and I was envious.

My life was boring, and I was getting restless. I wanted to go to work, and earn some money, and yes, I wanted to do something other than raising children. I found employment doing office work, but I found it hard to leave my babies all day. I lasted a month. I stayed at home for a few months, until I again got restless and bored, and looked for work.

I landed a job at a local accounting firm in Grande Prairie. It was during the tax season, so I was doing some simple tax returns. It was a good job, and they paid me well, but few months down the road a new fellow was hired. During a job evaluation, they discovered that I had only a grade ten education. They told me that they thought I was doing rather well for the amount of education that I had, and they were surprised at my ability. A month or so later, I was called into the new fellow's office and informed that I was being fired. I was furious. I walked out of there and said to myself, "I will never get fired from a job, ever, ever again! I will be so good at my job that people will be calling me, and asking me to go to work for them."

I found out later that the company was going broke, because they had sunk a whole lot of money into 214 Place, which was the first high rise apartment in Grande Prairie. It was hard to rent out the office space, so they were cutting back on anyone they could do without.

DAVE AND I HAD been married for seven years, and my discontent and boredom were starting to cause a distance between us. I was tired of not having a life, tired of the drudgery of nothing to look forward to, and tired of Dave's disinterest in me and the boys. I felt I shouldered the whole responsibility of everything, and at times I felt like I had four children— not three. I was constantly cleaning up his mess and the mess that the children made. We never went anywhere or did anything, and I started to think.

Dave had gone straight from his mother to me. He had lived on his own for about one month before we got married, but had never had to look after himself. I asked him to leave. I wanted him to go and live on his own for a while, have a temporary separation and give him a chance to experience the responsibility of caring for himself. I thought he might become more interesting, and maybe be more involved with the boys and myself if he didn't live with us. I guess I also wanted some space—space for myself, to do things that I wanted to do, and feel less burdened. It was February 1981. He moved out just before our eighth wedding anniversary.

He did well for himself. First, he moved to an apartment, then a few months later he bought a half of a duplex to live in. He met another woman and seemed to enjoy his new-found singleness. He was twenty-eight, handsome, and a good catch. There was no shortage of women who were interested in him. I continued to live in the house, and started to go out and meet other people, and even began to date a little bit. I was enjoying being single because at least I felt I had a bit of a life. In November 1981,

Dave and I went to court. He had decided to divorce me. The process was short and sweet, with no complications.

I met a neighbour lady named Ivy. She and I hit it off and became quite close friends. Ivy was a bit of an original. She was full of fun and tricks, a little bit on the chubby side, always trying to lose that final ten pounds. She was running one day during one of her exercise feats, wearing shorts and a T-shirt. "It was so funny, Loraine, I was running and this guy was riding his bike, looking at me, following me with his eyes and not looking where he was going. The stupid idiot ran right into the back of a car and flew ass over teakettle right over the roof!" She laughed.

"Laugh," she said, "I laughed so hard I peed my pants! You see," she continued, "I might be 28, but I still got it! Yeah!" She giggled so hard she couldn't even stand up!!

Ivy was a high school drop-out like me. None of us really had much to offer a potential employer. She told me, "Loraine," she said, "You can go back to school and get your high school, and if you have worked, you can collect unemployment insurance. They will pay for it. Why don't you try it? Go and see that counsellor there—his name is Laverne or something. He will tell you how."

I remember thinking, *If I want to be so good at my job that I will never get fired, what am I going to do? I really have no education.* I phoned the college and made an appointment.

Laverne was a lovely man, well-informed and encouraging. Yes, I could collect unemployment insurance, and there were even grants available to me to complete my high school education. I would have to go right back to grade nine for math. I needed to go to grade ten for physics, but biology, English, social studies, and chemistry, could be started in grade eleven. I could do some of the courses now, and do the rest the following September.

When I phoned my dad to tell him of my decision, he said, "You won't finish! You've never finished anything in your whole life."

When I called my mom, she told me, "It will be very difficult for you, but I admire you for attempting it."

When I told Evelyn, Dave's mom, and Bruce, Dave's dad, I did so in hopes that they would perhaps offer to look after the children sometimes for me to make it a bit easier. Evelyn said, "Don't expect any help from us. We're both retired now and I plan on spending all my time up at the lake. I don't know what Bruce is going to do, but he has his own plans."

I started to cry. I was very hurt, but I said, "I will do it with or without your help." I walked out, very upset. I had not expected that from them. They had always been so kind to me. I believe they must have been mad at me for asking Dave to leave. I didn't care. I was determined, and I would finish with or without help from anybody.

* * *

ABOUT A MONTH AFTER I started school, I met Leona. I had been watching her for some time, and she was in several of my classes. She was pretty, and seemed really smart, but appeared a bit aloof. She always was at the top of the class—especially in math. I thought she was either unfriendly or shy. I didn't know which, but I really wanted to meet her and become friends. I was sitting at a table alone one day when she walked by.

"Hello," I said, "would you like to join me? I will buy you a coffee." I don't even think she said anything to me; she just sat down. "What do you take in your coffee?" I asked her as I got up to go and buy it for her.

"Cream and sugar, but can you just bring it and I will put it in myself?"

"Okay," I said as I shrugged and walked off. When I came back to the table, and sat down, I said, "So what do you do for fun?"

"Nothing," she said as she looked me straight in the eye. Her response struck me as funny, and I started to giggle. She started to giggle too, and heads started to turn. She put her hand over her mouth, trying to suppress the laugh. "I have to go to class."

"Oh, me too," I told her. "We had better get going," I said, as we got up from the table. She went one way, and I went the other. *Maybe she would like to do some fun things?*

"Hey, do you want to go and see Loverboy?" Leona asked me one day as we walked out of math class together.

"What?"

"Loverboy—they're a band and are coming here for a concert. Haven't you ever been to a concert?" she asked, looking at me like I was some kind of idiot.

"Actually, no, I haven't. It's just not something that I do." I responded.

"Let's go. It'll be fun. It's this Saturday night, and I think I can get us some tickets. Let's do it, okay?" She looked so eager and excited about the whole idea that I couldn't resist her.

"Okay," I said, "I'll see if I can get a babysitter."

It was absolutely freezing outside as we stood in the lineup to get into the concert. I looked at Leona's feet. "Is that all you have to wear on your feet?" I asked, looking down at her flimsy little ballet slippers. "It's thirty below zero out here. Aren't you cold?"

"Oh, the lineup should get moving soon, and we'll be inside. I'll be okay."

The line finally began to move, which was good because it was very cold out, and no one looked very comfortable. We went in and found our seats. Good seats they were, too; we could see everything. Bryan Adams was the backup band, and he opened the show. I remember him and his raspy voice. I really don't remember Loverboy at all, whether I liked them or not, but I sure enjoyed Bryan Adams. He became famous after that, and I never heard much more about Loverboy.

College was fun, challenging, and exciting. *I'm just going to see how smart I really am,* I thought, so I worked hard and studied, and came up at the top of the class in just about every test. Three semesters of upgrading completed my high school education.

I needed to find a job for the summer. Leona had some experience as a cocktail waitress and had found employment. I wanted to do something outside. Ivy had already obtained a job doing grounds maintenance at the college.

"Come with me, Loraine," she said one day, as she grabbed me by the arm and pulled me along. "I want you to meet Pete. He's my boss and he's looking for more help around here. I told him about you and he wants to meet you."

Mmm, I always had a hankering for gardening. I even thought I might have a bit of a green thumb. I followed her.

"Loraine, this is Pete. Pete, this is Loraine, the one I told you about. She wants to work here with us."

"When can you start?" Pete asked as he extended his hand in greeting.

"Tomorrow?" I offered.

"Okay, we'll pay you $6.00 an hour," he said. "Be here at 8:00 in the morning. We start early because it gets hot in the afternoon."

"Scotty Poo! Scotty Poo! Come and meet my friend Loraine. She'll be working with us for the summer." Ivy hollered at Scotty as she dragged me by the arm to go and meet her protégé.

"Scotty, this is Loraine. Loraine, this is Scotty Poo!"

"Hi!" I said as I looked at Scotty's reddened, embarrassed face. He was young—very young and looked like a sweet, good-natured young fellow. We shook hands and hit it off. I was glad to be working with Ivy and Scotty all summer. There would undoubtedly be a couple of others hired for the job, and I hoped they would be just as much fun.

I loved doing grounds maintenance, but I was well aware that it would end in September. Pete, my boss, was very good to me. He knew I had applied for the Nursing Diploma Program, which was to start in September 1982. He promised to try to introduce me to the Director of Nursing, Rachael, who had been hired to organize the program.

It was a twenty-two-month, apparently very arduous undertaking, and it was the first of its kind at the college. I was quite excited about the whole thing. I had always wanted to be a nurse, and here was my chance! I sure hoped that I would be accepted. I had just completed three semesters of grueling upgrading. My marks were high, generally over ninety percent, and I had even successfully passed my Chemistry 130. That in itself was a feat, as I had not had any chemistry background.

Pete came looking for me one day. "Come and meet Rachael," he offered. "Loraine, this is Rachael, new Director of Nursing," he said.

Rachael reached out to shake my hand.

"Loraine has applied for entry into the Student Nursing program," he explained.

"Welcome, welcome," Rachael said with a charm and confidence that I hoped to achieve one day.

"Hopefully, I get accepted," I said. "I certainly have worked hard."

"We will have made our decisions in about two weeks, so perhaps you will hear from us," Rachael said.

"Nice to meet you," I said as I walked away, talking to Pete.

Two weeks later, I received notification that I had been accepted into the Nursing Diploma Program offered at Grande Prairie Regional College. I would graduate in 1984. "I got it! I got in!" I hollered as I ran out into the grounds maintenance coffee room. "I got in, look!" I yelled and showed my acceptance letter around.

"Congratulations, congratulations," everyone was saying as they alternately hugged me and patted me on the back. I was so excited I could hardly concentrate on work for the rest of the day.

The next day I talked to Leona. She said, "Me too, me too. I got into the Lab Tech Program at NAIT!"

We celebrated by getting together with a bottle of wine the following evening. It was a fun evening. We sat and chatted about our promising futures.

"I want it all," I said. "I want money, nice clothes, a decent car, and a promising life."

"I want it all, too," Leona agreed.

"Cheers to that," we said as we clicked our wine glasses together.

The following weekend, Leona and I both took some time off and went camping up at Twin Lakes. Leona and I were pretty good friends by now, and I discovered that she liked doing some fun things. We got our ex-husbands to look after our children, which was a great accomplishment in itself, because neither of them was ever very enthusiastic about playing the dad.

It was great! We were on our own, and all we had to do was swim, fish, lie in the sun, and explore the wilderness that surrounded Twin Lakes. And, oh yeah! Drink Southern Comfort! We found a place to pitch our tent after the long, dusty ride, so once that was complete, and our beds were organized we collected some firewood and got a fire started. Our weekend away had begun. We sat up late, laughing and talking, and drinking Southern Comfort. I think we overindulged a bit, but I just remember being really happy. I guess we must have fallen asleep at some point—or passed out. I am not sure, but the next morning when we woke up, it was clear, sunny, and cold. It always is in the mountains. However, we started a fire and had a few cups of expertly brewed coffee.

I had done a lot of camping with the boys and always looked forward to drinking my coffee by the fire in the morning before they woke up. It was always a peaceful and enjoyable break from my harried life as a single mom. Our plan was to do some exploring. We found something that looked like an animal trail and followed it. We were looking for access to the Kakwa River. We followed the trail up into some rocky areas that were quite steep. We were walking along chatting about nothing and Leona says, "Wow you sure move fast over this rocky trail—wait up!"

"Oh yeah!" I returned, "I'm just like a mountain goat moving over these rocks." Bang! Down I went and landed on my rear end, injuring my right leg as I did so.

Leona started laughing!

I didn't think it was very funny. My leg was hurting me, but the pain didn't last very long, and soon we were both laughing.

"That is what you get for bragging, Loraine," Leona said.

"Yeah! I guess you're right." We continued along the trail, and had a snack—never did find access to the Kakwa River, so turned around and went back to camp.

"Do you want to go fishing? Perhaps we can catch a couple of trout for supper," I said.

"We don't have a boat—how are we going to get out there into deeper water?"

"We can wade out there as far as we can and fish just standing in the water," I told her. I rolled up my pants and waded out, showing her what I meant. I cast my fishing line out with a worm for bait, and not two minutes later, I had a bite.

"I got one! I got one!" I exclaimed with excitement. I reeled it in. It was just pan-sized, nice for one person to eat—not two. "We need another one, or it won't be enough."

"Let me try, let me try," Leona begged. "You have to put the worm on though, I just can't."

"Okay," I responded.

She rolled her pants up and walked out into the water a few feet. "I'm getting wet, and I don't have any more pants or shorts."

"Well, cast your line out farther then," I directed.

She tried to cast a few more times. Nothing was happening, so she got frustrated and came into shore and took off her pants. She went wading out there in her underwear and T-shirt. She sure was determined to catch a fish.

I started laughing at her determination and stood on the shore, trying to get a photo. "Hey!" I yelled, trying to get her to turn toward me. "Smile." *Snap!* I got a really good picture of her.

After a few casts, I heard her bellow, "I got one! I got one! What do I do now?"

"Reel it in!" I yelled.

"I can't. You have to do it." I went wading out there in my pants and got soaking wet. I grabbed the fishing rod from her and began to reel it in, and we had the second fish we needed for dinner. We put on our bikinis and lay in the sun all afternoon, drinking Southern Comfort and relaxing. We had to leave the next morning, so were thankful that the weather was cooperating. It was a memorable and much-needed weekend. Now we had to go and face starting our first year of studying for our new careers.

CHAPTER 7

THERE WERE TWENTY-ONE OF us who began the Nursing Diploma Program that started in September 1982. We were a small group, so became a support system for each other, and shared the ups and downs. Our classmates almost became our family. We laughed and cried together, and we partied together. There were fun times and not so fun times.

Our first "lab" was bed making. The instructors were so particular that it was almost military. Our bed baths needed to be flawless, and our "vital signs" monitoring needed to be without mistake.

We learned to be compassionate, caring, and non- judgmental, and we learned how to relate to one another, as we learned to relate professionally, with our patients. It was a year of huge learning, and stress for me as I continually strived for top marks. How did I do it with three little boys? Well, I sent them all to bed at 7:00 p.m., then I studied and reviewed my daily lessons every night until 11:00 p.m. I refused to study or review on weekends, unless there was a looming exam, scheduled for the following week. I did not want my desire to become a registered nurse to take away from my children. I loved my boys deeply, and I enjoyed doing fun things with them, and spending time with them. They were still my top priority.

LEONA MOVED TO EDMONTON and was busy studying hard to become a lab technician. We communicated by letter and rare phone calls, but she was as busy as I was with her two children. Her family lived in Cold

Lake, Alberta, and she was very concerned about her brother, who was a drug addict, and very ill from his chosen lifestyle. She felt he was dying, and wanted to spend as much time with him as she could. She had also met Martin at the college, and she was quite enamoured with him. Martin proposed to Leona on Valentine's Day, 1983. Their planned wedding date was June 30, 1984, after Leona had graduated from NAIT. Martin was studying to become an engineer and work in the oil field. He was a smart and capable young man, and very much in love with Leona. I was kind of lonely, and with Leona being tied up with Martin and her children, I felt left out. It was a good thing that I was studying all of the time. By the end of the second semester, I was tired and burnt out. Sadly, we had lost two of our students, as the standards were very high, and it was difficult for some to maintain the marks required. I was ready for a holiday.

Louise invited me to meet her family and our mother in Yoho National Park, in August. The plan was to do some camping, hiking, and exploring. My mother really loved the outdoors. She had all sorts of plans as to how she was going to spend valuable time with her daughters and her grandsons. Mom loved hiking and was an active member of the local hiking club where she lived. She had learned all the ins and outs of being a good hiker and outdoors person, and was well aware of how to prepare oneself for a night or two of being lost in the wilderness.

This is the story that my mother, Dale Geils, wrote of her account of "A Night on the Mountain in Yoho National Park"

IT STARTED OUT AS an easy afternoon hike. We left Takakkwa Falls hostel parking lot at 1:00 p.m. on August 15, 1983, intending to hike to Emerald Lake via Yoho Lake, a distance of approximately six miles. We were a group of five; my son-in-law Jim, his son Eric, aged twelve, my two grandsons Jeffrey, nine, and Anthony eight, myself, and their dog Zimby. The children had all hiked many times before, and my son-in-law was an experienced hiker.

The trail climbs steeply for about 1 000 feet, and then levels off to Yoho Lake, a beautiful setting for a wilderness campsite where we stopped for lunch. It was almost 3:00 p.m. before we were on our way again. At the junction, the decision was made to try the trail from Burgess Pass area instead of the more direct route to Emerald Lake. It was a lovely day, and the scenery was truly magnificent. From this trail, we could look over the glaciers of the President Range or down to the vivid turquoise blue of Emerald Lake. All the views were impressive! As we went on, the ascent was steady until eventually, we came to a switchback section amongst some trees—a welcome respite from the heat. I was becoming anxious about arriving at Emerald Lake in time for us to be picked up at 5:30 p.m., as arranged.

As time went on and we continued through a fascinating area with interesting geological formations and a fossil bed, and I noticed that it was taking longer than we had anticipated. There was still no sign of the trail leading down to the lake.

The children were beginning to complain, so to keep them amused, I started calling the bear scare calls that I had learned with Skyline Hikes in Banff. I would yell, "High Up," and the kids responded with, "Low Down, Mr. Bear don't come around."

Jim and I found a broken sign, which could have been the trail down to the lake according to our map. The trail looked overgrown, as if it had not been used in a long time. There was considerable distance to go, and the children were getting tired. If we did not come across a more definite trail to the lake, we could climb up to Burgess Pass and then down into the town of Field. We would be late, most likely finishing our decent in the dark, but I had my flashlight and it was a good trail. We scouted a bit farther on without finding any further indication of a trail, so decided to head downward to Emerald Lake. It was a decent into a veritable nightmare!

The light bush soon gave way to dense, impenetrable forest growth, impeded by insurmountable barriers of deadfalls and windfalls. Any semblance of a trail was soon lost, and we were continually climbing over fallen trees, or crawling under them on our bellies. The progress was extremely slow. When we came to a steep gully, we had to make our way down to the creek bed, in hopes it might be easier going. It was steep and slippery. Jeffrey slipped and fell into the creek. Although the creek was not very deep it was deep enough that he got soaking wet. We used extreme care while we were trying to pick our way through, but that did not prevent increased number of falls between the five of us.

We were all getting exhausted! Especially the children, who were so tired they were literally dragging their feet. I knew we wouldn't be able to continue much longer and that it was only a matter of time before one of us would be seriously hurt. It was no longer feasible for us to make it out that evening, so we needed to find a place to spend the night before darkness came. We climbed up a bit from the creek bed and we were fortunately able to find a small slightly sloped area that was large enough to hold us all. We cleared out a small space, collected some wood to start a fire, and soon we had a blazing fire burning. We settled in for the night.

Jeffrey was wet, so I stripped his shorts off and used my sweatshirt as pants for him, by putting his legs through the sleeves. I gave him my spare pair of socks, put his boots back on, and dried his clothes by the fire. We had little food, but none of us had an appetite. Eric, with his incredible energy, regarded the whole thing as a great adventure. He went back and forth to the creek, filling up our water bottles, and was a willing helper with anything that needed to be done.

So we took stock of our position. We did have enough food and water, and were sure we could make it out the next morning without mishap. Jeffrey was the one I was most concerned about, as he had on only a summer jacket and was pretty miserable. Anthony had on a good sweater, over his T-shirt, and was wearing long pants. He never complained, and was a very good little hiker. So began the night. Neither Jim nor I felt sleepy. I had made a bed for the two little ones close to the fire and covered them with a flannel shirt. I sat beside them, rubbing their backs when they began to shiver with the cold. I wrapped heated stones in my swimsuit, and put them between the two of them, and they did manage well enough. I did try to encourage the dog to sleep between them, but he was so big and awkward that he just got in the way.

The three of us—Jim, Eric, and I—barely slept all night. We took turns tending the fire, and occasionally one of us would lie down and doze off for a few minutes. I had shorts on and my legs were cold. Eric was sick, and I could not get the boys to drink any liquid.

Finally, it became light enough to see. Thank God, there was no frost during the night, but it did get quite cold. I knew my daughters would have contacted the authorities, and they would come looking for us at first light. After consuming a modest breakfast of oranges, a peanut butter sandwich, and some cheese and a cracker, we drank some warmed liquid that I had heated up by dropping hot pebbles in a plastic cup, we doused the fire with water and headed out.

We slid our way back down to the creek bed again, and went on for a short distance only. We were forced to climb up into the trees when it became impassable. We continued in this manner, picking our way slowly over endless logs until we'd come to a steep gully or other insurmountable barrier. Then we had no other choice but to head down to the creek again.

I soon realized that far from renewing my energy, my night in the open had left me drained. It was an effort to continue to climb over logs and debris, my body felt like lead. Eric lost all his pep and kept lying down, saying, "I want to rest. I just need to sleep for a few minutes!" He needed us to urge him on, and Jim and I could barely urge ourselves on. I could tell that Jeffrey and Anthony were worn out. How long could we continue?

I had been blowing my whistle for three long blasts with an interval in between, but I was doubtful that anyone could hear. I was wrong. We learned afterwards that my whistles had been heard, and it was the first indication that the rescue unit had of our whereabouts.

About 9:00 a.m., we watched in frustration as a yellow helicopter flew directly overhead, unable to see us because of the dense bush. Soon after, it came over again, and this time we were down in the creek bed. Despite the frantic waving of shirts and jackets, they failed to spot us again. Still, I found it heartening to know that a search team was looking for us.

By about 11:15 a.m., the creek bed had levelled off and the going became easier. We could splash through the shallow water instead of avoiding it! I was still blowing my whistle when suddenly I thought I could hear a voice. I listened again! I did hear a voice! Jim was up ahead, and I heard him talking to someone. It was the park warden! What a wonderful sight he was! I felt like kissing him! He led us out of the last of the bush and onto the trail that encircles Emerald Lake.

We were almost home! We got to the parking lot and there were my daughters—Louise and Loraine—both looking like they had been crying. We were safe! A sight for sore eyes, they were, and so relieved.

About three weeks later, on another hike on the West Coast Trail, I met the chief park warden of Yoho National Park. He had been in the yellow helicopter that was searching for us, and he told me that if we had continued another 300 yards or so toward Burgess Pass, we would have found the trail leading down to Emerald Lake.

CHAPTER 8

JULY 2, 1984. I will never forget that day. I had spent the weekend in Edmonton at my friend Leona's wedding to Martin. I met her brother, Frank. She'd previously told me of him, that he was addicted to drugs, had spent time in jail for assault, assault with a deadly weapon, and assault with intent. He was the one she was concerned about, when we conversed on the phone during the final months of our medical training. He'd accumulated a lengthy record, tried the methadone recovery program without success, and at one time almost committed suicide.

He told me he walked with a rifle to the end of the road his parent's house was on, intending to shoot himself. He met God at the end of the road. He believed, being raised Catholic, that if he shot himself he would go to hell.

Something stopped him—the meeting with his maker? He had previously been accosted by a man in a parking lot in Cold Lake, who told him he needed to ask Jesus into his heart. He didn't want to listen at the time, but when he met God at the end of that road, he knew what he had to do. He got on his knees, begged God to forgive him of his sins, and asked Jesus to come into his heart and live his life through him. He became a new person. "Therefore if any man be in Christ, he is a new creature: old things are passed away; behold, all things are become new" (2 Cor 5:17 KJV).

His life changed. He quit the methadone program and with the help, of his new-found friend, Jesus Christ, he was healed from his addiction.

He was so excited about it, that all he talked about was Jesus, and the Bible being God's word.

Leona had mentioned this to me before. "What do you think, Loraine?"

"It sounds weird. I don't know what I should think." I hadn't met her brother yet, but when I did, I listened intently to him, throughout the weekend, as he shared his testimony and knowledgeably quoted the Bible. "For God so loved the world, that he gave his only begotten Son, that whosoever believeth in him should not perish but have everlasting life" (John 3:16 KJV). The scriptures he quoted resonated within me. I wanted it. I wanted Jesus to be the Lord of my life, too.

On my trip home, back to Grande Prairie, I was called by God. I had just been through more than three years of grueling education, I had a divorce behind me, and as a person I felt like I wasn't functioning well. My mind was riddled with feelings of guilt, shame, anger, stubbornness, and pride. As I was driving, these emotions were overwhelming, and I knew in my heart that Christ was calling me.

I said, "Wait! Wait! Lord, until I get to Whitecourt. I will pray then." I had to pee, just a bit when I left Edmonton, and I figured that I would be okay for a while.

The urge to void became stronger and stronger. I said, "Wait! Wait! Lord until I can pull over somewhere, like a public toilet or something."

The Lord responded, "You can pull over right here!"

Suddenly my lower abdomen was in excruciating pain! I couldn't drive. I couldn't bend. I could not concentrate on my driving! "Okay, Lord, okay!" I said.

I pulled over to the side of the road. There was a clump of bushes alongside, and I ducked in there and relieved my bladder. What a relief!! The pain was gone.

I went a bit farther into the bush and began to pray. I asked God to forgive my sins, and I asked Jesus to come into my heart and live his life through me. In my head, I made a decision to do God's will for the rest of my life, and live it according to how he wanted me to.

It was an amazing, relieving experience. I felt free, as if a huge weight had been lifted from my shoulders. The multiple emotions were gone. I was free of their complications, and I could not wait to get home to Grande Prairie and tell somebody about it.

> That if thou shalt confess with thy mouth the Lord Jesus, and shalt believe in thine heart that God hath raised him from the dead, thou shalt be saved. For with the heart man believeth unto righteousness; and with the mouth, confession is made unto salvation. (Romans 10: 9–10 KJV)

Believe and receive. That is what I did, there on July 2, 1984 at about 4:00 p.m. I began my new life in Christ. That's why that day is unforgettable.

The rest of the drive was a bit of a blur. The next thing I remember is quickly going to tell my friend Bev about what Christ had done for me. I was so excited I just couldn't stop talking about it. Now, along with the studying for the final exams of my nursing diploma, I felt driven to read the Bible and to get to know my new friend, Jesus Christ. I read and read. If I wasn't studying for my exams, I was reading God's word and praying. I prayed for everyone and everything, and experienced the growing closeness between myself and Jesus, my Saviour. He was like a friend, there with me all the time, to comfort me, guide me, tell me what to do, and tell what to think about. It was awesome! I loved it.

Soon my children began to play on my mind. I prayed for them constantly, that they would come to that place of salvation, and that they would share in my experience and give their lives over to Christ as well. I prayed for the rest of my family, my delightfully dysfunctional family. I wanted my dad, mom, my sister Louise, her children, and my brother David, even my step mother, Vicky, and my stepsister, Melody, to know what it was like to have Jesus Christ dwell in their hearts by faith. I wanted them to feel what it was like to be rooted and grounded in love. I wanted them to know the love of Christ. I prayed for Melody's children, Micah and Bethany, that they would meet Jesus sooner, rather than later, and I prayed for my ex-husband, Dave, and his parents and sister and brother. I wanted the best for them all, and I knew that the most solid way for them to achieve that would be to entrust their lives to Christ, and take their direction from him.

Cordell, my baby was the first one. Only five days after me, my little six year old son, bowed his head, folded his little hands and prayed, following my lead. He asked God to forgive his sins, and asked Jesus to come into his heart. He believed that Jesus is God's son, and that he died on the cross for his and everyone else's sins. He might not have had the full understanding, but there were tears in his eyes at the time and he truly meant what he prayed. I was thrilled! My son was the first person who was lead to the Lord through me and my willingness to share the love of Christ with others.

I remember being so excited that I phoned Frank. He was absolutely ecstatic. I told him about both of us. He was high on Christ that night, I tell you. After that I would call him every time I wanted to talk about something Bible related, or share some exciting experience with someone. He was a willing and enthusiastic listener.

My infatuation grew deeper with each phone call, and I wanted to see Frank again. I was off for the month of August, so I went to Edmonton. Frank, myself and the boys went to the observatory, and the three pyramids full of tropical flowers. It was a fun weekend, and the more I got to know him, the better I liked him. August disappeared quickly because I was in the process of moving to Manning, Alberta, where I had been accepted to start working as a registered nurse.

CHAPTER 9

SMALL TOWN NORTHERN ALBERTA was the place to be. Rural hospital nursing was what I wanted to do. Manning served an entire territory littered with oil rigs, logging camps, and hunting and guiding outfitters. Opportunities for adventure were there, and readily available. Emergency, maternity, medical, and long-term care were the departments that I was responsible for. The hospital consisted of nineteen inpatient beds as well as an emergency room, an ICU, and one labour and delivery room. The patients had a broad range of medical needs, requiring significant knowledge and organizational skills.

There was a rather large elderly population, so many heart attacks and other cardiac events occurred. One month there were nine. There was a newborn delivered about once a month, and because of the long-term care patients, the hospital was almost like a community centre. Visitors were allowed at all hours, and it was not unusual to have a card game of some sort in progress. None of us really minded; I certainly didn't because it helped introduce me into the community. It was an agricultural area and had been for a long time. Farm accidents were not unheard of, and I got to know many people and hear many interesting stories.

Manning was so far north that it was almost at the border of the Northwest Territories. My sons and I had found an old farmhouse to rent, several kilometres from town, seemingly in the middle of nowhere. The house was an old one, with a dugout for water supply. The water was an ugly brown, and the dugout was like a little swamp full of bloodsuckers and other nasty creatures. The boys had a great time digging around in the swampy water, catching them and happily showing them to me. Uugh! Swamp creatures are not my cup of tea. The house was riddled with mice, and at night you could hear them running around in the attic. We had a cat, named Randy, who managed to decrease the mouse population a little bit.

We also had a dog named Teddy. He was a big dog but friendly and playful. When we got him, he was just a puppy, and I trained him to come when I sang a song, "Me and my Teddy Bear, have no worries have no cares. Me and my Teddy Bear just play and play all day." He would come running every time he heard it. Teddy was a good buddy. He would accompany the boys to the school bus every day and be waiting there for them when they came back home. The driveway was about 500 metres long, and we were lucky enough to live amongst a huge herd of elk. They were always within close proximity of the driveway, so the boys threaded their way in and out of them as they walked to and from the bus. The elk were harmless, but I was also aware that they were, in fact, wild animals and I was happy that Teddy was always with the boys when they were outside.

Manning was a time in Jeff, Mitch, and Cordell's life, as well as mine, that we grew to better know our Lord Jesus Christ. Cordell had been baptized with me while we were still in Grande Prairie. Jeff was baptized the summer of 1985, in the Manning River, and Mitchell had so far not chosen to take that step. We were fortunate enough to find a wonderful small community church with a congregation that really loved the Lord, and an exemplary pastor, who was knowledgeable in the word and had a desire to encourage and enrich his congregation. We also made some good friends. My friend, Lindy Lou, and our families spent quite a bit of time together, swimming in the river and exploring. Lindy had three children, close to the same age as mine. Her husband was away much of the time because he was working farther north in a camp. She had the desire and the time to explore. We became good friends as we both sought the Lord for his will in our lives and became active in the church. We both sang with the music team, and Lindy taught Sunday school. It was a fun time, but I felt I wanted to move further in my career and work in a larger hospital, gaining more experience in maternity and emergency. I was still a new grad and eager to learn more.

* * *

I SECURED A JOB on the maternity/surgical ward, at the Peace River Hospital, so I bought a small house on the flood plain of the river. The house had recently been totally renovated. It was a large lot, with the back of the lot at the bottom of a cliff. *A good climbing cliff for the boys*, I thought.

It didn't take the boys long to make friends. I kicked them outside to play, and about an hour later, Jeff came in with another boy. "Hi Mom. This is Luke. He lives over on the next street."

"Hi Luke," I said, smiling at him. He was tall and gangly with a shock of unkempt black hair.

"Luke is going to show me some stuff," Jeff hollered as the two of them ran out the back door. As it turned out, there were many children in the neighbourhood close to my sons' ages. Walking around, exploring, and looking for the children, I met a kind elderly man who had a big productive garden, not far from us. He loved working in his garden and was willing to sell us his fresh vegetables. The Peace River Valley was renowned for its fertile soil, and there were several market gardens along the river.

Wayne and his wife Anne, were a wonderful elderly couple, who lived close to us and appeared to be quite friendly. They were interested in their new neighbours and invited us for tea. They knew Luke, and both loved children. Luke had brought Jeff over and introduced him to them. Wayne was an old cowboy, who enjoyed being called "Cinch," and Anne was very soft-spoken and kind. When we went over for tea, I shared what I was doing, and that I was looking for someone to look after the boys while I went to work. They quickly offered to care for them until I found a more permanent arrangement.

Luke wanted me to come over and meet his mother, Joyce, who was a single mom just like me, and worked at the local library. Luke had a little brother named Nick, the same age as Cordell. Nick was a nerdy-looking kid with red hair and glasses, but he and Cordell became fast friends and either my children were at Joyce's house, or her children were at my house. Joyce, Wayne and Anne were close friends, and they all attended the local Baptist church. Between the two families, I felt my children were in good hands when I had to go to work.

I started working at the Peace River Hospital soon after I got settled and had the boys organized. It was larger than Manning, with a full maternity ward and the ability to do caesarean sections. There were lots of deliveries because it was the main hospital that served the smaller outlying rural communities as well. It was not uncommon to have fourteen babies in the nursery at one time, so it was a great opportunity for me to learn. When I was unsure about something I had to deal with I always thought it best to ask.

"Pat," I approached my supervisor, "Maryanne seems to be bleeding quite a bit. Can you just come and look? It seems like more than normal, but I'm not sure."

"Massage her uterus, you idiot, and I'll come and look at her shortly," she yelled.

I ran back to Maryanne. I massaged her uterus as I had been taught, and the bleeding seemed to slow down somewhat. A few moments later, Pat came to check her. She grabbed my massaging hand, removed it, and took over, showing me how to do it properly. Then she called Doctor Torrence to come and examine her. When Dr. Torrence arrived he started giving orders.

"Start an IV drip, and give her some oxytocin," he demanded.

Pat got everything together and started the IV. I stood back and watched.

"Code blue. Code blue," I heard over the loudspeaker.

"We'd better go," Pat said, so I followed her down to where the code was. "Loraine get me a 5-cc syringe!" she yelled. I didn't know where they were, so was frantically looking around. Others were there, doing their part in the code, and I'd been chosen to fetch. I didn't know where anything was. This poor man was dying, and I felt I wasn't helping.

"Loraine, will you please leave," Pat demanded.

I walked out, relieved, but feeling very useless. I sure hadn't been much help. I knew that, and that was why she'd asked me to leave. I went back upstairs to maternity and checked on Maryanne. I was more comfortable in an area where I had more knowledge.

I WAS STILL A new Christian, as it had only been a bit over a year since I had made the choice to dedicate the rest of my life to my Lord Jesus. I was full of the joy of the Lord, and felt I was a woman of strong faith. I liked the energy that emanated from the various Pentecostal Assemblies that I had previously attended, so found the Pentecostal church in town, and we began to attend. It was great! I loved the live music, the boys could go to Sunday school, and I began to meet other people. Pastor Bishop was intent on helping me to settle in. I loved sitting around singing praise and worship songs with someone playing the guitar and several people present, joining our voices and musical talents. It was a time when I was very aware of the presence of the Lord. We would pray for each other, and others, and talk about our obligation to share the gospel message of salvation with people we knew, or even with those we'd just met on the street or during our daily activities. We would share testimonies and talk about what an awesome God we served, and how kind he was to us.

I met Molly there. She was a beautiful and talented guitar player and singer. She had an adventurous spirit, and her and I became friends. We spent quite a bit of time together, and I met some of her friends. Richard, a handsome charismatic Christian, who very much reminded me of Frank, also became my friend. These people were what was then termed as "Charismatic Catholics." They attended the Catholic Church and had asked Jesus to come into their hearts. It was a small group, and their intent was to minister to the Catholics and introduce them to a closer relationship with Jesus.

I felt my mission field was with my family, my patients, and my co-workers. I talked about Christ, my relationship with him, other people's relationship with him, and I shared the miracles that I had heard of, and some of which I even experienced. I tried to get a Bible study going within the hospital. The hospital was kind and accommodating. I was able to use the conference room for our first meeting. Several people said they would be delighted to come, and I was quite excited about the whole idea. My friend Leona was still a big part of my life, and I continued communicating with Frank, her brother. Both of them were very encouraging, and thought the Bible study idea was a good one. They said they would pray for me, and it, and with my blind faith, I went ahead. It was to be perfect. I got a lovely white table cloth, organized Bibles, workbooks, tea, coffee, and even made some baked goods to offer to the attendees. I studied the Bible daily, and knew what I wanted to share. I was well prepared. I remember sitting at the end of the table, praying and waiting for someone to show up. It was quiet and very peaceful. I waited and waited, for about two hours. No one came. The tendency to be discouraged was very real.

As I packed everything up to take home, I remember feeling disappointed. No, I am not going to be discouraged, I thought to myself. Perhaps everyone was just busy. But it tells me in the Bible:

> Go ye into all the world, and preach the gospel to every creature. He that believeth and is baptized shall be saved; but he that believeth not shall be damned. And these signs shall follow them that believe; in my name shall they cast out devils; they shall speak with new tongues; they shall take up serpents; and drink any deadly thing, it shall not hurt them; they shall lay hands on the sick, and they shall recover. (Mark 16:15–18 KJV)

Those are the very words of my Saviour Jesus Christ. The next day when I went to work and asked people why they didn't show up for the Bible Study. Everyone had an excuse. I decided I wouldn't try again to start a Bible study with my colleagues.

A FEW DAYS LATER, when I went into work, there was a young lady, in her thirties who was about five months pregnant. She started to bleed, and a miscarriage was imminent. I was to look after her on a one-to-one basis. Her name was Darlene, and she was critical. Because I was to be with her most of the day, I took the opportunity to share the salvation message with her. She was an avid listener and seemed to enjoy hearing about it. I was encouraged. Her baby had no heartbeat, so they were just waiting for her to pass the fetus. She had an IV and was being closely monitored by me and others, including Doctor Torrence. She started to have labour pains. The stillbirth was beginning, so she was moved to the delivery room.

It wasn't very long after that the stillborn was delivered, and she started to bleed profusely. Another IV was started, and the doctors were doing what they could. I was praying for her, praying for the bleeding to stop, as I stayed with her. All of a sudden, I looked and there was literally a river of blood, pouring from her vagina. I had never seen so much blood! It was pouring out onto the bed, onto the floor, and almost to the door. Maria, my nurse colleague, who had lots of experience, noticed Darlene had stopped breathing. Maria checked her. No heartbeat! She jumped up on the table beside the patient and started giving her CPR. The attending supervisor called a code, and it became chaotic. Again, I was the fetcher.

"Loraine get another two bags of saline. Call the lab! We need a cross-match! We need to give her some blood." I came back with an armful of normal saline bags. All I could do was pray, begging God not to let her die. She had a husband and a five-year-old daughter. Maria's CPR worked and Darlene started breathing again.

The doctor made a snap decision. "We have to take her to the OR and do and immediate hysterectomy! We have no choice. Call the OR and get them to prepare it—and make arrangements for her to be transported to Edmonton by plane after the surgery."

Maria and I quickly prepped her for the OR. The stretcher came to transport her down. We stayed to clean up, and by then, it was near the end of my shift. I did not know Maria very well, but I was impressed with her nursing knowledge and ability. She was always cheerful and happy, and radiated confidence. She was the kind of person that brightened up a room when she walked into it. She made people happy, and I wanted to be more like her.

About a week or so later, Darlene returned to the Peace River Hospital. She had apparently coded twice in the OR, but came back both times before being sent to Edmonton. Now she was on the road to recovery.

"Hi! I see you're back," I said as I walked into her room. "How are you? Do you remember me? I was with you when you delivered, and when you took that downturn."

"Yes, I do remember you. You were praying for me, weren't you?"

"Yes! Yes! I was."

"I think that's why I'm alive," she said. "You didn't want me to die, so I didn't want to either."

I was awestruck! God had listened to my desperate prayer, and answered it. My faith was strengthened that day. When I went home, I read the passage in the Bible that says, "And whatsoever ye shall ask in my name, that will I do, that the Father may be glorified in the Son" (John 14:13 KJV). I pondered on it for a while and phoned Frank. We had a long discussion about the whole situation, and his faith was also strengthened.

I experienced many things during my time at that hospital, working in the maternity ward. It was so busy that often the doctor did not make it to the deliveries in time. During the months that I worked there, I delivered several babies on my own. It almost became routine.

One night shift, there were three ladies in active labour. There were two labour and delivery rooms. The doctor on call was with one patient, there was a registered nursing assistant with another patient, and I was responsible for the other one. She and I were in her room, due to the fact that the delivery rooms were full. It was her second delivery, so I felt lucky. All the doctors and nurses said the second delivery for pregnant moms was always the easiest. I checked her; she was progressing nicely. The one poor doctor available was running from room to room, trying to manage all three. My patient felt the urge to push. I checked her again, and it felt different. I didn't think she was fully dilated. I wasn't sure what to make of it. I thought I would wait a bit.

She wanted to push again. I heard her holler, "I have to push!" and she did. I knew it was time for the baby this time, so tried to get the doctor. She was busy with her own patient pushing. All of a sudden, my patient pushed again, and out came the baby, bum first. It was a breech delivery. It came out fast and started crying immediately.

I thanked God that nothing was wrong. It was an easy breech delivery, and the baby was uncompromised. I knew what to do. Fortunately, the mom seemed to be doing okay as well. I put the baby on the mother's chest, and clamped the cord and cut it. I assessed the mother's uterus and her bleeding. She seemed fine. I pressed the call button, and another registered nursing assistant came in and took the message to the doctor. The doctor said she would come and check on everything when she was finished. Three babies were born within thirty minutes. Wow!

I ENJOYED THE ACTUAL maternity nursing that I experienced at Peace River Hospital, and I loved living there. It was beautiful right there beside the river, and I had made a wonderful friend, Molly. Molly and I seemed to have many things in common, the largest commonalities being our thirst for God and our thirst for adventure. I loved my relationship with my friend Jesus, and at that time, I felt that my faith was strong, and I believed that "I can do all things through Christ which strengtheneth me" (Phil 4:13 KJV) because that is what the Bible tells me.

When Molly called me up and asked me if I wanted to canoe down the Peace River with her, from Dunvegan to Peace River, I was more than eager to do it. Unfortunately, the Peace River was in flood, but neither of us was deterred. She was an experienced canoeist. I thought I was, but I was dreadfully wrong. The plan was for me to take Jeff and Mitchell with me in my canoe, and she would take Cordell in her canoe. We drove to Dunvegan, unloaded our canoes, organized life jackets and paddles, and launched. The river was high—and fast. I got in first and started paddling out into the river. There was a huge wave in front of me, and all I could think of was how much fun it would be to ride that wave. I paddled out, or tried. I was unable to control the canoe even though I was paddling as hard as I could.

Molly was busy getting herself going, and she assumed I was an experienced paddler and kind of ignored me. I was working hard, but could not get the canoe to face downstream. The current was too strong, and I really had no idea what I was doing. *Oh well,* I thought. *God will help me. All I have to do is ask.* I was totally unafraid. I knew that "God hath not given us a spirit of fear; but of power, and of love, and of a sound mind" (2 Tim 1:7 KJV).

Molly, finally, looked up and saw what was happening. "What are you doing, Loraine?" she asked in alarm.

"I'm trying to paddle out to that big wave so we can have some fun riding down it."

"What? Are you crazy? Here, let me help you." She paddled out to me, then went around to the side of the canoe that was facing the wave. "Don't you know how to do a J-stroke?"

"No, what's that?" I'd never heard of it before.

Molly stayed on the outside of me, paddling, and herding me in toward shore, talking calmly to me. "I thought you knew how to paddle a canoe. How about we all get in one canoe? We can leave the other one here, and I'll come and pick it up tomorrow. I'll take the stern, and you can take the bow. The boys can all sit in between us."

"Okay," I agreed, sensing the urgency in her voice. Looking back on it now, I was indeed an idiot.

My dad always said, "God looks after his idiots."

Molly probably hasn't thought much about it, but I do believe she saved some lives that day. I asked my sons if they remember how they felt. Mitch said, "I was terrified!" Both Jeff and Cordell agreed. I look back on that incident and I am ashamed and greatly humbled. It was great that I considered myself a woman of great faith, but it was a dangerous and irresponsible thing to do. The trip down the river that day, with all of us in one canoe, did turn out to be an enjoyable experience in the end.

CHAPTER 10

I LIKED PEACE RIVER, but the North was getting into my blood. I had an urge to go farther north. I loved the cold and the snow and was constantly mesmerized by the northern lights. To me, the North was excitement and unexplored wilderness. In the spring of 1986, I contacted the administrator of the hospital in Hay River, right up inside the Northwest Territories. I thought I'd like to live up there. We arranged for an interview, and he was kind enough to arrange accommodation for me and the boys so I could come for that interview. As a nurse, I had always got the jobs that I applied for, so I didn't think this would be any different. I put the boys in the back seat and our luggage in the trunk. It was a long trip, and I saw only a couple of other people on the road. It was very remote, but beautiful. I remember looking at the waterfall, near Hay River. It was still very frozen and very stunning! This was what I wanted—pristine wilderness to live in and enjoy.

With the three of them in the back, they were always fighting. "Don't touch me! Shut up! You're stupid! Are we there yet? When are we going to get there? Leave me alone! Wahhh! Jeff hit me! Wahhh! Cordell kicked me! Wahhh! Mitch pinched me."

I managed to put up with this continuous conversation and keep them from killing each other on the way up. Coming back home was a different story. I wanted to think. *Do I really want to move up there? I am becoming bushed. Is this a healthy way to bring up my children, in Northern isolation?* I had lots on my mind, and my patience was wearing thin.

Cordell was always a little shit disturber, and he and Jeff got into fisti-cuffs. We were on a gravel road in the middle of nowhere. I slammed on my brakes. "Get out!" I told Cordell.

He sat there.

"Get out right now!" I hollered at him again.

He started to cry and got out of the car.

I took off, leaving him standing there at the side of the road, all alone, in the middle of nowhere.

"Let me out! Let me out. I want to be with him!" Jeff hollered as he started to kick at the windows and doors.

My plan was to drive out of sight and let Cordell sweat a bit. Maybe then he would behave. I was shocked at Jeff's reaction.

Mitch was sitting there just stunned.

I drove a bit farther out of sight and stopped at the side of the road. I waited a couple of minutes, then turned around and went back.

Cordell was sitting at the side of the road, just sobbing his little heart out. I felt bad, but I told him he could get in if he behaved. He got back in the car, and the boys sat there in silence. The rest of the trip was much less stressful for me.

When I got home, I was able to ponder moving to Hay River. The administrator wanted an answer with the week. I literally grabbed myself by the scruff of the neck. *No! I think I'll move to Vancouver. I at least have family there, even if they are my delightfully dysfunctional family.* I talked to my dad, and he told me to see about finding a job. He and Vicky had sold their house in Squamish and bought a house in West Vancouver in the British Properties. He said we could live with them until we got settled.

I contacted the Lions Gate Hospital in North Vancouver, spoke to the administrator, and was advised to send my resume. I did and was called almost immediately to arrange for an interview. I just felt that I needed to be sensible. My boys needed to live in a larger centre where there were more opportunities. I needed to make an effort to get the North out of my mind.

It was summer, so I could take some time off work to go for my interview at Lions Gate Hospital. The boys and I would make a trip out of it. We'd camp along the way, stay at Dad's, have the interview, and then I'd decide whether or not I should move to Vancouver. I bought a big two-room tent—one room for the boys and one room for me. I also acquired a camp stove—what a luxury! We would drive through the Okanagan, take our time, and enjoy the trip. I was looking forward to it.

When I got dressed for the interview, Dad looked at me and said, "You look good, and I have a feeling that you'll get the job." I knew in my heart that I would. Interviews never bothered me. I was confident, and I knew that I was a good nurse.

I went to the interview and was offered a full-time position in gyne-cological surgery. The nursing supervisor asked, "When will you be able to start?"

"If I start in mid-October, that would give me the opportunity to move here and get myself settled, and get the boys into school," I said. Dad and Vicky had told me that they would care for the boys while I worked.

I think it was very stressful for my dad and Vicky to have myself and the boys living in the house with them. My dad was not young. He liked family, but not living in such close quarters. They were quite busy with caring for Melody's children, as well. Micah was six years old, and Bethany was two. My dad loved Bethany dearly. She was the light of his life. She had lots of energy and sometimes was quite a handful.

DAD ALWAYS TOLD ME, "I was there when she was born, and she was so little, I could fit her head in my hand. I remember her looking at me with those big brown eyes." I knew he loved her.

My dad was also very proud of Micah. "Micah is six years old, and he knows how to play chess. There is this big chess board at the Park Royal mall, and he goes there and plays chess for hours, with grown men. They like to play with him because he gives them a good run for their money, and he's only six!! He is a very smart young boy."

"Man, your boys sure fight," he would state with authority. "They never stop! Punching the shit out of each other constantly—I've never seen the like of it! One of these days, they're going to kill each other," he would remark with alarm.

Vicky didn't seem bothered by the boy's wrestling all the time. She had been raised with 4 brothers, so she knew about young boys, and their continuous fighting. She loved to feed them because she loved to cook for someone who appreciated her great cooking.

We lived there for approximately two months, until I got accepted into a co-op housing unit at Mount Seymour, in North Vancouver. It was a three-bedroom apartment on the main floor. It would do for the time being. The rent was subsidized by the provincial government, the housing complex was filled with new residents to Canada, and there were lots of children for the boys to play with. There was bush around and many secret places for the boys to explore. The children's favourite pastime was fishing. It was Jeff, Mitch, and Cordell, who introduced the neighbourhood children to the art of catching trout, and every time they went fishing, there was a trail of other children behind them. The boys loved North Vancouver.

We lived there for several months, but after a while, the thin walls and hearing the couple next door fighting all the time got on my nerves. I felt like I needed more space, so I looked for somewhere else to live. I found the top of a house to rent on 6th Street in North Vancouver. It was a beautiful place. I enjoyed having a yard to sit in, and a bit of privacy. I even had a patio! It seemed worth the $1 200 per month that I had to pay. I got an additional job doing private duty nursing to supplement my income, and another casual position in the emergency department in Squamish. My full-time rotation on the gynecological surgical ward, offered me two day shifts, two night shifts, and then five, six, and seven days off. These were the days that I would do the extra shifts of my other two jobs.

I liked the money, and it helped me pay back my student loan and my car. I was greatly in debt. My fridge was always nearly empty, but the boys did not go without meals. I cooked everything from scratch, and they ate as healthy and cheap as I could manage. Feeding them properly was always a challenge. Sometimes my dad would come over and look after the kids and bring some food. He was always ragging on me about how terrible I was with managing money, and comparing me with Melody. He felt she was much better at money management than I was, but I believe Melody did not have the expenses that I had.

Unfortunately, people with a lot of money, like my dad, cannot comprehend what it is like to not even be able to afford a cup of coffee, or to drive over to his house to visit because I didn't have enough gas. It was a very tough time in my life. I remember the calls because I could not pay all of my bills when they were due—threatening to take my car, my furniture, or anything else of value. One day, I drove my car over to the Royal Bank.

"Can I speak to the manager, please?"

The receptionist asked, "What is it about?"

"Can I just speak to the manager, please?"

The manager came out. I handed him my car keys, and said, "Here is my car. I can't afford the payments, so I am giving it back to you. I am tired of you calling me all the time!" Well! I tell you, did that cause a stir! All of a sudden I was Miss Important Customer!

"Oh no!" the manager exclaimed, "We can't do that! Come into my office, and we can see what we can do for you."

I was pissed off! I did not want the car because it cost too much. I believe my payments were about $300 per month. When we actually sat down and discussed it, he somehow, was miraculously able to cut my payments.

"$150 per month," he said. "How is that for you? Will it work better?"

I was shocked that they could do that. Why did they have to bug me all the time? Why didn't they offer that to me before?

"Sure, I think I can manage that." I signed the papers, and it was a done deal. *Whew!* I thought, *I'm glad.* I really did like my 1985 Ford LTD.

CHAPTER 11

MY RELATIONSHIP WITH FRANK, Leona's brother, was growing in leaps and bounds. We talked on the phone daily about the Lord and how good he was to us. Frank would share scripture after scripture with me. I would look them up, and we would talk about them together. I was quite devoted to my Christianity, and read and studied the Bible on my own. The boys and I went to a Pentecostal church on Broadway Ave in Vancouver. I enjoyed our time there. Jeff, Mitchell, and Cordell went to their respective Sunday school classes, and I attended adult Sunday school. I learned more about God's word, the Bible, and met many lovely people there.

I joined a hiking club in the North Shore and met several people who liked to hike as much as I did. I met some nice young men and women, but we all were just friends. At least I had people to do things with, and talk to, about something other than work. I did work many hours, so I spent most of my spare time doing some exploring around the area with the boys. North Vancouver was a beautiful area, and there were many places to go.

One day, when I was home, working in the kitchen, Jeff came running frantically into the house, yelling, "Mom! Cordell got hit by a car and I think he's dead!"

"Where?"

"Come with me," he yelled. I ran up the street after him, where I saw Cordell lying on the ground. I could see a fire truck, and Cordell seemed to be stirring a bit. I felt a sigh of relief. *He's not dead!*

A fireman knelt next to him and looked up at me. "Is this your son, ma'am?"

"Yes,"

"Well, the ambulance is on its way, and so are the police," he told me.

As I turned around I noticed a woman standing on the sidewalk crying her eyes out. There was a man beside her trying to offer her comfort. Her car was parked at the side of the road. A police car arrived, and the police-man quickly looked at Cordell, noticed he was already being tended to, and walked straight toward the crying lady. I could hear the siren of the ambulance approaching. When the ambulance arrived, Cordell was put in the stretcher and whisked away to Lion's Gate Hospital. I informed them that I would meet them there and ran home, phoned Dad to watch Jeff and Mitch, jumped in my car, and raced up to the hospital.

When I arrived at the emergency department, I could hear Cordell crying in pain. My heart was breaking, and I was trying to get a grip on myself. I did not know what injuries he had. I tracked down the doctor, who I actually knew. He was a young resident. I can't remember his name, but he seemed a nice enough fellow.

"Can't you give him something for pain?" I pleaded.

"No, we have to establish if he has a head injury before we give him something for pain. We are just waiting for an x-ray to be done," he explained patiently.

Tears freely flowed from my eyes as I watched my baby suffer. I didn't know what to do. I couldn't even pray.

Cordell had been skateboarding with his brothers. He flew down a steep alley out onto the street and an unfortunate woman smacked him with her car. I don't remember her name, but she was the one that was bawling her eyes out. She came up to the emergency department with a gift for him.

I felt sorry for her, and I knew it was not her fault. North Vancouver is extremely hilly and back alleys were not safe places to learn how to skateboard.

Cordell didn't have a head injury, so after that was established, he was given sedation and some morphine for pain. He fortunately did not break any bones, but he had a severe bruising injury on his hip, and the bleeding had caused a blood clot to form. He had to remain in hospital for several days.

My boys liked to wrestle. Jeff and Cordell got in a fighting match, and Jeff gave Cordell a swift kick in his injured hip. Cordell was in excruciating pain, and ended up back in the hospital for several more days. I tell you, that summer of 1987 was stressful.

ONE OF MY PATIENTS was an elderly lady who was quite ill. She should have been on the medical ward, but due to a shortage of beds, she ended up on the gynecological-surgical ward where I worked. I talked to her each time I went to work, and watched her steadily go downhill. She had ascites—her skin was yellow, her eyes were turning yellow, and she was starting to retain water around her middle. I was worried about her because her level of consciousness seemed to be getting lower.

One night shift, because I had the time, I went in to visit her even though she really wasn't one of my patients. She was barely responsive when I talked to her. I thought, *I never shared the gospel message with her! What if she dies? I must tell her!* I had learned that even sometimes when people are not seemingly conscious, they can hear you when you talk to them. I had my Bible with me, and I read her the salvation scriptures. "For God so loved the world, that he gave his only begotten son, that whosoever believeth in him should not perish, but have everlasting life" (John 3:16 KJV), and "For God sent not his son into the world to condemn the world; but that the world through him might be saved" (John 3:17 KJV). Also, "If thou shalt confess with thy mouth the Lord Jesus and shalt believe in thine heart that God hath raised him from the dead, thou shalt be saved. For with the heart man believeth unto righteousness; and with the mouth confession is made unto salvation" (Rom 10: 9–10 KJV.) I shared some other scriptures with her too.

"Do you want to ask forgiveness for your sins," I said to her, "and do you want to ask Jesus to come into your heart and live his life through you? If you do, squeeze my hand, and I will pray with you."

She squeezed my hand.

So, I prayed. I prayed for her healing, and I prayed for her salvation because I knew that was what she wanted. I had to go and attend to my other patients, so I left to go and do that. After that night, I was on five days off.

When I came back to work, I listened to report, and this lady's health had miraculously improved. I went into her room. She was sitting on her chair, and she looked like a totally different person. The yellowed colour of her skin was gone, and the yellowness of her eyes had disappeared. She was bright and alert.

"Hi!" I said in astonishment. "Do you remember me?"

"I sure do," she said.

"Do you remember me praying with you, and you asking God to forgive your sins, and asking Jesus to come into your heart?"

"I sure do," she repeated.

It really was a miracle, and I was high on the Lord. That night, I phoned Frank and told him about it. We had a great conversation, and I loved him even more.

ONE OF THE RARE times that I actually heard an audible voice from God occurred soon after that incident. I prayed and asked God to give me Frank for a husband.

He said to me, "I will give you Frank for a husband, but you must be patient."

I knew that patience was not one of my virtues, and I just felt that God was at work on me in that area. As Christians, we are constantly a work in progress.

In February 1988, the following year, I received a phone call from Frank. "Hi there," he said. "I'm in beautiful Valemount, BC at a conference. How are you?"

"I'm fine!" I returned.

"It's so beautiful here, and the conference is awesome, and I really feel the presence of God, and I phoned you because God told me I was supposed to marry you and I was wondering if you would marry me?"

I was silent—stunned! "Well," I said, "if God told you, you were supposed to marry me, I guess I'd better marry you. Yes, I will marry you!"

We were both so excited about the idea, and we talked forever, making plans, and what our life would be like together. I felt it must be God's will, and thought that if I married Frank, everything would be wonderful. I thought that if I married him, it would be the kind of life I wanted. He was quite the evangelist and was always sharing God's word, praying with people, and things were always good. I wanted to be a part of that, and I pictured us ministering together. I even thought we could minister as a family. I was excited about the whole thing. My desire was to do God's will and share the gospel message freely, without constraint.

* * *

FRANK AND I WERE married on July 30, 1988. Frank had come to visit me in Vancouver, and I had come to Cold Lake, Alberta, where he lived and where we were planning to reside. He met my family and friends, and I met his family and friends. Everyone seemed to think it was a good idea, and things were going well. Leona was my bridesmaid, and Frank's good friend, John, was his best man. Pastor Randy from the Cold Lake Christian Centre married us. This was the church that Frank had become a member of, and it was the church we would be attending after we married.

It was a wonderful ceremony. The presence of God was felt by everyone. My dad and Vicky attended, and Dad said, "Everyone that was there had light bulbs in their eyes."

Everyone was happy, and the music was all praise and worship. We sang, "I love you Lord," which is an awesome song and one I still hold very close to my heart.

We didn't really go on a honeymoon, but Frank's dad lent us his boat, and we took it across Cold Lake to go camping. It was a beautiful camp-site, right in the middle of God's amazing creation. There was no one about, only Frank and myself. We had a lovely fire in the evening and sat there discussing our lives, and what it would be like to live as husband and wife—and minister together. This was what I wanted. That night, it started to rain. We had planned on staying two nights, but by the morning it was stormy, and the rain was just pouring down. The waves on the lake were getting larger and larger. We figured we should pack up and leave while we still could.

As we made our way across the lake, the storm intensified. Frank didn't have that much experience driving a boat. It was a simple motorboat that his dad had used for fishing. Cold Lake is a large lake and there are times when the waves can become as high as five to ten feet. They were about five feet high as we launched into the water. Frank was doing okay at first, but then as the waves got higher and higher, he began to struggle to keep the boat under control. The wind was howling, and the rain was pouring down.

I remembered the story in the Bible when Jesus' disciples were in the same situation.

> And he was in the hinder part of the ship, asleep on a pillow: and they awake him, and say unto him, "Master, carest thou not that we perish?" And he arose, and rebuked the wind, and said unto the sea, "Peace be still." And the wind ceased, and there was great calm. And he said unto them, "Why are you so fearful? How is it that ye have no faith?" (Mark 4:38–40 KJV)

Anyway, I prayed and asked God to protect us, calm the storm, and guide Frank to the shore. We could see the shore by this time, not far away. We had a brief reprieve as we got closer to the dock. I jumped out of the boat into the water to grab the rope and help pull the boat in. The water was up to my chest. I hadn't realized it was so deep. With the waves, wind, and rain, it was difficult.

"Help me do this, Lord. Please? In Jesus' name," I pleaded. God gave me strength, and I was able to assist Frank to get the boat to the shore and dock it. No sooner had we secured the boat, when it was like all hell broke loose! The wind picked up, the waves got bigger, and the rain poured down even harder. We were thanking and praising God all the way home. We both prayed and thanked God for our home, and its warmth and comfort. That is how our marriage started.

THE FIRST TIME FRANK struck me was about two months after we were married. It wasn't that hard when he hit me on the arm, but I was a bit surprised by it. We were having a lively discussion, and I don't even think we were arguing. I guess me being the opinionated person that I am rather annoyed him.

I remembered Leona saying to me once, "With Frank, it is either Frank's way or no way." I put the incident aside and didn't think about it for quite some time. I was working at the Cold Lake Regional Hospital and was rather busy with work, and he was working for a moving company, moving furniture. I knew he was tired because he worked hard, physically, and he was putting in lots of hours.

I was quite broke, but was thankful that there was no mortgage payment on the trailer we were living in. Frank and his dad had worked very hard putting an addition, with a bedroom and a bathroom, on the trailer. Jeff and Mitch were sharing a bedroom, and Cordell had his own room. It was a small trailer for the five of us, but I figured it would be okay as long as we kept our personal relationship with Jesus first and foremost in our lives. I was happy, and the boys seemed to be settling in. I enjoyed the church and our involvement in it. The boys began to go to the church youth group, and Cordell was enrolled in the Christian school, run by the church.

Much time was spent with our friends, getting together and singing and praying. My friend Irene would come over and play the guitar, and pleasure us all with her beautiful voice. I liked to sing as well, and ended up as part of the music team. Our life was full, and I enjoyed sharing the gospel as much as I could while I was at work.

I did get into trouble once, when I shared with an older fellow about fifty, who was in with pancreatitis. I told him about Jesus, and his love and forgiveness, and he chose to ask Jesus into his heart. I prayed with him, and I prayed for his healing. He was high on the Lord after that—so confident that he had been healed that he signed himself out of the hospital. I did try to talk him into staying, but he wanted to leave. A few days later, my supervisor, Barb got a call from a hospital in Edmonton asking about him. Apparently, he was really sick, and I guess he thought he was healed, but he wasn't. I never saw or heard from him again, but I don't think he lived locally.

I was again working on the maternity/surgery ward, which had always been my favourite area to work. I remember assisting my sister-in-law Brenda to bring her son Jared into the world. It was an awesome experience that helped me get to know her better. When it came to my friend Leona, though, my supervisor Barb told me that I was too close to Leona, and she sent me off to the surgical ward. I remember being upset at the time, and so was Leona because we were both hoping that I would be on when she went into labour.

Leona was working as a lab technician at that same hospital. She had two baby boys, fifteen months apart, and she had been married to Marten for four years. Most of their married life had been spent in Cold Lake. She also had Julie and Curt from her previous marriage, so she was quite busy. I did feel like she was part of my delightfully dysfunctional family then, and I still do now. She is my best friend and has been now for many years.

FRANK AND I WENT on several trips with others in a group from our church. Frank was in much demand to share his testimony because he was very good and interesting to listen to. We went to the small town of Schell Lake, Saskatchewan. Cal was a fellow Christian at our church, and a friend of ours who was originally from there. His parents still lived in Schell Lake. We spent a couple of days there, staying with Cal's parents.

When the service was held, many people attended. We sang praise and worship songs, taught God's word, the Bible, and prayed for people both for salvation and for healing. I prayed for a young lady who had diabetes. I lay my hands on her for healing and bang! She fell to the floor. I will never forget the sound of her head hitting the floor. I was shocked! I knew she had been "slain in the spirit." I had heard of it before but never thought I would do it—actually, not me, but God through me. She woke up, unhurt and laughing. She felt she had been healed from her diabetes. It was a memorable event for me, but it has never happened since.

Some of the people in Schell Lake were very poor. A lovely young family invited us over for tea, after the service. They lived in a small house with mattresses on the floor to sleep on, and one couch. We were sitting on their couch talking, and I was reminded of my great desire to have a fur coat. I had recently visited Bonnyville, and walked into a store that sold fur coats. I tried on a white one—female mink, the fur was. I felt beautiful and rich, and this was a period in Christian history that prosperity was being preached. God wanted us to prosper, we were told by the sermons that were preached, by the Pastor of the church - and how would we prosper? We would prosper by giving more and more money away.

These people gave us $20 to help with our ministry. I did not even want to take it, but I was encouraged to because I should not deny these people the blessings that would accompany the gift that they so willingly gave. Their gift was accepted by all, and as I walked away, I thought, *Oh yeah, I'd look great in my white fur coat that cost $7 000, sitting on their worn and tattered couch, accepting their $20 donation.* I didn't buy that fur coat, even though I had seriously considered it, nor have I desired a fur coat since. It was a successful trip, and all of us came back to the Cold Lake Christian Centre and shared our many testimonies. Frank became even more in demand. He had lots of invitations to come and speak.

At home, he continued to be somewhat abusive. He was having difficulty with the boys and would beat them up when he fought with them. My boys never struck back. Once, he was outside having a fight with Jeff and I heard him say, "You know I could kill you." He punched Mitch in the face when he was only twelve, and all Mitch did was cry—and bleed from the nose. Frank got into it with Cordell more than once, as well. I did nothing, and I regret it to this very day. I was trying to be a submissive wife, as I was taught by sermons at our church, and as I thought the Bible told me to be.

Things were not going well. One fall, we were cutting birch trees on the property for Frank to sell for firewood. I had a rope on a log, trying to drag it out from the pile. I gave the log a jerk. The log flew up and the end of it hit me right in the cheek. It whacked me pretty hard, and my cheek swelled up and became black and blue.

At church the following Sunday, Frank's very good friend Blair came sidling up to us and said, "I see you have given your wife a lesson in submission." I denied it, and so did Frank. He didn't do it, but I didn't think it was very funny, nor did Frank. I never liked Blair—he always seemed to have an ulterior motive for everything. He and his wife were considered pillars of the Cold Lake Christian Centre, but that didn't make me like him any better.

Frank and I were invited to Taber, Alberta, to speak at a church. Generally, he would share, and I would take part however I could to be helpful and supportive to him. That night, while in the motel we were staying in, we were arguing about something, and Frank actually started pushing me around so hard I fell. I didn't want it to deter me from the evening of sharing and preaching at the church we were at, so I put the incident aside and focused on God and what he wanted us to accomplish that night. There were people who would need prayer. There were people who would need someone to talk to. There would be people who wanted to ask Jesus into their hearts and live their lives differently. I had to pull myself together and get on with it.

Being a nurse, I was used to listening to people and their problems. One gentleman, a deacon of the church we were speaking at, shared with me that he was molesting his daughter. He did not want anyone to know, but he asked me to pray for him. I prayed with him, and for him, and he asked God to forgive his sin, and he asked Jesus to come into his heart. He really did not want to sin any more. He knew it was wrong, and he wanted me to pray for strength for him to resist this temptation. I shared this scripture with him: "Submit yourselves therefore to God. Resist the devil, and he will flee from you" (Jas 4:7 KJV). After I shared that, I prayed as he asked, and I could see in his face that he was excited about his new-found relationship with his Savior, Jesus Christ.

CHAPTER 12

BECAUSE FRANK HAD A previous criminal record, and because he was having many requests to speak both in Canada, and the United States, Pastor Randy told us that it would make it easier for him to cross the border if he could get his record sealed. He suggested that we apply to have it done. We felt that this was what God wanted us to do, so we went through the bureaucratic process of filling out the appropriate papers and finding the needed documentation. It took about two years in total, but after that, Frank was free to travel in and out of the country as he pleased.

IT WAS 1991, AND there was a change happening in our relationship. We had been married for going on three years, and we continually talked about going to Bible school. As we were both avid fans of Kenneth Hagen, we seriously considered Rhema, his school in Tulsa, Oklahoma. Frank and I wanted to get into ministry and go full force for God.

We were aware Jeff was growing up and planning his future, and soon would be gone from home. Mitch and Cordell still had a couple of more years before they would graduate, and Cordell spent most of his time at his best friend Ryan's house.

Things were changing in the church. Pastor Randy's wife, Jill, was doing more teaching, and it seemed like the whole attitude of the congregation began to shift. As a congregation, we began to follow Kenneth Hagen and Kenneth Copeland quite closely. Gloria Copeland, Kenneth's wife, was a very attractive lady whose blonde hair was always well-styled, and she always wore beautiful clothes. They had a television ministry that many of us watched. The women of the church were involved in running the Christian school, teaching Sunday school, and organizing banquets. They were also responsible for assuring that the church was clean and accommodating for anyone who wanted to drop by. The congregation was growing by leaps and bounds, and there was even a short-lived attempt at a local television ministry within the Cold Lake and Bonnyville area.

I remember a particular evening service, when I looked around at the women in the congregation. Many of them had bleached their hair blonde and wore it like Gloria Copeland. They all had on beautiful, stylish clothes, and I thought, *They are all turning into Gloria Copelands!* I knew the preaching style was changing. There was much about women and how their devotion to God and/or Jesus should play out. A "good Christian woman" would love and support and be obedient to her husband. She would always look perfect and behave perfectly, in every situation. She would serve and serve and continue to serve, and put her relationship with God, through Jesus, at the top of her priority list—even above her family.

I believed this until one day my friend Emma told me she had wanted to have a party for her son's fifth birthday. Pastor Randy had approached her and advised her that she was needed for ministry in the church that day and should cancel her birthday party plans for her son. Emma was an awesome woman who loved the Lord. She taught at the Christian school, taught Sunday school, and did many other things to support the church. I am sure she gave most of the hours of her day to that, not leaving many hours left for her family or herself. I was not in agreement with Pastor Randy's advice, but Emma was. She agreed that she should cancel her son's birthday party.

That incident spoke to me, and I began to see what was happening. It was slow and insidious. I was devoted to reading my Bible, so I knew what God wanted of us. I did not believe he wanted people to be used and abused and taken advantage of. There became a hierarchy with the frequent banquets. The "lower" people, or the ones not considered mature enough to minister, were expected to be servants to the "higher, more mature" Christians. Much was demanded of the women in the congregation. The men's time was consumed with meetings, planning, and organizing ministries.

Much of the focus was to bring in money for the different ministries that were in the planning process. Pastor Randy gave himself a raise to $5 000 per month and gave Jill a salary of $1 200 per month. I felt it was rather excessive, but it was voted in by the members of the church. Frank was a member of the church, but I had not yet made that commitment. I was beginning to have many concerns about the changes that were being made. I approached Pastor Randy about my concerns in a congregational meeting. I was informed that I had a "rebellious spirit."

My friend Leona's son Joshua had been diagnosed with a severe congenital heart defect that combines four structural anomalies of the heart. She was devastated Joshua would have to undergo more than one open-heart surgery. She was advised by some very mature Christians in our church that she should have enough faith that God would heal Joshua. This kind of thinking had begun to penetrate people's attitudes. She and her husband Martin were going through a very rough time trying to deal with Joshua's diagnosis, and it led her to feel abandoned with no support from the people she thought were her friends. I questioned it, but I thought that perhaps I did have a rebellious spirit, and the ones who thought that she just needed to have enough faith were right.

Frank expected me to read my Bible all the time or to be praying or talking to people. I felt I was with people all the time, and sometimes I just wanted to let my hair down and relax. I loved to watch *The Golden Girls* on television. I would laugh so hard I would get tears in my eyes. Frank would come home and catch me watching the show, turn the television off, and chide me for wasting my time. He would often come home from work and go straight into our bedroom and pray in tongues. Sometimes, he wouldn't even join us for supper. One evening, when he was in a particularly foul mood, and I tried to encourage him to join us for dinner, he got so angry he took the spaghetti that we were eating and threw it all over the floor. I was stunned at his action, but patiently, saying nothing, I cleaned up the mess. The boys were embarrassed and I was mortified.

It seemed like our relationship was becoming very tense. I was not sure what to do about it, so I just read my Bible and prayed as much as I could. Things continued to deteriorate within our relationship, but I continued to hope for it to improve and trusted God that He would get me through these difficult times. I thought that if Frank did not have to work so hard, physically, he would not be so disrespectful of me. I knew he was tired, and I knew his job of moving furniture made him sore everywhere. I hoped that once we went to Bible school, things would change. One night, though, I was fast asleep and I woke up with him punching me in my back and saying, "I can't sleep! I can't sleep! Why are you keeping me awake?"

I was so shocked. I couldn't believe he was acting like this! I had a few bruises, but wasn't really injured. *Is this abuse?* Then I thought about my friend Lindy Lou in Manning. Her husband was abusive, and he frequently beat her up. She told me he'd even broken her nose once when he punched her, and he'd fractured two of her ribs another time when he was beating her. *No, this isn't really abuse.* So again, I set the incident aside and tried not to think about it anymore.

* * *

IN MAY 1992, I was determined to be what God wanted me to be and do what he wanted me to do. I wanted to attend Bible school and learn how to minister properly. In November, Frank, myself, and Cordell arranged to go on a mission trip to Mexico with a team from our church. There were young people as well as a variety of adults. We were to leave on Christmas Day and return January 6, 1993. Everyone was extremely excited about the trip. I began to prepare for our mission trip by spending more time reading the Word and in prayer. I made the effort to spend time with Christian friends and acquaintances to learn more, and to become more confident in my ability to be effective as a missionary. I had wanted to be a missionary from the time I was a kid. I remember I said to my mom one day, "When I grow up, I want to be a nun."

She replied with, "You can't be a nun. You're not Catholic." Well, that put quite a damper on my ambitions then, but now I had the chance.

We arrived at Mexico City airport on time, but no one seemed to be able to speak English. Praise God! When we came out of the baggage area, we saw a gentleman holding a sign saying, "Frank - Halleluiah!" He was a sight for sore eyes—and he could speak English. We were picked up and taken to the apartment where we'd be staying. We needed a rest, as it would be a busy trip.

The Mexican people were friendly and helpful. I noticed the importance of children to the Mexicans. They loved them, and they were always being hugged or held. Many looked dirty and unkempt, but most of them looked happy and healthy. Not so for animals, though. There were stray dogs everywhere, looking starved and sick, with sores on them. Some of them walked with a limp due to swollen and infected-looking legs. Some of the men even seemed to take delight in being cruel to the dogs. You could observe them kicking the dogs, purposely on their sore legs, then laughing. Others would shoot them in the face with pellet guns. I had a hard time with that. Out and out cruelty to animals was prevalent, everywhere you looked.

Poverty was very real, when we began to look around. Yes, there were child beggars on the streets everywhere. We were told not to give them money, and apparently there was a revolutionist camp that the children were from. The revolutionists were farmers who asked for more money from the government. The government refused and threw them into jail as political prisoners. The people at the camp were families of the farmers, and they were demanding that they be released from jail.

We were shown the homes that people lived in. Some had no walls, or only three walls. Some never even had roofs! The scenery was lovely, but tarnished with garbage and rubble. One has to witness such poverty to believe it.

On December 28, 1992, we were picked up by bus to undertake an eight-hour drive up the side of a mountain to our final destination. The driver got lost, and didn't know his way around Mexico City. We all thought that was pretty funny, but he eventually found his way. We were driving along fine until our ears were traumatized by a loud, horrible whistle. It was the brakes—they were shot. We cautiously continued until we came to a town where a mechanic was able to look at the bus. It was about a two-hour job, so Frank and Alex, our interpreter, got together and began to preach the message of salvation. It was exciting! Six people were led to the Lord. Alex got their names and addresses so he could pass them on to Amistad Christiana, a church in Mexico City, so they could be followed up. Cordell and the other young teenagers busied themselves with a basketball game with some young-looking Mexican children and teens.

Once the bus was repaired, we continued our drive up the mountain to Huautla, through the pouring rain. There was a thousand-foot drop to our right, and a thousand-foot cliff rising to our left. The road was narrow and winding, and the windshield wipers did not work. The driver had to stop frequently to wipe the water off the windshield so he could see. All of a sudden, the bus stopped. The road in front of us had washed out.

"I think I can get the bus by on the left here," the driver informed us, "but you should get out, in case I don't make it through." We got out of the bus, and I could not believe what he was going to do! There was a mere trail, not even wide enough to accommodate the bus. We got together and prayed for his and the bus's protection as he moved slowly forward. We were all watching with bated breath, praying for his success. Slowly, cautiously, he wormed his way across the washout. He made it!

"Yeah!" We all cheered. Praise the Lord! Halleluiah! We walked across the narrow path, uneasily looking down at the thousand-foot drop. We arrived safely at 5:30 a.m.

December 29, 1992, I woke up well-rested, and had a hot shower, followed by a long walk with two other members of our team. We came upon a badly crippled little boy, and gave him a few coins. We did pray for his healing, but he did not understand, and we did not have our interpreter with us. The rest of the day, we walked around town, handing out tracts and invitations for people to come and see the film *Jesus* that would be shown that evening. Everyone was very receptive to the gospel and wanted to come to the movie. Every day we found three or four people who wanted Jesus to be their Lord and Saviour. Some days it was even more.

The next day we planned on going to another small village of about 2500 people. In the morning, we jumped into a Mexican Chevrolet and drove through the mountains, admiring the beautiful scenery. When we arrived, we began to walk the streets praying, and sharing God's love to the villagers. There were at least seven people who gave their life to the Lord, and many others who came forward for prayer, and healing. God was reaping his harvest in Mexico.

January 1, 1993, was to be the big day. Frank and I were scheduled to go to Teotitlán to preach in the jail. Frank had previously spent time in jail, so was quite excited about being given the opportunity to go and share God's love and message of salvation. It was a successful mission. At least twenty-three people gave their lives to the Lord, and many came forward for prayer and healing. I met my first murderer there. He had eleven more years to serve for murdering his wife. He asked Jesus into his heart and truly wanted to live his life according to how God wanted him to. He was a genuine convert, and it made me very aware of the fact that God loved that murderer just as much, maybe even more, than he loved me. It gave me a new perspective on the gift of salvation and God's extensive mercy. Over two hundred people gave their lives to the Lord on that trip to Mexico. It was an amazing, eye-opening experience, and a trip I will never forget.

CHAPTER 13

ON JANUARY 14, 1993, when I met with my program manager, she demanded my resignation. I was shocked, and I didn't know why she was demanding it, but she told me I could have done more with some of my patients. It was a new job, with a different type of nursing, where I'd been visiting people in their homes. I felt hurt and angry, and was convinced I was wrongfully dismissed. I approached the union, but they were unable to help me because I'd only been there ten months, and I was still on probation and could be let go at any time.

My life spiraled downward, as did my relationship with Frank. He was angry with me and told me I deserved to be fired because I was a lazy bum, so he stated that he was not going to give me any money for anything. I didn't know what to do. I still had to feed my children and pay for other expenses. I knew I could probably collect unemployment insurance, but I also knew it would take about six weeks to get any money from them.

It was the middle of winter, and Cold Lake was very cold. I was pretty good at cooking from basics, but I still needed to be able to buy the basics. We lived three miles from town. How would I get gas for my car? I went to church with Frank the following Sunday, and went up for prayer. I had to learn to trust the Lord for my needs. I needed wisdom, guidance, and direction because I didn't know what to do. I had a bit of money in a savings account, but it wouldn't last very long.

Frank's father, a kind and gentle man, lived very close to us, and I believe he was aware of what was going on. He would commercially fish for whitefish in Cold Lake, and generously share his catch with us. We lived on fish, homemade bread, and garden produce that I had frozen the previous summer. We lived on part of a quarter section of land that was marked out by gravel road. Every other day, I would go and walk around the back roads for miles, collecting bottles and cans so I could put gas in my car and buy some basics like milk, butter, flour, sugar, and salt. I managed to feed my children adequately, but I don't think that they were aware of how I got the money.

Frank generally went over to his parents for dinner, and rarely ate with us. He would just come home after he'd eaten, go into our bedroom, and pray in tongues. He became more and more abusive. He would get angry at nothing, then start choking me and chucking me around the bedroom. My children could hear the ruckus, and they would cry, but they never interfered. I was glad, in one way, because I did not want them to get hurt.

My sister-in law Brenda phoned me one day and asked me to come over because she wanted to talk to me. She said, "Loraine, the Holy Spirit has told me that Frank is abusing you and using physical violence against you." Brenda always claimed to have discernment of the spirit. "I had to deal with that with Lawrence [Frank's brother] and I tell you, he had to be delivered of it, and so does Frank. In the meantime, you have to do whatever you can, to avoid being beaten up by him."

I listened to her and thanked her. I wasn't sure what to do, so I thought I'd go and speak to Pastor Randy about it.

"Well, if you were more submissive," he said, "he wouldn't have to beat you up!"

I was shocked at his reasoning, but thought perhaps he was right. I was beginning to fear Frank, though, and I would run away from him or disappear when he drove down the driveway. I certainly hadn't expected this when I married him.

He became quite cruel to me. "You are like something that crawls out from under a rock. I am so ashamed of you. If you divorce me, I'll give you $10 000 and that is all."

Divorce had not even entered my mind. I didn't want to talk about it, to anybody because I was ashamed. Frank was a really good preacher, and many people came to know the Lord through his testimony. I didn't want people to be aware of his actions because then, perhaps, they would not come to that place of salvation and ask Jesus into their hearts. I was protecting God, Jesus and the reputation of the gospel.

I look back on it now and I think, *How stupid is that? God created the world, and raised Jesus from the dead, so we human beings would have a bridge to heaven. Do I think God needs me to protect him?* It was a dark time in my life.

JEFF WAS GRADUATING FROM high school, and he was almost nineteen. He had his driver's licence, and was a good driver, as he had taken formal lessons to learn how to drive properly. One day, he asked me if he could borrow my car to go out for the evening. He'd borrowed it before, but Frank didn't want me to lend it to him.

"It is my car," I said, "and I will lend it to him if I want to." I told Jeff he could have it.

Frank was furious with me and he beat me up pretty bad. He choked me until I couldn't breathe and yelled at me as he spit in my face. He picked me up and threw me across the room. It was the worst beating I had ever received from him.

I knew, as a registered nurse, that in an abusive relationship, the abuse does not get better; it only gets worse. That night I slept in the living room on the couch. I spent some time in prayer and read my Bible for comfort.

The next morning, Frank got up early to go to work. I got up early as well and confronted him. "If you slap me, punch me, choke me, or abuse me in any way again, I am going to charge you with assault. You have a criminal record for assault. Your file will be re-opened again, and you will go back to jail and lose your privilege to cross the border freely. Remember, I'm the one who went through all of the rigmarole to get your records sealed. I mean it, Frank. Don't you ever, ever touch me violently again. Is that clear?"

"You wouldn't," he said.

"I swear on this Bible that I will."

He was upset and stormed out of the house. Things settled down for a while, and he was at least decent to me.

* * *

IN THE BEGINNING OF May, my friend Emma contacted me and told me that the children in the church's Christian school had won first prize in the regionals for their radio. They were going to Flagstaff, Arizona, to compete in the internationals. She was to go with them, but we needed to fundraise.

What an exciting venture, I thought. *Well, we need some money to do this. What can we do? What can we do? A walk-a-thon! We can do a walk-a-thon! Those kids need exercise anyway.*

"What a good idea!" Emma told me. Let's get started." We contacted the local radio station, and the local newspaper—then we all began to walk the streets to get sponsors. It was a competition! We knew that wasn't really the point, but it was fun to compete, and we all did well. We collected $3 000 to help them on their way. A garage sale was the next lucrative venture—$700 was made that day.

Emma asked me to go with them as a supervisor. She'd spoken to Pastor Randy, and he was in agreement. Frank didn't want me to go, but I thought it would be fun. Cordell, Katy, Cory, and Olivia would be going, and Emma and I would be there to supervise the children. The plan was to meet up with another Christian school group from Caroline and travel with them, in their van. I didn't really like the idea, but I thought I should try to be more positive. I just hoped that it would be a good crew, since we had to spend twenty-four hours a day with them for about two weeks.

In 2 Corinthians 12:9, KJV, it says, "God's grace is sufficient for thee," the "thee" being me—not really, it was Paul, but it applied to me as well, and I needed all the grace I could get from God. We met with the other people from Caroline and began our journey down the road.

Trevor was driving with his wife Vanessa accompanying him in the front seat. It was an old van, adapted to accommodate many children. Benches had been built all around the back, and that is where the children all sat. Emma and I and one of the students shared the back seat.

We loved to look out at the scenery, and it was lovely!! As we drove, we were treated to seeing buffalo, elk, deer, ducks, and porcupines. We made our way to Yellowstone National Park, with thinking that we'd camp at one of the campsites there. I had never been there before, and I knew the children would be amazed at what was there to see. By the time we arrived, it was so dark we decided to stop in at the hotel by Old Faithful. It was far too expensive, but the gentleman at the front desk gave us directions to a parking lot where we could park for the night and get some sleep in the van. It was pretty crowded, but we did all manage to sleep.

It was beautiful and sunny when we woke up, so we went to check out the steaming, bubbling pools, and the paint pots. Old Faithful erupts every 72 minutes. I guess that's why it is so appropriately named. We were all reminded of how awesome our Creator God is. Some people have the audacity to say this earth, with its marvellous, creative formation was an accident. I guess our job as Christians is to tell the truth to everyone who will listen.

We continued on through to Utah, admiring the desert flowers. They were so bright—fluorescent almost. I liked the desert. It had its own magnetic beauty.

We arrived in Flagstaff about 2:00 in the morning, and Vanessa found us this filthy, dirty motel room that we were all to share. I was not impressed. Vanessa seemed to do whatever she wanted, with no consultation with the others. She was only 21. How was she to know everything? Her husband, Trevor accommodated her every whim, and I found that extremely annoying. I felt like beating the crap out of her. I went for her! Stupid bitch!

Emma grabbed me, held her arms around me, and would not let me go. Vanessa was, of course, totally unaware. Emma knew me, and with the help of God, held me back, guided me away from the group, and let me verbalize my frustrations to her instead of beating up Vanessa. "You are not behaving like God's daughter," she reprimanded me.

I knew I wasn't, but I didn't care. I'd had enough of Vanessa.

Emma said, "Just avoid her, and let me deal with her. I think that would be better since she annoys you so much." I was happy with that, as Emma was much more tactful and patient than me.

The next morning, we registered at Northern Arizona University, and then took a trip to the Grand Canyon. It was awesome! The children amazed me with the way they related to each other, just like brothers and sisters, and they didn't even fight! They were entertaining and pleasant, and I really enjoyed being their chaperone. We were all glad to be at the university where we were staying, and noted that the dorms were much cleaner and more pleasant than the filthy motel. The stay at the university was enjoyable and educational.

The kids did reasonably well. Karen, one of the girls from Caroline, placed fifth in the dressmaking category, and fourth in the artistic painting that she submitted. I was proud of them all. When the awards were complete, we left for home, with an anticipated stop in Las Vegas.

We arrived about 12:30 that night. It was exciting for the children and us. There was a steam bath, and a Jacuzzi, and we were in a gaudy but elegant room. That night, even though it was late, we decided to take a swim in the rooftop pool. The next morning we got up and did some exploring. Pornography littered the streets. "Don't you kids even look at that stuff!" Emma demanded. There were flowers and fountains and statues everywhere. The whole area is like a fantasy land.

Cordell was tempted by the gambling, and every time he went past a slot machine, he was compelled to drop a coin in, in hopes he would win. Of course, he never did, but he got pretty sneaky about it and managed to continue when my back was turned.

When we left Las Vegas, our goal was to get to Great Falls, Montana. Vanessa wanted to drive all the way home. What a joke! She was still pissing me off with her stupid ideas. When we arrived in Great Falls, we found a decent hotel that had some available rooms. It was a Best Western, and of course Vanessa wanted us to find a cheaper place. We drove all over without success. I finally spoke up and said, "Look, this is a waste of valuable sleep time, and propane, it is ridiculous, just to save a couple of bucks. Let's find a hotel and go to bed." We went back to the Best Western and spent the night.

The next day we were anxious to get home. Trevor asked Vanessa to drive the van so he and Emma could organize the finances for the trip. "I could drive the van," I offered. "I've done it before, pulling a trailer, and I certainly know how to drive."

"No," both Vanessa and Trevor said.

"Vanessa can drive," Trevor said.

"Oh, okay, I just hope she knows how to drive while hauling a trailer," I returned. Then I took my spot in the back seat, and pouted. I was angry. She was 21, how could she have the experience that I had driving? However, I decided I wouldn't argue. Everyone was a bit anxious to get home.

Vanessa had not even driven for a kilometre when the trailer we were pulling began to fish-tail. It was windy and flat, and we were on a divided highway. The fish-tailing became more and more pronounced, so she panicked and slammed on the brakes. We slid across the highway and began to roll.

"Jesus help us!" I hollered.

The van went over, and over…

The first thing I saw when I came to was a big guy who looked like a truck driver pulling out the windshield glass with his bare hands. There was complete silence.

"Is everyone but me dead?" I asked myself.

The big truck driver was shouting, "Is anyone injured? Is everyone okay?" The silence continued until Vanessa started to cry. She was hanging upside down in the seatbelt in the driver's seat, and Trevor was also upside down. The van was in shambles!

Slowly, the children in the back started moving around, saying, "I'm okay. I'm okay." None of them had been wearing seatbelts, and the back of the van was totally destroyed.

Cory had landed on my head when the van rolled. Emma's glasses had flown off her face and the lens was stuck solidly between the widow and the door. She had banged her head and did not feel well at all. Ambulances arrived and insisted on taking us all to the hospital to check us out. I was ever so glad we were inside Canada because I was not sure any of us had insurance for injury in the United States.

The drivers kept asking, "Does anyone have neck pain or chest pain?" I was quite concerned about Emma. As we were being transported to the hospital, I began to feel the chest and neck pain. Cordell was crying because his arm hurt so much. I feared that his arm might be broken.

Everyone kept talking about the accident, and I wished they would all just shut up about it. The van was a write-off, and everyone who saw it, and us, was absolutely astounded that we were not killed or severely injured.

I knew in my heart that it was because of my prayer, "Jesus help us!" just before I must have passed out. The Bible states, "Whosoever shall call upon the name of the Lord shall be saved" (Acts 2:21 KJV).

Emma was able to contact Pastor Randy, who kindly informed all of our family members of the accident. He also contacted the Pastor of the church in Caroline, who, accompanied by his wife picked us all up and took us to a hotel that Pastor Randy had organized for us to stay in for the night. Another van was arranged to transport us all back to Cold Lake the next day. I am sure we were all happy to be home. Cordell's arm was not broken, and as far as we all knew no one else had broken anything.

CHAPTER 14

ON JUNE 30, 1993, we went to Edmonton to see Phil Driscoll at *Word Explosion* at Victory Christian Centre. Phil was a talented musician and one of my favourites. His music had soul, and his praise and worship seemed to be straight from the heart. I truly felt part of his devotion to God. He encouraged us all to "Boldly go forth and declare the word of God." Mitch came with me and enjoyed the concert very much. Sadly, though, I felt that Mitch appeared to have a block in his personal relationship with Christ.

The other thing that saddened me was the fact that Victory Christian Centre seemed to be getting consumed by the spirit of greed. There were several calls for donations. One in particular, struck me: "If you have an extra car that you can do without, you could donate it to the church and I can assure you that God will bless you for it." There were three collections that day, and I could tell that Phil Driscoll was not impressed.

I felt the Victory Christian Centre was using Phil to create wealth, and I had noticed that at some other church services there had been more than one collection plate going around. People were donating thousands of dollars to the church—not only Victory Christian Centre but other churches as well. It appeared that a "wave of greed" was filtering into churches that had started out wanting only to share the love of Christ and the message of salvation. I found it somewhat bothersome, but thought perhaps I could be wrong. After all, no one else seemed to say anything about it.

Frank and I continued to travel about, attending social functions, and sharing the gospel message with everyone who would take the time to listen. I felt that I was quite shy and did not interact with people that well. I had prayed about it and asked God to help me with the problem. The more I talked to people, the easier it became to share what I believed.

I'd been having quite a bit of pain in my neck since the van rollover accident, and had been seeing the chiropractor. It was discouraging. An X-ray confirmed two compression fractures on C-6 and C-7 of my vertebrae. I guess those were from when Cory had fallen on my head.

Frank stated angrily," I told you not to go on that trip! Now look at you, going to the chiropractor." It was as if I was sinning or something. I could just choke the bastard sometimes! Oh well, I felt that I was going through a time of trial, when it was necessary that I actually apply God's word to my life. It wasn't easy, but I knew that God would help me through.

Frank began travelling back and forth to Edmonton. He was planning with Blair and others who were in Edmonton to begin working under another pastor who was leading at Victory Church on the Rock. They were encouraging Frank to move there and help them get the church off the ground. Frank didn't consult me or even let me know what he was planning. He had begun to make arrangements to move there and had an idea to buy a trailer and live in it there. He just told me that it was what was going to happen.

Our relationship spiralled downward again. I did not want to move. I hated the city. I didn't even know any of these people except Blair and Cathy, and I didn't like Blair one bit. Frank did not consider me, and continually told me, "Get off your ass and work!"

EXCERPT FROM MY JOURNAL, JULY 14, 1993

I called Cathy, and she explained to me that the Victory Church on the Rock would not be flakey, and would be founded on God's Word. She shared with me about the other churches in Edmonton such as Victory Christian Centre, which was having a "School of Prophesy" and a "School of the Holy Spirit" which is not scriptural at all. She shared with me that in fact, they were falling apart, as was "The Vineyard Church," which was emphasizing God's grace. She felt, obviously among others that the spiritual condition of Edmonton was poor. I could understand what they wanted to do, but I would have liked to be a part of the consultation process.

"I don't want to live in a mobile home in Edmonton! I hate mobile homes, and I hate cities and you never even asked me. This is my life too you know!" I expressed to Frank. "If you insist on moving to Edmonton I want a house, a proper house! We can take out a $30,000 mortgage on this place and use it for a down payment—and easily get a house!" I continued.

He was furious with me, and stated, "Anything I ever want to do, you come against me." "I will never get a mortgage on this place—ever." He makes me so angry. He always says he is going to do this or that and shares testimonies about it in church and never bothers to discuss it with me. It is like I don't even exist. He says, "I am going to do it! If you don't like it leave!" Frank and I had several discussions and/or arguments about moving to Edmonton. However, it did not happen.

EXCERPT FROM MY JOURNAL, AUGUST 1, 1993

Well I will write about the last four days, and how my life has changed so drastically and so quickly. Wednesday night, July 29, 1993, Frank and I had a fight and he beat me up for the last time. It started because I asked him not to unplug the curling iron while I went and picked up Cordell. He jumped off the bed, and ripped it out of the wall and started yelling at me because of the cost of electricity and the fact that it might short out. I apologized profusely and went on my way. He did settle down somewhat. When I came back after Bible study that day, I noticed he had knocked the phone over and it wasn't working. I said to him, "Just in case you are interested, you broke the phone and you will have to get us a new one."

He began to flip out, yelling at me and saying all sorts of things to me. He pushed me around and wouldn't leave me alone. He threw me against my desk, pinned me there and spit on my face several times. Then he reminded me what a bitch I was and told me to stop it.

Stop what? I asked myself. I wasn't doing anything, or saying anything. He was the one doing all the yelling! At that moment, I realized how much he hated me, and how much he really believed what he was saying.

"All you do is sit on your ass all day doing nothing! I work my ass off all day and you don't even appreciate it. You disgust me, and I wish I never married you!" He hauled me into the bathroom, and threw me in the tub and started to smash my head against the tap—he smashed it so hard that it actually bent the tap downward. I did not feel pain at the time, and I think that is God's grace. I felt like I was going unconscious, and he let me go, and left the room. Later, he "humbled" himself and begged me to forgive him. "I can't believe I acted like that!" he pleaded. "I couldn't sleep, and I was so tired," he continued. I did forgive him and told him so, and suggested that he go to bed.

The next morning I was sitting in bed on the couch, where I had slept the previous night, drinking my coffee. I remembered what I had said to him the last time he beat me up. I had sworn on the Bible that I would charge him with assault, and screw up his chances to go preach down in the United States.

What can I do? I asked myself. If I don't charge him with assault, he will beat me up again … and again … I knew about spouse abuse. He is a good preacher, I thought, and so many people have been led to the Lord through his testimony.

I simply cannot destroy his reputation, and God's reputation, and the message of salvation. What can I do, Lord, what can I do? I asked God. I decided to pack up and leave. Frank had gone to work, and I knew I had to be out of there before he came back. Cordell helped me pack, and I gave all of my furniture that I had brought into our home away. I borrowed Leona's truck, distributed it out to the ones who said they would take it and I left.

Cordell was upset, and sobbing. "Mom, you know it is just his job," he said tearfully. My heart went out to my poor little sweet pea. He could not say goodbye to his friends, and he knew his life would change, but he did not know what it would be like.

"I will not put up with physical abuse from anyone! You know it has been *going on almost ever since we married. I don't want you to grow up thinking it is okay – it is not!"*

He was depressed all day, but he was able to pull himself out of it by the end of the day. Cordell was amazingly resilient. He continually astounded me, by his cheerful demeanor, no matter what was happening in his life. We drove as far as Whitecourt, and took a room for the night. Our fifth wedding anniversary was July 30. My plan was to drop Cordell off at his dad's in Grande Prairie and continue on to Chetwynd and Smithers, where my sister lived, and told me I could stay with her for a while until I got myself organized.

* * *

I LEFT CORDELL WITH his father, but no sooner had I driven out of town than a wave of loneliness hit me. I tried very hard not to cry. I loved my kids—my sons were my life. I wasn't sure if I could do this. I was depressed all day and couldn't eat. I drove as far as Chetwynd and got a motel. I had called my dad while I was still in Cold Lake, and asked him to put $500 in my bank account. He did, thankfully, because that is where I got my money to pay for the move. My dad was happy I was leaving Frank, and stated that he and other family members had their suspicions about what was going on.

I checked into my room, went for a walk in the bush, and spent some time in prayer. I love praying; talking to God is so comforting to me. I felt better after that and was thankful for the sense of His presence. Praise His holy name! I arrived at my sister Louise's safe and sound, the following day, and was feeling much better. She was happy to see me, so we celebrated my "escape" with a shared glass of wine.

I had always loved my sister, Louise, but she was also the most annoying and maddening person I'd ever had to deal with—except my dad. She was comforting, caring, and great at offering me wise council. Louise had spent most of her years doing what she could do to improve the world socially. She was an advocate for the community, an advocate for the poor, and supported policies and politics that agreed with her beliefs. As a people person, she had dealt with many situations, similar to mine, with other women, young and old. I was happy to be living with her for the time being, and I felt that God had led me in that direction.

Frank phoned me and I talked to him for a long time. He was high on the Lord, and claimed that he had been slain in the spirit twice and that the Lord had done a mighty work in him. Being slain in the spirit refers to an experience wherein you are so focused on worshipping God that you kind of pass out. When you are seemingly passed out, God does a mighty work inside of you.

He told me, "I vowed before God that I would never yell at you or hit you or push you around again. I love you and I did not realize how much until you walked out on me." He wanted me to come back. He promised to be the best husband ever.

I was sorely tempted but was also very aware of the honeymoon phase of an abusive relationship. I loved him, but I also wondered if his hardest would be enough. I wanted Frank to prove himself faithful—to me and to his Lord, Jesus Christ. I guess I needed some time. I pondered on it. Perhaps in six months or a year, we could try again for a successful marriage. I wanted him to go to Edmonton and follow his heart. We would keep in contact, and I would monitor the situation until I believed, with all my heart, that he would never beat me up again.

On August 3, 1993, Frank phoned me again, begging me to come back. He had gone to Lethbridge for a convention. He told me he wept before the Lord and was totally broken. He promised marriage counselling. He said he knew where he went wrong and would fix it at all costs. He asked me to go to Hawaii with him, and told me he would fly down and pick me up to go.

He was so sincere. I told him I would go back. I called my dad and told him I had decided to go back to Frank. Dad was very angry! He demanded his $500 back and told me, "All I can do is hope for the best, but I tell you, Lorainy, if Frank hurts you again I will kill him!

"I mean it, Loraine. I don't care about prison or anything. I am already old, and I don't care. I won't let him hurt you again!"

My poor dad, I thought, remembering all the things us kids had put him through.

Later that night, I phoned the boys and told them that I had decided to go back. Mitch told me he wanted to stay with his dad and so did Cordell. I was kind of hurt and taken off guard. I advised them to take a bit more time to think about it, but I did think that perhaps it would be best for them.

Frank phoned me again and told me he would not fly down to get me. It was too much money to spend and wasn't necessary. He had plans. He would accept a new job that had been offered to him, which would mean he wouldn't have to work so hard.

EXCERPT FROM MY JOURNAL, AUGUST 6, 1993

I woke up this morning very angry! Last night I was walking and could not understand how void of emotion I was! I was thinking about going back to Frank and moving to Edmonton and I thought, I don't want to do this. Then, I was lonely, and missing my husband. I was angered at my volatile personality. One day I want to do one thing and the next day it is completely different. I was thinking about how none of my friends in Cold Lake had tried to contact me to see how I am doing. I was thinking how everyone was so concerned about Frank—not me. I was thinking about how Blair told Frank that if I didn't come back, he was free to marry again. Sometimes it seems like I don't even exist or that I am just there—like an old couch. I don't want to go to Edmonton amongst all of Frank's friends and start all over. I realize now that I was pressured into moving back and making a decision.

I DIDN'T GO BACK. September 1994 I got my decree nisi from Frank. He had chosen divorce. He got re-married in October 1994 and the following summer, he had a brand new baby boy. I have not seen him or spoken to him since, and I must admit that I do not have any regrets.

CHAPTER 15

WITHIN A COUPLE OF weeks of arriving in Smithers, following Louise's advice, I hooked up with the Bulkley Valley Backpackers, a well-established hiking club. Hiking was my therapy. The more kilometres I put on my feet through the alpine terrain, the happier I was. My first excursion was up the McCabe Trail in the Babine Mountains. There were eight of us, and it was pouring with rain. I didn't care, because the fellowship and exercise were just what I needed. I had decided to leave Mitchell and Cordell with their dad until they graduated from high school. I think it was a good decision because it gave them stability and me some freedom. When they were finished school, they were free to come to Smithers to live if they chose. I would be glad to have the company.

Louise had a partner who had a small forestry contract to plant trees. She felt I could probably be hired and have some gainful employment for the time being. I talked to Les, and he hired me right away. I was looking forward to working with him because it would get me into the mountains, and I would even get paid for it! I wanted to check out the country and do some of the fun things that I'd always enjoyed before I committed to a full-time job.

My dad was going to arrive soon, and I wanted to spend some time with him. He had been busy with his new family for several years, and I had not seen him since my wedding to Frank. I anticipated the three of us sitting around together, having a couple of shots of whisky, and discussing politics. It was usually most enjoyable, and informative, as long as dad didn't over-indulge in his whiskey consumption.

I stayed with Louise in Telkwa for six weeks, then found my own little house in Smithers. I loved my sister, but could only live with her for short periods. She was always trying to convince me that her way was right.

Toward the end of the summer, I was still having difficulty with my separation from Frank. I needed somebody to talk to, so walked into Mountainview Pentecostal Assembly one day, and asked to talk to the pastor.

George Richmond, an elderly gentleman, was about the same age as my dad. He sat and listened to me for quite some time as I told him my story about living in Cold Lake with Frank and the abuse I suffered. He was the only Christian I talked to that told me not to go back. He said, "God doesn't expect you to stay in an abusive situation like that; you need to move on."

I appreciated his counsel and followed it. I began to attend the church, as I needed to be around Godly people and needed to learn how to continue to develop my relationship with Jesus Christ. George and I became good friends, as I found him a wise and patient man who knew his Bible thoroughly, and lived Christianity as it should be lived. I met some wonderful Christians at that church, and I learned more and more about God's word. There was an adult Sunday school class for ladies that I attended, and there were often two services on Sunday, the evening service being full of praise and worship.

I was alive again and began to grow in my personal relationship with Jesus Christ. I enjoyed having my little house to myself as it was conducive to further developing that relationship. I had time to read God's word and pray without being interrupted by somebody else's schedule. It was peaceful there and quiet. I could live in my own routine. I even had access to the Perimeter Trail from my little house.

One day, when I went for a walk around the trail, I was thinking about myself and thinking about God, and why he made me the way I was— rebellious, independent, opinionated, and confident. I knew I would never, ever fit into the confining role of a good Christian woman and wife. I said to God, "God why did you make me like this if I am not supposed to be like this?" I don't recall him answering me, but since that moment, I quit feeling guilty about who and what I was.

In September, I was hired as a casual RN to work in the maternity and surgery ward. The people that I worked with were mostly outdoor people who enjoyed the adrenaline rushes. They did lots of hiking in the summer and river kayaking, as well as taking up skiing when adequate snow arrived in the winter. Many would go on long canoe trips farther north, or explore in uncharted territory for weeks and even months. They were exciting and interesting, and I longed to be a part of their adventures. However, most of them had already established relationships with people, had their own friends, and had already been there and done that whenever I suggested we go somewhere or do something. I felt that I had arrived too late. I had already found my way around on the many trails in both the Babine Mountains and on Hudson Bay Mountain. Sometimes I hiked alone, and sometimes others would go with me. The Babine Mountains were my favourite because they were beautiful, remote, and difficult to access. I purchased everything I needed to hike, backpack, and camp overnight, and made good use of the equipment by going out as frequently as I could.

The rest of 1993 went by quickly. I worked many hours in the maternity ward, as that was where my experience was. I enjoyed that it was a busy place and lots of babies were born there. Because of the experienced pediatrician who lived in Smithers, even difficult deliveries took place at Bulkley Valley District Hospital. When the head nurse told me she remembered when my sister Louise arrived from the Telkwa Pass by helicopter in 1975 to have her first child, it made me feel at home. By January 1994, I had become quite friendly with many of the doctors and nurses who worked there. Julie-Anne had started work, and Bal was hired. There were now three male nurses: Lynn, Wayne, and Bal. They were lots of fun, and I actually looked forward to going to work every day.

Early in the spring of 1994, Melody came to visit. She stayed in Telkwa, and Louise took her on a tour of the area. They drove to Hazelton—an extremely scenic drive. Melody spotted Mount Roche de Boule. "I looked up at that mountain, and I started to cry! And Louise started to cry too! I knew then that I needed to move to Smithers." Melody applied for a position at the hospital and was immediately hired. She had previously worked in the emergency department at Royal Columbian Hospital in New Westminster and had also worked in emergency in Hawaii when she and her husband Wayne lived there.

She had returned to Vancouver when she and her husband separated. Wayne had decided he wanted to marry another woman. Melody was devastated—and angry! She told me, "I went into his office, and nobody said a word as I walked into where he was. I entered his client room and I literally attacked him! I kept punching him and kicking him until I was absolutely exhausted. He never fought back. Then I walked out, feeling better, and he stayed in Hawaii and I went to Vancouver to live."

I admired Melody after she told me that. She was some gutsy woman! She did what hundreds of women feel like doing when they are challenged with that very situation.

As spring turned into summer, Louise, Melody, and I discovered many absolutely stunning landscapes during our exploratory hikes. Ted, one of the doctors at the hospital offered to show me around, and he took me on a couple of the most interesting, but enduring, and difficult hikes I had ever experienced. It was during one of these hikes, that he asked me if I would be interested in looking after his farm while he went to the Caribbean for the winter to spend time sailing his boat.

* * *

I STILL WANTED TO hike the Chilkoot Trail in Alaska. It was the summer of 1994, and as I was working casual only, I thought I would try to take some time off and just do it. My mom was coming to Smithers for a visit, and she was always up for a bit of adventure. She didn't feel she was physically able to undertake the grueling journey, but was happy to stay in Skagway on her own for a few days while Cordell and I hiked the trail. Cordell was more than willing to accompany me. His life-long dream was to be rich, so he decided that he would pan for gold in the creeks and rivers along the way. He purchased a gold pan and a shovel.

I said, "Well, if you want to do that, it is fine, but I am not packing that pan and shovel. You have to do that yourself." We endured the dusty ride up Highway 37 toward Alaska, and got to Skagway, unscathed. We settled into a little motel for the night and planned on leaving in the morning. The next day it was pouring rain. We made our way to the beginning of the trail, and my mom dropped us off then took the vehicle back to where she would be staying.

It was raining so hard, I felt like bailing. Cordell wanted to go, so we headed out through the dripping evergreens toward our first camp. The weather began to clear a bit, then became overcast again, and it rained some more. When we arrived at Sheep Camp, we were pretty wet, but we cooked a hot meal on my little camp stove and settled in for the night. The next morning when we woke up, it was beautiful and sunny. We piled out of bed, had a cup of coffee and some breakfast, packed up, and began hiking again. We had 33 miles to cover in four nights and five days. There were others on the trail, but we very seldom ran into them, so would have a quick chat, mostly discussing the trail and the weather, and continue on our way.

I dreaded the so-called Scales, as they had a reputation of being very difficult, but when we came upon them, I must admit I was a bit disappointed. It was a rocky, steep grade, obviously meant to climb carefully on, but it was not as high as I expected, and Cordell and I climbed it without effort or incident. This was apparently the most difficult leg of the journey. My feet and ankles became excruciatingly painful, and it felt like my boots were too tight. Cordell was cheerful and happy, even though he was packing his gold pan and shovel. I began to get cranky. Not expecting pain, I was caught off guard, unprepared. The hiking became difficult, and I needed frequent rests. I managed to get through the day by praying, "God please give me strength, and help me get to our camp tonight, in Jesus' name." The scenery was stunningly beautiful and made for a good distraction from my pain. We both rested well that night, and the next day was a bit easier.

At the end, we caught the White Pass & Yukon Railway train back to Skagway. When I weighed my pack, it was 48 pounds, and Cordell's pack was 36 pounds. He never found any gold, but it wasn't for lack of trying. He brought the pan and the shovel back, hung it on the wall of his home, and ever since it has been a bit of a joke in the family.

Jeff had arrived in Smithers the previous year at 18 years of age. He said, "I remember because I went to a coffee shop every day for five days, waiting for my nineteenth birthday to arrive on October 7. That's where I met Chad and all of my other friends. My first job was burning those slash piles that they burnt every year in the fall. I remember getting picked up at Petro Can every morning. I had to be there quite early.

"After that, I did a bit of this and a bit of that, worked part-time at the pool, but could not seem to get permanent employment."

That first year for Jeff in Smithers was a difficult one—"The Launch" I called it. It is always stressful when you can't get a proper job, or a place of your own.

Jeff stayed with Louise for a few months, but he had gotten into drinking and smoking pot, so was a bit of a handful for her so she kicked him out. He was young and foolish, and trying to make his way in the world. He stayed in Smithers, working when he could but was still unable to find permanent employment.

He finally got an extended temporary job with Tyee Forestry, doing compassing. He managed to find himself a place to live, but to help pay the rent he acquired a couple of roommates. "Those idiots just used me, and they wouldn't pay their part of the rent." His job at Tyee lasted for several months, and he liked it, but I knew that he had to start preparing himself for a career. I asked him what he wanted to do.

"I want to be a mechanic," Jeff said.

"Okay," I agreed, "that is a good profession to get into because you will never be unemployed again, ever. I will see what I can find out." I did some searching, and found a pre-apprenticeship program in Prince George at New Caledonia College. He applied, was accepted, and was to start in January 1995.

CHAPTER 16

I HAD HEARD FROM someone that there was a lovely set of lakes just outside of Houston, not far from Smithers. Nanika Lakes could be done in two days or longer if you wanted to take your time. A magnificent waterfall marked the end of the journey. I asked Jeff if he would do it with me on the Labour Day Weekend. He was happy to, so I borrowed a canoe, packed up a tent and sleeping bags, and enough food for the weekend, and we embarked on our adventure. It was a bit of a long drive along dusty gravel roads, but it was well-signed, and we found the first lake quite easily.

Jeff proved to be a capable and strong paddler, so while he manoeuvred the canoe from the stern, I paddled strongly from the bow. It was kind of a cloudy day when we started out, but there was no rain. We paddled through the first lake quickly, and as we landed at the dock on the other side, we noted a little white creature poking his head out from under the dock. It was a weasel, already with its winter coat. He was cute and curious and followed us a little way, then disappeared into the bush. Jeff carried the canoe, and I carried the two packs through the first portage of 1 500 metres. The huckleberries were everywhere; we just had to stop and eat them because they were so sweet and delicious. We didn't want to hang around too long, though, in case a bear came around.

We got to the second lake, which was the lake we would camp at overnight, and launched the canoe. It was long and narrow and had good fishing.

"Look at all the fish jumping, Mom," Jeff said.

"Yeah, perhaps we can catch a couple for supper to roast over the fire tonight," I said. We continued up the lake until I spotted a likely spot to set up the tent. "Over there!" I directed Jeff as I pointed to a beautiful little clearing on our right. We paddled over and set up camp. We started a fire, as it was getting toward supper time.

Jeff grabbed the fishing rod and paddled out to where all the fish were jumping. He cast his line out. "I got one, Mom!" he hollered from halfway across the lake. I looked up. "See," he yelled as he held it up for me to look at. I gave him a thumbs up, as I was enjoying a rare shot of whisky to warm up and I did not want to talk.

"Look at that, Mom. I got another one," I heard him say again.

"Have you got enough for supper yet?" I yelled. "I'm getting hungry."

"Think so," he said, as he pulled in another smaller, but still edible fish. We had brought rice in hopes of catching fish, so I cooked the fish up over the fire, and added a bit of rice to complete the delicious meal.

After eating, we sat at the fire, looking out at the lake and watching the sunset until it became dark. It was beautiful! We had not run into one other person. It was just me and my son. We settled into bed.

"Hope no bears come around tonight," he said.

"Me too," I said, "but if they do, we'll run down to the lake and jump into the canoe, okay?"

"Alright," he mumbled. Jeff was asleep in a minute, but I lay awake, enjoying the quiet and the scattered night noises. This was heaven for me; I liked nothing better.

The next morning, we woke up and it was cloudy, but it looked like it would be clear by the end of the day, so we broke camp and got back into the canoe. We had two more lakes to cover, and our plan was to camp at Nanika Falls that evening. The next portage was 500 metres, and the final portage was 2 500 metres. Jeff packed the canoe both times and we got to the last lake. The rain began to fall. We thought it would clear up, but it rained harder and harder as we paddled, and it was getting cold and windy. The waves were picking up on the lake, and we were trying to paddle closer to the shore, but it was difficult because the wind kept washing us up onto the too-shallow water, where it became almost impossible to get back out into the deeper water. We finally made it to Nanika Falls, and I thanked God that my son was so very strong.

We pitched the tent and the rain came down even harder. Everything became wet within minutes. The clouds were low, and there was no end in sight.

"I think I see a building over there," I said. "Let's check it out. Perhaps we can get in out of the rain." It was an old tarpaper shack, with two tattered, mouse-ridden bunkbeds in it, and it smelled strongly of oil. At least we could get out of the cold. Jeff noted that there was an old barrel stove, so he gathered some wood and managed to get a fire going. The cabin filled with smoke. We opened the door and the one tiny window to let the smoke escape, ran out coughing, and then went back in. The fire was going quite nicely so we hauled our equipment in and hung it up to dry the best we could.

We huddled in the cabin that night as the rain turned into snow and the wind picked up to roaring storm levels. It was so bad outside that I didn't even want to go out and look at it. It was scary, but we had food, coffee, and I had a bit of whisky left that we shared. We were safe.

We slept that night, even with the wind whistling around the cabin, but we were very tired. I was ever so thankful that we weren't in the tent. When we woke up the next morning, it was raining pretty hard and we could see that it had snowed during the night.

"We have two choices, here," I said to Jeff. "We can stay huddled up in this cabin for another night, and hope the weather clears, or we can jump in the canoe and go for it. It's at least an 11-hour paddle. What do you think?"

"Let's go for it," he said.

"Okay, are you up for it?" I had proper clothing on, but Jeff had chosen to wear his leather jacket. I knew he would become cold and wet, and his leather jacket would weigh him down. We got in and began the difficult task of paddling back to the truck. We paddled as it poured. The wind was against us and the rain turned into snow, which began to accumulate on the shore.

Jeff was cold, and I could sense him shivering in the back. I prayed, "God, please get us back to the truck. I'm worried about Jeff getting hypothermia." When we got to the 2 500-metre portage. Jeff was tired, but still able to pack the canoe. He seemed to warm up a bit as we hiked. By the time we got onto the next lake, it was still snowing but the wind wasn't quite so blustery. There was no sign of anyone else in the area. I thought, *We are truly alone out here, and this is looking more and more dangerous. Thank you, Lord, for watching over us and giving my son and I strength.* I prayed.

We made it through the next portage, and launched ourselves onto the next lake. It was raining, and both Jeff and I were chilled to the bone. Jeff was shivering as if he would never stop. At the final portage of 1 500 metres, I was afraid for Jeff. He was staggering, struggling not to fall, and was so cold and so exhausted, I was afraid he would not make it.

"Only one more lake," I said, "and it's only a small one. Then we'll be at the truck."

Our packs were soaking wet and very heavy. I couldn't carry them both any more. Jeff's leather jacket was soaked and heavy, sagging on his thin body. He could barely walk, but he picked up the other pack, loaded it on his back, heaved the canoe on his shoulders, and soldiered on. As I watched him, I prayed, "Please, Lord, don't let him fall or get injured, in Jesus' name." When we made it to the final lake, we dumped our packs into the canoe and paddled toward the final shore. At least the wind had died down, but the pouring rain continued.

When we got there, I climbed out of the canoe, fumbling for my keys, and ran up the bank to start my truck. It needed to warm up for a couple of minutes. I hollered at Jeff, "You get in the truck and I'll unpack the canoe. You need to warm up."

He staggered up the bank, and literally crawled into the truck. His shivering was uncontrollable. I unpacked the canoe, threw our packs into the back of the truck, and pulled the canoe out of the water. Then I hoisted it up on my shoulders, climbed up the bank, and left it beside the truck and before climbing in.

I was afraid Jeff would need to be taken to hospital. When he warmed up a bit, he helped me load the canoe, and we drove off. The truck heater was up as high as it would go and about halfway to Houston his shivering settled down. I felt reassured that he would probably be okay. I thanked God again for helping us to arrive safely back to the truck.

CHAPTER 17

WHEN TED LEFT FOR the Caribbean and I moved into his house, my life changed. I was now a "farmer," even if it was only temporary. I was thrilled to be given the chance to care for Ted's twenty-three cows. They had all been bred, so the calving would begin at the end of February. He would be back at the end of the following April. I knew it was a big responsibility, but he had been very particular about showing me everything that needed to be done, and how to do it. He even wrote it all down. There was a back – up plan for the cattle in place that he had arranged, with nearby neighbours. It would be a great opportunity for me.

Fortunately, I had a good stock of firewood, as it was the only source of heat. There was a wood furnace, as well as a wood stove, the kind of stove that if you lit a fire in it, you could cook and bake and even warm up water. I had always been intrigued by living like this; however, even though I stoked the furnace before I went to bed, by the time the morning came, it was pretty cold in the house.

I would get up in the morning, get my coffee started, light the fire in the stove, and stay in bed, reading my Bible, until the house warmed up. Then I would get up and start up the old tractor, get some hay to the cows, and make sure the watering trough was working properly. There was an electrical gadget that would warm it up enough to thaw it so the cows would be able to drink when they wanted to, and there was always a lineup at the trough.

In 1994 and 1995, minus twenty was common in the winter, and the temperature would frequently drop to minus thirty. The cows didn't really have a barn, but there was a covered building with open sides that the hay was stored in to stay dry. The hay was piled around the greater part of the outside of the building, offering a dry, sheltered area for the cows to go into if they so choose, but they grew winter coats to keep them warm.

The management at Bulkley Valley District Hospital was very understanding, so I was able to choose my shifts according to my convenience. I loved what I was doing, but it was a lot of work. Mitch had graduated from high school in June of 1994, and had begun to work at Earl's in Grande Prairie. After working there for a while, he realized that it was a bit of a dead-end job. He was up for a change, so came to my assistance in early December. I was thankful for his help. He learned how to drive the tractor, so sometimes fed the cows in the morning, leaving me free to work more hours. He was also helpful with getting the fires started so that when I came home from work, I didn't enter a freezing cold house. It was a large house with four bedrooms, so there was plenty of room for both of us, and I had really missed him while he had been living with his dad.

Christmas of 1994 was memorable to each member of my delightfully dysfunctional family, as Dad and Vicky came up for Christmas. "That was the best Christmas ever!" my dad would exclaim with a smile. "The kids were outside sledding, and we all were together. We had a great dinner, and a good party afterwards. Unforgettable," he would say. I remember brisk discussions, and my dad having a bit too much to drink, and doing a Ukrainian dance with my son, Mitch. It was fun! Twenty-five years later, when I asked everyone who was there what was so "memorable" about it, the answer was always the same: "I can't remember anything specific. I just remember that it was a lot of fun."

As 1994 turned into 1995, I began to watch the cows more carefully, and I refused to work any more than four hours at a time at the hospital. The cows were getting fat, and there were no signs of ill health, but it was very cold. Ted had also told me that he generally lost two to four calves every year, so he did not want me to feel bad if that actually did happen. I remember thinking, "I'm not going to lose any!"

The old saying in Smithers is "March comes in like a lion and goes out like a lamb, or comes in like a lamb, and goes out like a lion." February 28, as the day went on, the wind began to howl and it was snowing so hard it was difficult to see. I was concerned because I knew that one of the cows was about to calf. In the late afternoon, Mitch and I went outside to check on them. They were all milling around, mooing, as if they had nothing else to do. Obviously, they were somewhat unnerved by the blizzard, but all in all seemed okay. I looked around and saw one of the cows had isolated herself from the rest of the herd and was looking uncomfortable. I watched her for a few minutes, and pointed her out to Mitch. "See," I said, "she's going to be having that calf tonight. We had better keep an eye on her." In the cold, if the calf was left unattended and wet, it could quickly die.

We walked back to the house, intending to check later. It was still snowing heavily and the wind hadn't settled down. After we finished supper, I bundled up. "Brrrr! It's cold out there," I hollered at Mitch. "Come on, let's go check on that cow."

"Can I finish watching sports?"

We always watched the news and I knew Mitch liked to watch the sports part of it. "Okay, I'm just going to head out there. Come out when you are ready and I'll see you out by the hay barn," I said to Mitch as I wandered out into the blizzard.

I could hear the cows in the near distance. I made my way out, cautiously because it was terribly slippery, and I hated falling. I shone my light amongst the cows, then I saw it. The shiny wet, brown little calf, was struggling to stand up in the wind, bawling for his mother. "Mitch, are you there? Can you hear me?"

"Yeah! I can, I'm coming," Mitch shouted.

I could do nothing but wait for him. It was pathetic watching that little calf struggle. I peered through the darkness, trying to see the mom. "There she is, Mitch. Hurry up, we need to get that calf out of the cold."

"I'm coming. I'm coming," Mitch said. I could just see his dark form through the blinding snow. When Mitch arrived, he surveyed the scene. "What are we going to do, Mom?"

"We'll have to carry him to the hay barn. At least he'll be out of the wind. Then we'll have to try to convince his mom to follow." We walked over to the calf.

"Do you think we can pick him up?" Mitch asked me.

"Well, we can try," I said. "You get on one end and I'll get on the other." Mitch wrapped his arms around the calf's head and shoulders, and I wrapped mine around his hindquarters. The little calf was heavy, but between the two of us we got him off the ground. "Let's walk past his mom so she can smell him. Hopefully then she'll follow."

We squeezed our way through the cows as they were all milling about, trying to crowd together to keep warm. We went to the mother and nudged the calf under her nose. Then we beckoned her to follow us. She was hesitant, but took a few steps. Slowly but surely we fought our way through the cows and almost made it to the barn. "Hang on, Mom," Mitch encouraged me. He was much stronger than I was and it took all of my effort and concentration to get that calf inside.

"Whew, we made it!" We laid the calf on the hay and tried to encourage it to stand up. "Mitch, can you go and try to get the mom in here, please, and I'll try to get this calf standing up?"

"Okay." He ran out the door, grabbing an old board from the ground. Moments later, I could hear them coming. Mitch herded the mother under the roof and in amongst the hay bales where her baby was. The calf continued trying to stand, and when his mom came through the opening in the hay, he wobbled up. His mom began licking him, and finally allowed him to have his first feed. With the feed, you could almost see the strength flow into him.

What a relief, I thought, *that was a lot of work.* We watched the pair for another half hour or so and made our way back to the house. "Let's call him Normand," Mitch suggested.

"Sounds good to me," I said. My plan was to name all the newborns.

We were just about to sit down and relax in front of the television when

I jumped up. "We have to tag him!" I ran downstairs to get the tagging kit. "Come on, Mitch. I might need a hand. I've never done this before."

He got up and put his jacket on again, and out we went. We had to put matching tags on the mom's and baby's ear. I went through the directions in my head as I pictured Ted demonstrating how to do it.

"Make sure both tags have the same number and colour, and put them on this thing like so, and squeeze the handles together. You only have one chance, so you need to make sure it's correctly placed," he had advised me.

The animals never even flinched when we pierced their ears for the tags. #1 was the number of the first calf born on the farm in 1995. The next morning when we woke up, it had stopped snowing, and the wind had gone elsewhere.

The month of March passed quickly. The calves were born one right after the other. I monitored them all very closely, and there were no difficulties except for Dalphine. I named Dalphine after my mother, but the more I watched her, the more I thought she was either retarded or blind. She kept walking into the fence and the hay piles, and appeared constantly confused. Physically, she seemed healthy enough.

Then came the birth of Theodore! Ted had warned me about his heifers. A heifer is a cow that has never had a calf, and he had said that if you breed them with too big of a bull, they could have trouble delivering. Theodore's mother was a heifer and had been in labour for a long time, not progressing. I phoned Ed, my backup plan, and expressed my concerns to him. "Get her into a stall in the barn and we'll come over and see what is going on." Ed was a neighbour and an old cowboy who had been raising cattle for decades. A few minutes later, he and his wife arrived with his equipment. He looked at the cow. "She's stressed, not doing well. Let me check her."

She seemed to be weak, tired, and struggling to remain standing. It was a horrid sight. "I think we're going to have to pull the calf," Ed observed. He waited a few minutes until he could see the feet coming out. His wife was with him, so between the two of them, and me helping as much as I could, he wrapped the chains around the calf's ankles, and proceeded to try to winch it along to delivery with each contraction. The cow was bawling loudly, and I was trying not to cry.

Slowly, but surely the calf was being assisted out. With every pull of the winch, it moved forward a few inches. "Pull! Pull!" Ed said. Finally, the calf came, falling on the hay on the floor. The mother staggered, almost fell, but managed to stay on her feet. I pulled the caul off the calf's nose and cleared his nostrils so he could breathe.

He tried to get up, but couldn't. "Sometimes, when you pull a calf," Ed said, "they cannot stand for a while because of the effect of the chains around their feet."

"I'll give it physio," I offered.

"You could do that, and it might even help," he said jokingly.

I don't think he thought I would. I was a registered nurse and I knew about physio, so planned to give the calf's legs physio three times a day until it would stand. I would have to bottle feed it as well. When I was twelve, I used to stay at my friend Janet's place in Pemberton, BC. Her dad had three hundred head of cattle, and he showed Janet and I how to give the newborn calves injectable antibiotics. Each calf received a needle soon after birth. He'd also shown me how to milk a cow. Thirty-one years later, I still remembered how it was done—or at least I thought I did.

Ted had some bottles and nipples stashed away for such an occasion, so I collected them. I found a clean bucket and placed it beneath the cow. "Put your baby finger on the bottom of the teat first, then one finger at a time, up toward the top, grasp it, and squeeze," he'd said. It worked! Milk began to squirt out into the bucket. I filled the bucket about a quarter full, then prepared the bottle, and put it in Theodore's mouth. He started to suck – he was starving! I extracted more milk from the cow, but I had no idea how much to feed him. I would just keep it going until he did not want it any more. I would have to feed him several times a day, as well as doing physio three times a day. I was going to be a busy lady.

I phoned the hospital, told them what was happening, and asked them not to call me for three days. I would keep them posted about how things were going with Theodore. Heather, the head nurse, was very accommodating. Morning, noon, and night, I patiently massaged all four of Theodore's legs, then I would try to get him to stand up. The first two days, he was still crippled but seemed to be getting a bit better. The third day, I massaged and massaged, and tried to get him to stand. I was lifting him, or trying to lift him, and all of a sudden he was able to bear weight. I had been leaving him and his mother in the stall, as I was hoping that perhaps he would get up on his own, even if I wasn't there. He didn't, but with my help that third day he was up and trying to suck on his mother. I was elated! I had done it! I could relax—for a few days, anyway.

CHAPTER 18

MARCH WAS ALWAYS A tough month in Smithers. One evening, Mitch was downstairs in the basement. "Mom, I'm not sure what is happening, but the walls downstairs are really hot—so hot that when I touch them it burns."

"What?" I exclaimed. "Show me!"

"Look outside, Mom. There's an orange glow!" He pointed out the window. I looked out, and sure enough, he was telling the truth. I ran down the stairs, and as I ran, I could hear the fire roaring in the chimney. I wasn't sure what to do. I phoned Kathy, the neighbour across the road from me. As she was on the phone, she went to look out the window. "Loraine," she exclaimed, "you're having a chimney fire. There are flames coming out of the top of the chimney!"

"What do I do? What do I do?" I didn't want to burn Ted's house down. If I did, I'd never forgive myself. "Open the door where you put the wood in, quickly throw a cup of water on it, then shut the door."

"Okay, I'll have to get some gloves. It's really hot." I was scared. The house was all made of wood, and if it blew, it would blow quickly. Mitch and I would be dead. Shaking, I told Mitch to get outside, and watch the top of the chimney. I wanted him out of the house—just in case. "Please Lord," I prayed, "don't let the house burn down, and please surround us with your shield of protection, and do not allow us to come to any harm, in Jesus' name, amen."

I followed Kathy's direction, opened the door quickly, and threw one cup of water on the fire. I phoned her back.

She was watching the chimney from her window. "I think it has gone down a bit," she said encouragingly. "Go throw another cup of water on it."

I filled another large cup and ran back down the steps. It was so hot— and the walls were still hot. I opened the door quickly again and threw the second cup of water on the fire and ran back up the stairs.

Kathy had remained on the phone. "It's gone from the chimney—but you might want to throw some more water on it. Just be very careful, and whatever you do, don't put any more wood on the fire for a long time!"

I called my dad and told him what had happened. He had grown up with wood heat, and knew the dangers. "You are lucky, Lorainy," he said. "That neighbour of yours gave you good advice, but you're going to have to be careful. Don't put so much wood on the fire. And your chimney probably needs a good clean."

I felt a bit relieved and was always glad to get some advice from him. He was a wise man. I made arrangements to get the chimney cleaned the next day.

Toward the end of March, it warmed up, as it often did in Smithers at that time. The snow began to melt, and whatever had previously fallen as snow turned into rain. It was wet and muddy and water was flowing every which way. It was the time of year when you couldn't count on the weather. There were still ice patches to be aware of, and it could be hot and melting one day, and then freezing the next. March was always like that, and everyone, I'm sure, was happy to see April.

I was sitting in the kitchen, sipping my coffee one morning in late March. "Is that water I hear running in the basement?" I listened again. "Crap, I hope I'm not having water or sewer issues." I ran downstairs to check.

The water was up to the top of the bottom step. My eyes and ears were drawn toward the sound of a waterfall. Water was pouring through an open window, collecting on the floor. I looked up and noticed that there was also a river of water running all along the side of the house. Half of it was pouring through the open window and the other half was flowing by.

"Oh no! What an idiot I am!" Mitch wasn't there. I was all alone. I felt like crying as I took in the flooding all over the basement floor. "How am I going to clean it up?" I had dealt with fire, and now flooding. I didn't know what to do.

Maybe this is just too much for me? I had the cows to check and feed, I had to go to work, and I had to figure out how to clean up this horrible mess. I was too lazy to find my rubber boots, so I rolled up my pyjama bottoms, took off my slippers, and walked over to shut the window, hoping that it would at least slow down the waterfall. It did, but I knew it wouldn't last very long. I had to divert the water somehow away from the window. I quickly got dressed, found my rubber boots, and grabbed the nearest shovel.

I started digging a ditch away from the house. There was a bit of a downhill bank, running toward a field, so I was hoping to divert the flow that way. Strategically placed rocks and boards would protect the window somewhat, at least until some of the ditch was dug. I worked steadily for about two hours until the water was flowing well away from the house.

Now all I had to do was get it out of the basement. Sump pumps? Had Ted said something about sump pumps? I couldn't remember, but fortunately, he'd written everything down, so I went back into the house to find his directions. There it was, written clear as a bell. He'd created a detailed sketch of the sump pumps and drawn a map of how, and where, to set them up and turn them on. What a lifesaver!

I ran down the stairs with the book in my hand, reviewing the directions. I found the pumps where they were supposed to be, and turned them on, intently listening for them to start to purr! Thank God, they worked. The basement got pumped out as much as it could, but there remained some puddles, which I mopped up with a bunch of old rags. I found a couple of fans to dry it out even more. *Whew,* I thought, *another crisis resolved.* I was exhausted.

I STILL HAD TO monitor the calves closely, so I made my rounds daily. I realized, too, that I needed to castrate the little bulls, and I had to do it soon. The older they got, the harder it would be. I phoned my neighbour, Kathy. "I think we need to get the bulls castrated," I said, "so I was wondering when you think you could help me do it? I know you're busy with your sheep, but the longer we procrastinate, the harder it will be."

"Let me see," she answered. "I can't tomorrow, but the next day I think I can, if you can have everything ready by about 9:00 a.m. I'll come over and we can at least get started."

Two days later, we met in the field. I had all the equipment, and again, Ted had written the instructions down quite plainly. I'd reviewed them and felt that I could actually do this. Kathy and her husband had castrated sheep before, but I wasn't sure if they'd ever done cattle. I had never even seen the procedure before, let alone done it, so I appreciated her expertise.

"Let's do Normand first. He is the biggest and will probably be the hardest to do," Kathy suggested. We made our way into the herd so we could find Normand and herd him off to the side.

"You hold him, and I will do the castrating. Then you can see how it is done," she suggested.

"Okay!" I went around to the front of Normand to hold his head and shoulders.

"I'll tell you when I'm ready—we have to do it quickly," Kathy said.

"Grab him now and hold him as tight as you can!" she hollered at me.

I wrapped my arms around his head and shoulders, using my whole body weight to my advantage, and held him down.

Kathy was quick. She had the elastics around his testicles in seconds.

Normand was not amused. He started bucking his hind end up and fighting with me to get out of my grip. I went flying.

"Oooh!" I heard Kathy gasp.

I landed hard on the ground. When I opened my eyes, my face was centimetres from a pile of fresh cow poo.

"Are you alright?" Kathy asked

"I think so," I mumbled, and she started to laugh. I couldn't help but laugh too, just thinking about what a sight I must have been. My face was covered in mud, and one of my boots had flown off. The front of my clothes were covered in mud, poop, and water. I was a mess!

IT WOULD SOON BE the beginning of April. Thawing had been steady, and mud and dampness were everywhere. I watched the calves, looking for any odd or seclusive behaviour. This was a critical time as far as their health was concerned. When animals are unwell, they tend to isolate themselves and find somewhere to rest where they won't be bothered.

One day, I noticed two calves that were lying quietly by themselves while the rest of the babies were running around wrestling with each other. I went over to the closest one, and sat down beside it, talking to it quietly. I wanted to figure out what was going on. It didn't jump up and run away as I would have expected. It just lay there, kind of dull and not really responding to my gestures.

I'll come and check on this little calf later, and see if she's still here in a couple of hours, I thought. I walked over to the other calf. It was a little bull and he didn't try to get up, either. I knew in my gut that something was not right. I would have to give them some penicillin—even if it was just in case. I searched out Ted's medical kit and read and re-read the directions and doses. I was used to giving needles to people, not cows. I gave the penicillin as prescribed and both the calves improved greatly. I found two more calves that were acting the same, and gave them the penicillin shots as well. They recovered. I was keeping my vow to myself, "I will not lose even one calf."

My goodbye adventure was the final straw of the experience of being a farmer. I was driving into town in my 1985 Ford LTD, and I arrived at the stop sign on the intersection of the Old Babine Lake Road and Highway 16. I was in a hurry, driving fast, and there were still ice patches on the road. I came to the stop sign, stepped on my brakes … and I kept going, out into the traffic.

There was a loaded logging truck speeding down the hill toward me on my left, threatening to collide with my driver's side. On my right was a Bandstra freight truck bearing down on me, heading right into the passenger side of my car. A half-ton had just gone through the intersection, turning right, and its wheels were spinning. Vehicles were all around me that could have easily crushed me.

I had a flashback to when the van had flipped and rolled. I hollered, "Jesus help me!" The Bible states, "For whosoever shall call on the name of the Lord shall be saved" (Rom 10:13 KJV). I focused and tried to listen for direction from the Holy Spirit.

I remember cranking my wheel to the right. I managed to squeeze between the Bandstra truck and the logging truck. The man in the half-ton had stopped spinning and managed to steer to the side, out of everyone's way. Both big trucks sped up, frantically trying to give me space.

I slowed down, trying to stay in a straight line and trying not to slip on the ice. I made it, thanks to teamwork. I just kept driving, and so did the trucks. It was too risky to stop, or even slow down, because of the ice.

I drove to Melody's house in town and phoned my dad. "I've fought fire and flood and life and death, and I'm exhausted." Tears were rolling down my face, and I was sobbing my heart out as I told my dad what had happened. I think, at that time, I had reached my limit of endurance.

"I think you deserve a glorious hero's badge," he told me. It was kind of a family joke that Dad always said when someone in our delightfully dysfunctional family did something noteworthy. He actually had one that he'd made out of cardboard. "Yeah, I probably do," I said, as I finally regained my composure and successfully regaled him with my adventures.

TED RETURNED FROM THE Caribbean toward the end of April. I stayed on at his house for a couple of days just to catch him up on the winter's activities and then I moved on to house sit for another friend. He was happy with the way I had handled things, and offered me a calf. "You can choose whichever one you want, and I can either take it to the auction and sell it, and give you the money, or you can take it home with you. Your choice, and you pick." he said.

I thought about it, and chose Yvonne. Yvonne was a beautiful reddish brown colour, and she had a gentle personality, and I had grown rather attached to her. Because I didn't have my own home at the time so I asked him to auction her off and give me the money.

CHAPTER 19

WITHIN A MONTH OF Ted's return, Dad and Vicky had arranged to move to Smithers. I was elated! I loved my dad, and still leaned on him for some things. The previous fall, Melody's children joined her in time for school. Melody, Micah, and Bethany had been living with Dad and Vicky, since Wayne left, so when Melody decided to move to Smithers, they missed the children very much. It was the only time in our lives that we all lived in the same place. I was looking forward to spending time as a family, even if it was "My Delightfully Dysfunctional Family."

Dad and Vicky found a house to buy, and we helped them to move in. I'd been looking for a house since I'd moved there, but couldn't find one that seemed to fit. I moved in with Melody, because if I lived with her, I could save money and continue to look for my own place.

Brian was the real estate agent who was trying to find a place that would suit me. He was very helpful, but sometimes I felt I'd never find the right place. If I couldn't find a house, I was thinking about buying a piece of land and having my own house built. Brian took me to several places, and in our travels I got to know him, and he became a good friend. He was an enthusiastic skier and hiker, and so was his wife, Kim. Both had been in Smithers for many years, and knew their way around. I was happy to hook up with them and their local friends just so I could see and do more.

One day, Brian phoned me up and said, "I may have found a place that you might be interested in. When would you be free to come and look at it?"

"Perhaps tomorrow. I'm not working. What's a good time?"

"How about ten o'clock?"

"Great! I will see you then," I said.

The next day, he picked me up, and we headed out. "It is one and a half acres of riverfront property, but it is long and narrow. I think it is about 80 feet by 800 feet or something," he said.

My curiosity was aroused. *Sounds interesting—just what I always wanted.* We arrived there quickly as it was only about fifteen minutes from town.

The property was covered in trees and underbrush, but we carefully wove our way through the tangle and walked all around the perimeter. It was right next to the river, and the river was high, as it was early spring. I was impressed! Living by the river—just as I always wanted to? I told Brian that I was interested, but I had to talk to a couple of people.

I called Ted and asked him to come and have a look at it. I figured he was knowledgeable enough to give me an informed opinion. We went there, and walked around, and I showed him where the river came up to.

"What are you going to do with this, Loraine? It's all bush, it's hilly, and there are old rotten logs and tree and brush piles everywhere."

"Build me a house and live here," I retorted.

"It's lots of work. You're going to have to clear it, level it, and organize power, sewer, and a well. Why don't you just buy a nice house in town, where all of that is already done? It would be so much easier," he advised.

I took his words to heart, and thought that perhaps he was right. Could I really do it? Could I really organize it all? I was a registered nurse, and I had some savings, but I knew that I would have to do much of the work myself. I was over forty, gainfully employed and physically fit. The trees on this property were old spruce and cottonwood, so large that it took three people to wrap their arms around them. I had my work cut out for me. Of course I could do it!

We left and I asked a few others. They all told me the same thing. After all, I was over forty years old, and most women my age did just that—bought a house or a condo in town. I wasn't most women. I was me, and the thought of living in town, whether it be a house or condo, was not appealing at all, especially when I felt I had a chance to build my dream home.

Then I thought, *I'll ask my dad what he thinks. He'll give me good advice, and he knows me well.*

I called him up. "Dad," I asked, "I have found this piece of property that I'm interested in. Would you mind coming and looking at it with me, and see what you think?"

"Sure," he said. "I always like looking at property investments. Let's go and have a look." We went there the next day, and I showed him around, and shared my plans with him. "Do you think you can do this? It's a lot of work, but it's also a nice chunk of land."

"Yes, I do, Dad," I said.

"Well, I would say to you to try it out, and see what you can do with it," he told me.

Yes! Yes! I would. I had a vision, and I knew in my heart that I could create something, and I even loved the fact that I was starting from scratch. I could do whatever I wanted. It was amazing to have that freedom, to make my own decisions, and create my own oasis. I sat there for a while after my dad left. Birds were flying around, and squirrels were chattering away. It was beautiful and sunny and I could hear the river flowing past my back yard. Ha! Ha! – My back yard. I was in heaven!

I phoned Brian. "Brian I am going to buy that property by the river. I talked to my dad, and others, and I think I am going to go ahead. So, what is the next step?" I asked.

"Well you need to make a formal offer, so when can you come here, so we can do up the paperwork?" he asked.

"Now," I returned, "can we do it now?"

"Well I have another client that I need to do a showing with, but after that I am free, how about 2:30 this afternoon?" "Okay I will be there," I said excitedly.

At the suggestion of my sister, I hired Adam, to clear and construct. He would knock the trees down by machine, and I would cut them up with the chainsaw for firewood. When I came to monitor the progress the day Adam began clearing, I saw a war zone. Fallen trees were scattered everywhere and he was clearing the land along the roadside. I wanted to live by the river. I went running in there. "No! No!" I yelled, "I don't want this part cleared. I want it left in bush. Stop! Stop!"

Adam stopped and came to talk to me. "It's okay, we are just clearing as much as we need. We are trying to level it so we can put the driveway in and give us access to the area where the house is going to be!" he explained. I settled down.

"Okay, but don't clear any more than you have to out here. I want my driveway to have bush on both sides." I told him. I wandered around a bit and then left. When I came back to check again, I noticed that he had constructed a rough driveway right to the back of the acreage, and he had not cut down any more trees. I drove my truck up the driveway, sat in it and looked around. Some of the larger trees by the river had been knocked down, and there were disorientated squirrels running here and there. Three bewildered looking moose were standing in the southwest corner of the soon to be yard, observing the destruction. I sat in my truck, intrigued and overwhelmed. I backed out of the driveway and went home. I would come and check again in a couple more days.

I moved in to my house in September of 1995. It was a simple house, my dad called it "a Loraine House." It was eight hundred square feet with two bedrooms, one bathroom and a kitchen/dining/living room area, and I had a Bay Window looking out toward the river, and Hudson Bay Mountain. I had a "million dollar view," according to some neighbours and friends.

* * *

As the fall of 1995 unfolded itself to winter, I continued going to Mountainview Pentecostal Assembly, where I had first spoken to George Richmond. I enjoyed the music, the services, and absolutely loved the ladies Bible study on Sunday mornings. There was a gentleman named Mike there whom I had previously met through Margie, one of my neighbours when I lived in my little house on First Avenue. I'd spent quite a bit of time with my neighbour, and Mike was often there when I visited her. He seemed like a fun-loving guy, and he was always smiling, happy, and talking about God's word frequently and knowledgeably.

Mike followed me out of church one Sunday. "Do you want to go out for coffee? I know a great place to go. We could even have brunch if you are hungry."

"Well I am, so I will," I answered.

"Let's go in my truck," he said, "and I can drop you back here afterwards."

I climbed into his truck and we drove off to the local steakhouse. It was a popular local venue, but we found a seat, and ordered the buffet. As we sat and chatted he said, "So, tell me about yourself, like how and when did you arrive here?"

I didn't want to go into too many details about my failed marriage. "I've been here since the summer of 1993, and moved here from Alberta. My sons moved here as well, within the last year, and so did my stepsister, and my dad and stepmom.

"My sister Louise has lived in the Smithers area since 1971. She's an old hippie. Ha! Ha! She moved here with all of the other old hippies back then. She and her boyfriend lived in the bush out at Telkwa Pass for a number of years, trying to live off the land."

"How did they do?" he asked. "Are they still living out there? Are they still even together?"

"No, unfortunately, her boyfriend was killed in a single-vehicle accident between Smithers and Telkwa some years ago," I said. "She's living in town now, and working for the Friendship Centre here. She has two sons, one still here in school and the other in university at UBC."

"What about your sons?" he asked.

"Well, there is Jeff who's almost twenty-one, Mitch who's nineteen, and Cordell who's seventeen and still living with his dad in Alberta.

Cordell was here in the summer visiting for a while but has now gone back because of school.

"What about you? Have you ever been married? Do you have children? What about your parents and siblings?"

"No, never been married, don't have kids. I have a brother who lives in Venezuela. He works in the oilfield there as a diamond driller. I have a sister, and my parents live in the Burns Lake area, actually Takysie Lake."

We chatted for over an hour, had a good brunch, and then I told him that I'd better go home. He drove me back to the church and I picked up my truck and left. We became close friends after that and began to spend more and more time together.

When I worked at the hospital, I worked twelve-hour shifts, either from 7:00 a.m. to 7:00 p.m. or 7:00 p.m. to 7:00 a.m. Because Rosie, my dog, was penned up all the time I was away, I had to take her for a walk at the beginning of my shift, and also at the end. One morning, after working a night shift, I took her for a walk around the "dog poop trail" as it began to be known. It was November, and it was extremely icy and slippery. I had her on the leash and as I tentatively walked across a large frozen puddle she bolted, trying to run after a sassy squirrel.

I slipped and fell to the ice. "My knee, my knee!" I hollered. "Owww!" There was nobody around to hear me. The searing pain tore through my knee and I could not get up. I lay there, unable to move. I held on to Rosie, who stood there looking at me, trying to figure out why I was lying there moaning.

My knee was hurting so bad. *What am I going to do? No one is around, and it is early. Nobody will even be coming by for at least an hour. I can't lay here for that long. I'll freeze.* I had to get up and at least try to walk. I spotted a sturdy-looking stick not too far off.

If I could just get over there and get that stick, I might be able to stand. I dragged my throbbing knee toward the stick. I reached for it, pulled myself up into a sitting position, and sat for a moment to catch my breath and wait for the pain to abate. Rosie instinctively knew something was wrong, so kept very still, watching me closely, so as not to add to my distress. I slid on my rear end to the edge of the frozen puddle, so I wouldn't have to stand on the ice. I did not want to slip again.

"Come here, Rosie," I coaxed. "Let me use you to help me get up." Rosie positioned herself while I leaned on her back and tried to stand. I got up on one foot, but could not bear weight on my injured knee. *I have to. I can't hop on one foot all the way home.*

I was about a kilometre from my place, but there were other houses closer. Perhaps I could knock on their doors and ask them to help me. "Lord please help me to get there," I prayed. The stick was helpful because I could put my weight on the stick and minimize the weight I had to put on my injured right leg. I managed to make my way slowly. Every step was excruciating. When I got to the houses, I was too embarrassed to knock on their doors. I didn't even know these people.

"What if they think I'm a nutcase and refuse to answer the door?" I asked myself. Rosie was great. She never left my side and let me lean on her back to help myself get along. No cars came by. It took a long time, but I made it home.

I got into my house and sat on the couch, revelling in the warmth and comfort. I managed to get Rosie locked into her pen and get myself undressed and into my bed. My knee was just throbbing. I was hoping that if I lay down on my bed and put a pillow under my knee, I would be able to get some badly needed sleep. I was so tired. I'd just worked all night, and now this.

It didn't work. Nothing seemed to help. I knew I had been seriously injured, and felt I needed to go to the hospital. Should I phone an ambulance? No! I was too embarrassed.

I phoned Mike. "Hi Mike, I injured my right knee this morning when I slipped on the ice while I was walking Rosie. It really hurts, and I have to go up to the emergency department. Can you pick me up and take me there? Please!"

"I'll be right there," he answered.

I was thankful. I couldn't stand the pain any longer, and I needed some Demerol, or something. When he came, I didn't even bother getting dressed. He carried me in my flannel nightgown, wrapped in a blanket, to his truck and drove me up to the hospital. Afterwards, he said, "That's when I fell in love with you. You looked so vulnerable and helpless, I couldn't help it."

It was a good thing I went there. I had a torn AC tendon. The doctor told me I should go to Prince Rupert and get it repaired, but I felt I couldn't afford to take the time off work. My dad and Vicky offered to let me stay with them for a few days until I was able to care for myself. I thought that was a very good idea, and Mike offered to go and look after Rosie for me.

It was kind of fun being cared for. Vicky loved to cook for someone who enjoyed a good meal, and that was me. Dad kind of hung around, talking to me, and offering advice, and the household had many people coming and going. Dad and Vicky had been in Smithers only a few months, and they'd already made many friends.

"Hey hi Roger," I heard dad say as he answered the door bell, "come on in."

"Hey Vicky, Roger the Lodger is here." He yelled.

Vicky came hurrying out of the kitchen.

"Hi there, would you like a sandwich and a cup of tea?" she asked him.

"Sure – that would be wonderful," Roger returned.

"Roger, come and meet my daughter, she is laid up for a while so is staying here. Loraine, meet Roger the Lodger, Roger, this is Loraine," he said as he introduced us.

Roger came over to the couch and shook my hand. I had never seen him before, so I thought that perhaps he lived out of town and didn't come into town very often. I nodded off to sleep. I woke up to the sound of the banging door, as Bethany came running in.

"Hi Grandma," she greeted. "I am home from school so I came over."

"Do you want a sandwich?" Vicky asked her.

"No," said Bethany, "I just want to watch T.V."

Melody refused to have a television in her house so it was a real treat for Micah and Bethany to come over to Grandma's and watch T.V.

"Hi Bethansnoo," dad hollered.

"Dad why do you always call her that?" I asked with disgust.

"Because when she was little, she always had these greenies running from her nose, and the name just seemed to fit." He told me.

Soon after that Micah arrived from school.

"Do you want a sandwich?" Vicky asked him.

"Sure, mom is working so she won't be home until later. "Hi Auntie Loraine how are you doing?" he asked me as he came into the living room. Vicky soon arrived with one of her huge sandwiches.

"Here is your sandwich, Micah," she said as she passed it over to him.

"Thanks Grandma," he said as he headed out the door.

"Where are you going?" she questioned.

"I got basketball practice," he yelled.

"Don't you even have time to sit and eat your sandwich," she asked.

"No I will talk to you later," Micah hollered as he raced down the driveway.

My sons, Jeff, Mitch, and Cordell would drop by daily to check on me, and Vicky always offered them a sandwich. She became famous for her sandwiches, and all of the grandchildren would drop by just to eat.

CHAPTER 20

MELODY WAS SETTLING INTO Smithers quite nicely, as were Dad and Vicky. Melody had met Dudley, a well-known local character and heavy-duty mechanic who was a single dad with seven children. Being a single dad with seven children could be very attractive to a woman, or very unattractive. Melody was very attracted to Dudley. Apparently, Dudley had seen Melody at the local coffee house one evening and, liking what he saw, asked his friend, "Who is that woman over there?"

"Oh, that's Louise's sister who moved up here a year or so ago," his friend responded.

Dudley knew Louise, so phoned her up and asked her about Melody. Soon after that, Melody and I decided to go to the spring mud dance, which occurred every April out at Driftwood Hall. It was a popular event with a band, dancing, and several games that included mud. It was a celebration of the arrival of spring!

I noticed that Dudley was following us both around. He was an excellent conversationalist, and getting to know new and interesting women was not foreign to him. He was fun, friendly, and entertaining. He danced with both Melody and I, but mostly with Melody.

After that, he and Melody were inseparable. Dudley became a large part of our family and he, and his children were welcomed at our family events. Vicky always loved children and would have been happy to have more. Having Louise's, mine, Melody's, and Dudley's children around made her day. Vicky was never lonely, living in Smithers, and talking to her now, she feels it was the most fun time of her whole life. Dad was always making jokes about their grocery bill. "We fed lots of people in Smithers," he would say, "and I'm sure our grocery bill was over $800.00 per month, but I'm just happy that we could afford it."

Melody and Dudley loved the music scene, and would always attend the Kispiox Music Festival, which generally took place around the end of May. Dudley was also largely involved in the Midsummer Music Festival in Smithers that took place every July 1st weekend. At that time in Smithers, the music scene was very busy. There were coffee houses where people could sing and advertise their talents. There were monthly concerts that would take place at the Della Herman Theatre, thanks to the active arts and music community. Mark Perry was popular and a historian in his own right. He wrote musical renditions about what living in an isolated northern community was like. I always thought of him as somewhat of a legend. He'd been raised in Smithers and knew some interesting stories of major events that occurred there, such as plane and helicopter crashes, and other incidents where well-known local people were killed or injured. He wrote songs about those events, but he'd also write about celebrations, such as marriages or births, and he even created a song or two about his own family members. All in all, he gave a pretty good history of the community and its people.

* * *

MIKE AND I CONTINUED to see each other throughout 1995 and into 1996. I noticed he was becoming rather possessive and nosy, wanting to know everything I was doing and who I was with. I didn't think too much about it because I was so attracted to him and loved him, despite his issues. He was kind and adoring (every girl likes that), and he became a big part of my life. We discussed marriage, but made no commitment to one another. I began to feel suffocated and needed to get away from him, just to think things through.

A friend of mine had a teepee in a remote area of the Babine Mountains. It would be warm and isolated, perfect for the state of mind I was in at the time. The first weekend of March 1996, I flew up there accompanied by my dog Rosie, the helicopter pilot Carl, and my friend Doug. Carl and Doug would stay only long enough to ensure I would be safe and warm for the weekend. I couldn't wait to sit by myself at the fire, and enjoy the clear, sunny, relatively warm winter afternoon. Dusk arrived. The stars began to twinkle up above and moonlight flooded the landscape. Winter silence surrounded me with peace and quiet. The hot rum I was sipping on warmed me, and I was content.

When morning dawned the next day, the sunlight woke me up, shining through the hole in the top of the teepee, offering another flawless day to enjoy my solitude. Coffee sounded good. Lighting up the Coleman stove, I put on the pot. Soon the smell wafted through the air, tempting my nostrils, and my palate. Nothing is quite so good as the first cup of coffee in the morning. I couldn't believe how warm it was outside and was anxious to start the day.

Rosie was already out, running around, doing her thing. I knew she was impatient to get going and explore the mountainsides and hunt for her favourite meal, the voles. With breakfast out of the way and a substantial lunch packed, I strapped on my skis with skins, and started out. I made my way cautiously up the cliffs and along the snow overhangs. To risk injury would be foolish. A few more feet and I would reach the top.

I thought about the glorious downhill run on the other side. The skins would simply be removed, and I would ski down through the untouched and ever-abundant powder, leaving only one pair of ski tracks—mine! The primal feeling of being the only person for miles around was exhilarating! Over the top and down, faster and faster I went, the wind blowing my hair back and burning my face. I felt wonderful, euphoric, and exuberant! I looked ahead to see where I would end up, turning to the left and to the right again to slow down my speed. I spotted my landing at the bottom of a rocky little gully and accelerated, veered sharply to the right and put on my brakes, spraying powder snow all over Rosie. The bewildered look on her face when she shook herself made me laugh. What a day! This was great!

I sort of knew where I was and thought that if I could just get over the next hill, Reisiter Lake would come into view. It was a magnificent azure in the summer, but even in the winter, white and covered in ice, it would be a striking scene to behold. Up and up, I continued. It was steep and beginning to tire me. Finally, puffed out and exhausted, I reached the top, skied along a short flat area, and then I saw Reisiter Lake and the blue glacier that was just beyond the north corner. I sat on a wind-blown rock, overlooking the massive valley. How matchless it was, in its overwhelming beauty, and I had all day to enjoy it.

To the northwest, a small wisp of a cloud floated lazily in the sky, blowing gently toward the east. It was a comfortable-looking cloud, seeming quite at home. I unpacked my lunch, ate it slowly, and took my time sipping on the hot tea. As I ate, I gazed at the scenery and pondered on life in general.

I was a free spirit, and I couldn't stand being suffocated. Mike was too possessive, too in my face, and he squelched my creativity. I laughed. "Squelched my creativity" sounded like something out of a book. I would have to talk to him about that. It was true, though, and if I did marry him, I could end up divorced in a couple of years. No, I couldn't go through another divorce. I would talk to him when I came down from my getaway.

Attaching my skis to my feet, I prepared to ski along the ridge bordering the lake valley. There was a scenic loop that would take me back to my original tracks, and lead me home to the teepee. Peering at the sky again, I noted that the cloud seemed quite ominous and not so comfortable-looking! Gut instinct told me to hurry back. Being used to the mountains, I was familiar with the velocity with which the wind could pick up and the clouds could come down, surrounding the unsuspecting skier, causing total disorientation and loss of direction. Many mountaineers had died this way. I continued in haste, for I did not want my ski tracks to be blown away. Getting lost was not an option. The wind was picking up, and I could feel the temperature drop. The clouds began to catch up to me, threatening to overcome me. It became a race, me against the wind and clouds.

I hollered at Rosie and told her to stay with me. She ran a bit ahead of me. *Should I trust my dog to help me find my way back?* She seemed to know where she was going, and I remembered all the Walt Disney movies I had seen as a child that showed the dog as a hero, leading someone home. Maybe she did know her way back. She was running ahead of me, and I was skating my skis furiously, trying to keep up to her.

I was scared, cold, and tired, and wished that the teepee was just around the corner. I knew it wasn't, but I had to keep my head. Sense of direction and caution in my skiing was foremost. It would be fatal to suffer an injury at this time. Down the hill I flew, to the first valley where I'd stopped. Quickly fastening my skins to my skis I began the uphill climb. My tracks were barely visible, and Rosie was like a white ghost fleeting in and out of the encompassing cloud. It was an arduous climb, but when I reached the top, exhausted and short of breath, I could look down and see the teepee, dark and tall, through the blowing snow and thick cloud. Time was of the essence.

Darkness was closing in, and soon visibility would be nil. Skiing would be better than with the skins, so I removed them, and began my decent. Carefully navigating the gullies, cliff edges, and snow overhangs, I went slowly and cautiously. Rosie was beside me, and I followed her tracks. She would know if a snow overhang was going to collapse, causing an avalanche. It was almost dark, and the wind was howling mercilessly down my neck and in my ears. I was so cold. My hands were frozen and I could not feel my feet. There it was, suddenly appearing before me like a castle from a fairy story, the teepee, dark and black in the surrounding dusk, offering at least some shelter from the wind.

The pellet stove kept blowing out. Thank God for the Coleman. At least it was reliable. I warmed my hands and feet and made some hot tea. It made me feel better and warmed me up a bit. I tried to light the pellet stove again. This time it took, but only produced minimal heat. The wind continued to howl and it was snowing hard—a literal white-out blizzard.

The teepee was flapping in the wind with such force that I feared it would blow right over. I climbed into my sleeping bag with my hot water bottle, warmed by the Coleman stove, and called Rosie over to lie beside me and keep me warm. The snow was filtering down into the teepee from the hole in the top. I was somewhat warm in bed, but instinctively knew that the temperature had dropped severely. Fortunately, I did get some sleep.

The next morning, the teepee entrance was drifted over, so I had to dig myself out. It was still blowing outside and snowing. *How is Carl ever going to manage to fly in here to pick me up?* I thought. If I had to stay another night, I knew I could very easily freeze to death. I was stuck! Stranded! Brr!

I had never been so cold in my life! I had to light the pellet stove. Even if it only produced minimal heat, it might be enough to keep me from freezing. I was unsuccessful. For some reason, it just wouldn't take. Constant shivering made the muscles in my neck tense, causing me to suffer a headache and neck pain.

I put Rosie on the leash and we walked around outside, always in sight of the teepee. The only way I could keep warm was to move continuously. We walked and walked for what seemed like hours. Exhaustion was my constant companion, but I knew Carl would at least try to fly in and retrieve me. He was probably worried.

I prayed, "Please, Lord, just give us a small break in the wind and snow, so the helicopter can fly in to pick me up. Please, Father, in Jesus' name, amen." Rosie and I continued to walk in circles.

About one o'clock in the afternoon, I thought I heard the sound of a helicopter. *No, just imagining things.* A few moments later, I could hear it again, closer this time. I listened intently. Yes! Yes, it was! I knew Carl would try, even if the chance of success was minimal. I quickly went to the teepee and threw my belongings in my pack. I heard the chopper come closer. There was no time to spare.

The wind continued to howl and blow, but the clouds seemed to be lifting, allowing for clearer visibility. You could see only a few hundred feet, but I thought it might be enough. I ran down to the landing area with Rosie at my heels. The yellow and brown machine appeared, hovering unsteadily just below the clouds. I waved wildly! Carl landed, and I ran, crouched down, as he opened the door for me. I threw in my gear and climbed in. Rosie jumped right over me into the other passenger seat. Our seat belts fastened and our ear muffs in place, we began to lift. "Did you know that it's minus twenty-nine?" Carl asked over the radiophones.

"No," I said.

He turned the heat up to full blast and I relaxed, allowing myself to warm.

Mike was happy to see that I was okay when I arrived back home, and the rest of my family members were relieved. I guess they did some good old-fashioned worrying about me, way up in the mountains in the freezing cold.

My dad said, "I knew you would be alright. You're my daughter and you're made of tough stuff." My dad always had great faith in my ability to do anything, and he always encouraged me to follow my dreams.

CHAPTER 21

I TALKED TO MIKE about my feelings regarding him being so possessive and always wanting to know what I was up to. I did not break up with him, though, because I still was madly in love with him. He was a fine Christian man of good reputation, and I felt that this was what I wanted. I wanted a Christian man, one I could pray with, talk to about my relationship with Christ, and maybe even do some mission work with. He knew the Bible quite well, and I enjoyed discussing it with him. He was also very devoted to his personal relationship with Christ. It was a kind of relationship that every Christian woman like myself desires. I thought that it was God's will that I marry him, so decided to go ahead with it.

FOR MY BIRTHDAY IN May, he bought me an engagement ring, and we set a date for September 7, 1996. I liked his family, and he seemed to like mine. Unfortunately, when my mother met his parents when I invited them over to my house for tea, she despised them.

"What's wrong with them, Mom?"

"Stupid Americans, I can't stand them—never could. Their accents and the fact that they are so full of themselves makes me ill!"

I was stunned! My mother had never shown such disdain for Americans before. I was familiar with my mom's comments such as, "Oh, I don't like Catholics," or "I don't like the Baptists—or the Pentecostals," but I'd kind of ignored those comments and thought, *Oh, that's just my mother—whatever!*

My mom escaped to the bedroom for their visit, feigning the need for a nap. She was not happy with my choice for a future husband.

Mike and I continued to plan the wedding. I asked Louise if she would be my attendant.

"No," she said, "Mom and I are going to Scotland during that time."

"What!" I retorted. "You knew that was when I was going to get married. Why did you plan on going to Scotland then?"

"We don't want you to marry Mike. He won't make you happy, and Mom doesn't like his family, so to save arguments and bad feelings, we decided to go to Scotland then," she informed me.

I was surprised and quite hurt. I asked Melody if she would stand up for me, and she agreed. Dad and his new family would all attend the wedding. We wanted to have the ceremony at Mountainview Pentecostal Assembly, but the pastor at that time said he would be unable to marry us because I had been previously divorced. He suggested I get the pastor at the Evangelical Free church to marry us. Pastor Dwayne was happy to, so the arrangements went ahead.

At the church for the rehearsal the night before the wedding, Mike met me at the door. "I can't go through with it, I just can't," he said.

"What," I cried, "Why?"

"I'm sorry, but I can't accept your past, and I don't feel it is right for me to marry you. I don't think it will work. I'm sorry!" He put his arm around my shoulders and led me to my truck, supposedly to save embarrassment for me because I was crying. He knew me well enough to know that I hated for anyone to see me cry.

I was shocked!

"This is not really happening," I thought to myself. Cordell noticed that something was going on, and climbed in with us.

"What's going on, Mom?" he asked. Mike told him, and Cordell also began to cry. He was very upset. He liked Mike.

"I'll take care of all the cancellations," he told me kindly as he stepped out of the truck and left me to my tears with only my son to comfort me.

I was devastated, humiliated, and so ashamed. Cordell and I drove over to my dad's, and I was bawling my eyes out.

"Mike dumped me at the altar!" I cried. "What am I going to do?"

"Come on, Lorainy. Dry your tears, go and get yourself dressed up and I'll take us all out for dinner at that new place in town. I hear it's quite good."

"Come on you all," he hollered at the rest of the people in the house. "Get yourselves dressed up. I'm taking us all out for dinner. You can order whatever you want. Vicky, get Louise on the phone, and call Micah. Tell them we're all going out for dinner!"

Later, Dad told me that he'd actually begged Mike not to marry me. That is what my dad did for me. He told Mike, "She's a free spirit, and you are too possessive. You will destroy her. She has committed herself to that marriage, and she won't back out come hell or high water, so you need to be the one to back out." Somehow or other he got Mike to agree, but I also think Mike, himself was having second thoughts.

When I went to work to break the news, one of my colleagues offered to tell everyone for me. I was more than happy to give her that responsibility. I was unable to do anything. I took a couple of weeks off work, and every day, one or more of my work colleagues would phone me and invite me on a hike. I hiked twenty to twenty-five kilometres a day for the whole two weeks. Hiking and/or other physical activity had always been my crutch for combatting stress.

* * *

BY THE SUMMER OF 1997, all my children had moved to Smithers permanently—or so they thought. Jeff and a friend decided to share a townhouse, and Cordell and Mitch decided to share a townhouse, both in the same building. They all seemed to be content and preparing to settle down. Jeff had established a career in roofing, and was working pretty steadily, and he loved it. Joe, his boss, and the owner of the roofing company paid him good money, and Jeff was able to work pretty independently. I think that was the initial draw. Mitch was cooking at the Hilltop and getting involved in the local music scene. Cordell had been hired by Tyee Forestry, the same company where Jeff had previously worked. He liked that job; it was exciting for him as he got to explore the local wilderness and learn how to plot logging blocks. Sometimes he was away at camp for a few days, but most of the time he was home every night.

One late afternoon, I was expecting Cordell to come home, but wasn't sure when. I heard a helicopter flying over, which wasn't unusual, but this time it sounded really close. I ran outside to see what was going on, and I could see the helicopter lowering itself for a landing on the sand bar in the middle of the river. I watched it because I wasn't sure what was going on. *Oh my goodness,* I thought, *I hope Cordell isn't injured!*

When it landed, Cordell jumped out with his camp gear on his shoulder, waving and hollering. "Hi, Mom!" The river was still high, so he had to take his shoes and pants off and wade across the channel that divided the sand bar from my yard. He kept his gear dry but waded through the current up to his waist. The pilot watched him until he successfully crossed, then waved to both of us and up the chopper went up and was gone.

"MOM, LET'S ALL GO for a picnic and a hike on Sunday," Cordell said. "I found the coolest place. It's a creek with a waterfall, and you can climb up the waterfall and then jump down into a pool of water. It's so cool, Mom. Let's go," he implored.

"Sounds interesting. I'll ask Dad and Vicky if they want to go. Vicky is always looking for interesting places to see." I was intrigued and really wanted to check it out. "Cordell, you call Grandpa and Vicky and ask them. They might be more inclined to go if you ask them rather than me. I'm up for it."

"Okay," he said as he went to the phone. I continued making the beds.

"They're into it, Mom," he told me excitedly as he ran into the bedroom. "Micah and Bethany want to come, and they talked Grandpa and Vicky into going as well. They want to take two vehicles, though, which means we can take Rosie if we want to."

"Well, Sunday it is then. Mmm! We'll have to make a picnic lunch. Okay!" I said.

Sunday came around, and it was a gorgeous fall day. We all climbed into our two vehicles and headed up Highway 37. We drove and drove some more. I was driving, and Cordell was with me in my truck. Dad, Vicky, Micah, and Bethany were behind us in Dad's van. I looked in my rear view mirror—Dad was flashing his lights. He wanted to pull over, so I began to look for a place to stop. We both parked, and he hopped out of the van.

"How far is it? If I'd known it was this far away," he said, "I wouldn't have bothered to come."

Cordell got out of the truck.

"Dad's wondering how much farther it is, Cordell," I said. "Do you know?"

"Not much farther—maybe just around the next corner? I have to watch for a road to the left. It is a small road that we can drive down a bit," he said, "but then we need to park and walk."

"Okay, let's get going," my dad said. We all got back into the vehicles and headed up Highway 37 again.

Cordell was watching closely for the turn. "I think it's up here, Mom. Yes, it is. Put your flicker on so Grandpa will know."

We turned in and found a place to park. Dad followed us in his van, and when he had parked, we unloaded everything and began to walk down the trail. We could hear the waterfall. It sounded like a pretty big falls. We came to the end of the steep rocky trail, and the waterfall was right there in its full glory!

Cordell stripped down to his shorts and waded into the water. "Come on, Micah!" he hollered. "I'll show you how to do it." He started climbing up the base of the falls. It looked a bit dangerous to me. "It's alright, Mom. I know exactly where to go." He made it to the top, and sat in the water for a few minutes, calculating his next move. All of a sudden, I heard, "Yahoo!"

I could see Cordell falling down toward the pool. "Please, Lord, protect my son from injury, in Jesus' name," I prayed.

Splash! He landed right where he wanted to. "That was fun, Mom! Do you want to try it?"

"No, I think I'll pass," I said as I watched Micah climbing up the falls in Cordell's footsteps. Micah made it to the top without incident. I could see him up there, looking cautiously down at the pool, stroking his chin, and planning his strategy. He sat there for a long time, just watching the water, and looking.

We were all watching with bated breath. My dad hollered at him, "You don't have to do it if you don't want to." Dad turned to me. "Micah is like that, you know. He doesn't do anything without thinking about it. He's very cautious, and he won't do it if he doesn't feel comfortable."

I relaxed a bit. Bethany didn't want to do it, I was too nervous, and the water was too cold. Nope, I would be happy if Micah did it. I wanted some lunch.

"There he goes!" Cordell hollered.

I looked up to see Micah falling downwards toward the pool of water. Under he went. "That was awesome!" he said, as his head bobbed up out of the water. "I did it! I did it!"

We all gave him high fives. "Good for you. Now, let's eat," said my dad. We all sat down and enjoyed our picnic lunch. It was a good day for some of my delightfully dysfunctional family, although I felt a bit sorrowful that everybody wasn't able to be there.

CHAPTER 22

WHEN I ASKED BETHANY, several years later, about her experience in Smithers, she said, "I remember the times when Mitch took me fishing, and I liked that, but I felt I didn't fit in anywhere. I had some friends but I was Gothic, which wasn't very popular with the school kids. They didn't really understand what Gothic was."

I'd spent some time with Bethany when she was younger, and she attended church with me several times. I even remember the day when I stood up in church and shared that Bethany had asked Jesus into her heart. When asked, she stood up and said, "Yes I did," but now when I ask her about it she doesn't remember.

When Bethany was thirteen, Vicky took her to the Ukraine to meet some of her relatives. Vicky said, "She was such good company, and so helpful. You know, in the Ukraine everyone is so happy to see you, and of course there is very little money, so they insisted that we stay with them in their homes rather than a hotel, and Bethany never complained. She didn't mind sharing a bed with Grandma. She was just so good—a very good travelling companion."

Bethany said, "It was great to discover your roots, and how colorful the Ukrainian people were. I felt very connected to the land and the people right away. Every night there was lots of food on the table, and I had the best Ukrainian sausage that I ever tasted!

"They were so good to us. One of the relatives even wanted to give me her wedding pillows—her most valued possession!" she exclaimed. "I couldn't take them though because they were big, and it would have been hard to take them on the plane.

"They were all so generous; they just wanted to share everything. It was a great trip—the highlight of that European excursion that Grandma and I took." After that, they toured England and Scotland, staying with friends of Vicky's, and they went to Paris for a day. This was the beginning of Bethany's travels.

The following summer, she joined a group of high school students who were planning a trip to Nepal. It was a yearly event organized by the school, where the students would go to Nepal and do some charitable work. A registered nurse was required to accompany the students, so Melody volunteered to go along. "At least that way I could keep an eye on my daughter," she said. "It was a good thing, too, because while we were over there she got drunk on rice beer. She was so sick that the porters were carrying her on their backs, and praying over her. I was worried."

Bethany said, "I got drunk on rice wine, then I got dysentery—I guess there was something bad in the wine that I drank." She was 14 years old. After the time spent in Nepal, Melody thought, *Since we're in this part of the world, we can take the opportunity to go over to India. Why not?* She and Bethany went to Northern India where the Dali Lama lived, and where the Tibetan Buddhists had been exiled. Melody began to develop an interest in Buddhism. They stayed there for two or three weeks, and headed home.

"Things went downhill after that," Melody said, referring to Bethany's wild and crazy period. "Did you know that she hitchhiked to Terrace for a rave party?" "Can you imagine? She hitchhiked on the Highway of Tears where all those Aboriginal women and girls went missing. She is dark enough, and she could easily be mistaken for an Aboriginal person."

When I asked Bethany about it, she said, "It was okay. I got two rides, but after the first ride, the people had to go the other way, so they let me out on the side of the road. It was getting dark, and I was a bit nervous, so I started praying for God to protect me—then an indigenous family picked me up. It was really weird, though, because there were kids in the car too, and there was complete silence. No one was talking at all. Actually, it was kind of creepy. Then, they dropped me off at a gas station in Terrace, and I found out that it was forty-five minutes out on the other end of town. Thank God that the lady who was working in the gas station was just getting off work, and she offered to take me out there." Bethany got a ride back to Smithers with some friends of hers.

I thought, *God answered her prayers and protected her. God is so faithful! "And it shall come to pass, that whosoever shall call on the name of the Lord shall be saved" (Acts 2:21 KJV).* I believe God saved Bethany that day. Bethany never hitchhiked again, although she continued to be a handful according to her mother.

Melody told me, "I called Micah, crying, and said to him, 'Micah, Bethany is so bad I don't know what to do with her.' I didn't really know what to do, but I was doing meditation, and Bethany came with me to a meditation retreat at Hollyhock on Cortez Island for a few days. The instructor there thought that Bethany was a natural, and offered to arrange for her to go to a Buddhist Monastery in Myanmar [Burma]. She was looking for excitement and adventure, and it was just exciting and adventurous enough for her to agree to go. So she went."

Bethany was up at 4:00 every morning for meditation and prayer. I asked her, "If Buddhists consider it wrong to kill anything, what do you do about mosquitoes?"

"Oh, we just brush them off. They aren't as bad as the ants, though. I had lots of ants crawling through the cracks in the floor of my room, so I put some tape along the cracks. It did help some, but you just put up with it," she informed me. The monastery worked well for Bethany for a time. She remained there for six months in total, learning about meditation and Buddhism as a religion. When she came back to Canada, she went to a private girl's school in Winnipeg until she graduated.

Micah fit into the Smithers lifestyle like "a stocking on a chicken's lip," my dad would say. He made friends and established himself in the community. He enjoyed school and was always a willing partner for a hike because he loved the surrounding mountains with their alpine meadows and challenging trails. His other interests were the same as any other teenager. He liked to go out with his friends and partake in activities of which his mother would not approve.

One night, Micah wanted to go to a movie with his friend Mike.

Melody said, "No you can't go and see that movie, it is too risqué for someone your age. Find another one."

"Well okay I won't go anywhere then; I will just stay at home and be bored." Micah said grumpily.

When Melody returned from work, Micah was not home as he had said he would be. She phoned Mike's mom, and found out that he had gone to the movie after all. Melody was angry he had lied to her. She went to the theatre and walked down the aisles until she spotted Micah. It was difficult in the dark, but she bravely stepped into the row of seats behind him.

"Excuse me, excuse me please," she said to the moviegoers as she pushed past. It was Micah, sitting there, intensely watching the movie. Melody looked over at Mike, Micah's friend. He had a big smile on his face as he was watching the lurid scene on the screen. Melody looked at the screen, didn't like what she saw, and angrily grabbed Micah by the shoulder and said, "We are out of here."

Micah, not wanting to create a scene, humbly stood up, and followed his mom out of the theatre, absolutely humiliated!

"Mothers can be so mortifying," Melody said in retrospect.

My dad always said that he thought Melody was a good mother, and he approved of the ways she disciplined her children. "She doesn't spank them or yell at them, but she grabs them by the shoulder, and I tell you, when she does that, they sure come around to her way of thinking."

Micah graduated from school in Smithers and then went straight to university at UBC to pursue a career in geography. After his first year, he returned to Smithers and began his own Student Works Painting business. He did very well and established a reputation for being reliable and affordable, and the students who did the actual painting were highly recommended for their craftsmanship. Micah said, "We were almost too busy." After he completed his second year of university, he continued with the painting business for another summer, and then went to Australia for one year as an exchange student.

Geography was a good profession for Micah, as he loved to travel and explore different countries. Unfortunately, travelling is very expensive, so he found a way to get someone else to pay for it. He taught English in both South Korea and Japan, and did some work as a tourist guide in between. Forever seeking more excitement and adventure, he found himself in Dawson City, working for a local gold mine. He discovered why gold is so expensive—the miners have to work themselves half to death to leach it out of the ground. Micah decided that he wanted to pursue teaching as a career, so he moved to Ottawa, went to university there, and got his master's degree in teaching. He soon found his way back to the Yukon.

The North has a way of grabbing you and hanging on desperately. Micah taught in Whitehorse at the college for a couple of years then, tiring of that, decided to start his own business. He opened up a place called The Watershed, which was a family-friendly coffee house during the day and a lively, fun pub at night. When he fell ill and needed some surgery Melody flew up there to help him out.

"What did you actually do?" I asked her.

"I did cleaning, serving at the counter, and even some cooking. Whatever had to be done that Micah couldn't do, I did."

I laughed, "Remember that judge when I had to go to court for Cordell and he said, 'What mothers won't do for their sons.' Well, I was mortified when he said that, but he does have a point."

Micah's most noteworthy accomplishment, according to him, was in 2014 when he hiked the Pacific Crest Trail. "You can't forget that," he said. "It took me five months!"

CHAPTER 23

In 1998, while I was still working at Bulkley Valley District Hospital, I was offered the opportunity to go to BCIT to complete some courses so I could work in the operating room. It was a new challenge for me, and I enjoyed working alongside the surgeon, assisting him with his various surgical procedures. I was still working casual, so had a bit of freedom to take some time off work, and I decided to go to India. I did not know when, or how, but I knew that was what I wanted to do. Going to India and working with the Mother Theresa organization in Calcutta had always been a bit of an item on my bucket list.

Since the fall of 1997, I had decided to be more diligent in my quest for that intimate personal relationship with my Lord Jesus Christ. I had been a bit off track since Mike dumped me at the altar in 1996, and had become involved in a couple of relationships that I regretted. I decided one day that I'd had enough of people who wanted to hang out with me but tried to convince me that their value system was better than mine. All I discovered when I seriously considered their idea of right and wrong, was that I was tempted to be drawn into sin, and I was not very happy with myself.

I was reminded that the Bible says, "If we confess our sins, he is faithful and just to forgive us our sins and cleanse us from all unrighteousness" (1 John 1:9 KJV). It is always good to refresh one's memory. So I did just that. I got down yet again, on my knees, and begged God, to forgive my sins. I knew he had. After all, that is why Jesus had to die on the cross—so our sins could be forgiven. He was the ultimate sacrifice. I felt a new surge of life flow through me—a new beginning. I knew in my heart that God loved me, and He had a purpose for my life.

I had found a new church following the breakup with Mike. He had continued to go to Mountainview Pentecostal Assembly, and I just could not bear to go there, even though there were many people there that I cared about. I began to attend the Alliance Church. I joined the worship team, got to know several people, and felt that was where God wanted me to be.

I had heard of a missionary couple attending our church who returned from India the previous summer. I knew in my heart that I had to talk to them. Her name was Alison, but I cannot remember her husband's name. When I introduced myself to her and began to question her about her time in India, I got so excited and felt in my spirit that I was supposed to go there. I thought that perhaps next year I would do that. While I was driving home, after that conversation, I thought, *What is stopping me from going now? Is it my two dogs, Rosie and Robin?*

Well, if I allow them to, my dogs will run my life! No, no, I did not want that. When I got home I phoned Steve, the gentleman from whom I'd bought the dogs, and asked, "Do you know anybody that might want to purchase my two dogs? I want to go to India, and I feel this would be a good time to sell them, if anyone is interested."

"As a matter of fact I do," Steve said. "There was a woman who just phoned me yesterday who asked me if I had any dogs for sale. She lives in Princeton, and has a business running dog sleds. I can call her and see if she is interested."

"Please do," I implored. I prayed following that phone call, "Lord if you really do want me to go to India, please urge that woman to buy my dogs, in Jesus name, amen."

The next day, Steve called. "She has offered to pay you $600.00 for both of them – do you want to sell them?"

"Yes! Yes! I do," I told him.

"Okay, I am planning on going down there tomorrow with two of my dogs. I can come and pick yours up and take them with me if that will work out for you."

I couldn't believe it! Praise the Lord! I guess he wants me to go to India. I began to plan my trip in my head. I already had a passport, but I knew there were other papers that I would need. I was going to be busy for the next while. I needed to arrange transportation and accommodation. My new-found friend, Alison, was very helpful. She gave me the phone number of the YWCA in New Delhi, and told me about arranging train transportation in and around India. She warned me of the do's and don'ts and told me about all of the immunizations that I needed to get into the country legally. Things were moving along quite fast for me.

This planned trip opened many doors for me to share the gospel with the people I interacted with on a daily basis.

EXCERPT FROM MY JOURNAL, JANUARY 31, 1998

I went skiing with my friend Ron, and I shared my testimony with him. He said he was interested, and he wanted a religion that was more personal.

"What is more personal than a one-to-one relationship with our Lord Jesus Christ?" I asked him.

"Well, that is why I am kind of interested," he answered.

I also shared about my previous mission trip to Mexico with the surgeon that I worked with. He was questioning me, and listening so intently I ended up being late on my lunch break. I felt a bit guilty about that. It is all falling together. I am so excited! Oh yeah, I did cut my trip down a bit and I will be back in Smithers on May 8, 1998, rather than June 6, 1998.

EXCERPT FROM MY JOURNAL, MARCH 29, 1998.

When I finally arrived in India, I got off the plane and collected my baggage. I walked outside looking for the cab booth that Alison had told me about. I could not see it. I began asking directions from anyone who seemed like they might be able to speak English. There were mostly men. I saw only one or two women. The men were following me about giving me confusing directions, and volunteering to help me, when I asked them where the cab booth was. Alison had told me only to go to the pre-paid cab booth because she said if I hailed a cab down on the street I may not get taken to where I wanted to go. It was dark out, as I arrived about 10:00 p.m.

One young fellow who was trying to help me said, "You have to trust somebody." I realized he was right, so accepted his offer. I followed him, pushing my shopping cart filled with my baggage, and soon I found myself down some sort of blind alley with six men following me and pretending they wanted to help. I realized what was happening, and I sharply turned my shopping cart around, hollering "NO!" very loudly. I aggressively pushed my cart through them all. They stood there stunned, and blankly staring at me as they parted to let me through.

I prayed, "Please Lord, in Jesus' name please guide me and direct me to the cab stand." I got to the entrance of the alley, looked to my left, and I could see it! Praise the Lord!! Thank you Lord for showing it to me," I prayed as I followed the lights. I managed to hire a cab, and was safely driven to the YWCA, where I had arranged accommodations.

My room at the YWCA was somewhat like a jail cell. It was totally concrete, with a window that had bars over it. A single bed stood in the corner, and there was a concrete shower with a rusted shower rod and worn-out curtain. A shared toilet was down the hall. The good thing about it was that it was cool.

The next morning I took a walk outside to see what New Delhi looked like during the day. There were cows wandering freely on the roads—they even had the right of way with the traffic. Piles of cow manure flowed on to the street from the sidewalk. Up the street to my right was a thin, naked little girl playing happily in the manure pile. She appeared to be about six or seven years old and looked like she may have come from a family, parked in a tent, on the other side of the sidewalk. It was suffocatingly hot and the stench of manure, mixed with diesel fumes, was overwhelming.

I was happy to return to my jail cell. At least it was cool there, and it didn't smell.

I had obtained a ticket to go to Dehra Dun for April 1, and on March 31, I planned on going to Agra to see the Taj Mahal, so I knew I had to do a bit of shopping. I asked the attendant at the front desk to get an auto-rickshaw, to take me around and show me a few things in the city.

Appropriately clothed , I joined several others and hopped onto the bus to take a trip to Agra and see the Taj Mahal. It was a fun ride, and I made a point of going about the bus, trying to talk to people. I felt I was in India to share the gospel, so I figured that I had better get on with it. I went around the bus with my Bible in my hand, talking to everyone who would listen, sharing the salvation scriptures and my testimony. It was most exciting!

When I was finished talking to the other bus passengers, I went back to my seat and prayed. "Please, Lord, all of these people who have heard the gospel today, open their hearts and minds to receive it. Thank you for giving me the courage to speak, in Jesus' name, amen."

I sat there for a few minutes and one of the other passengers, a gentle, humble-looking man came up to where I was sitting, and asked, "May I please join you? I am interested in what you are talking about, and I want to hear more."

"Sure," I said as I moved over to give him room.

"You seem so excited about your relationship with Jesus, and I want to ask Jesus into my heart. I am a Jesuit priest, but it seems like what you are talking about is so much more."

I went through the salvation scriptures with him—John 3:16, Romans 10: 9–10, as well as 2 Corinthians 5:17, which states, "Therefore if any man be in Christ, he is a new creature: old things are passed away; and behold all things are become new." Then I asked him, "Do you want me to pray with you, to ask Jesus to come into your heart?"

"Yes, I do," he said.

"Okay, I will lead you through the prayer. You can repeat it after me if you like. How does that sound?"

"Okay," he said, and we repeated the prayer. "Lord, please forgive my sins. I want you to live your life through me, so please Jesus, come into my heart and help me to be what you want me to be. Thank you that you died on the cross for my sins, and thank you for forgiving my sins, in Jesus' name, amen." His name was Ricardo Gomez.

My time in India had its ups and downs, and even though I doubted at times that I was within the will of God by being there, I look back on it now and remember that Jesuit priest with whom I prayed. I remember thinking, *You know, Lord, trust You to send me all the way over to India for even this one man—this Jesuit priest, who was so moved by my testimony and enthusiasm that he could not help approaching me and questioning why— resulting in his salvation. There was joy in heaven that day, just like Jesus says in Luke 15:7, "I say unto you, that likewise joy shall be in heaven over one sinner that repenteth, more than over ninety-nine just persons, which need no repentance."* God did close the door for me to go to Calcutta. I was unable to get a train ticket because all the trains were booked due to a religious celebration that I was unaware of. The rest of my trip is a story on its own.

* * *

DAD AND VICKY HAD always been quite social. They got to know several people in Smithers, and often had dinners with as many as eighteen guests. Gudrun, an old friend of Melody's from Bella Coola who had moved to Smithers, became a large part of Dad and Vicky's life. She and her two daughters spent lots of time with them. Dad and Vicky loved children and were particularly fond of little girls, so it was almost like they adopted Melanie and Anya. Their house in Smithers became a refuge for many, and even some people that they did not know very well. Both Louise and I became concerned about the impact of all of the activity in their home. Dudley and Gudrun were always there, and others seemed to be constantly coming and going.

I found it increasingly difficult to have a visit with Dad without anyone else around. He was showing evidence of health problems, like shortness of breath with activity, and having some difficulty walking. Vicky was having some health issues as well. She always seemed to have a cough, and I thought that perhaps all the activity in the house was not conducive to their wellness. I was even beginning to think that people were taking advantage of them. Free food, free booze—why wouldn't all of these people come over to spend time with Dad and Vicky? When either Louise or I mentioned it, my dad would angrily say, "All you girls are worried about is your inheritance."

Louise told me that Marilyn was staying with Dad and Vicky. Apparently she was having marital problems and needed a place to live for a while. Louise said, "I went over to visit her just to talk to her. I suggested—I thought kindly suggested—that perhaps her presence for such a long period of time, might be a bit stressful for them, as they were both experiencing health problems. I suggested that she might want to look for another place to stay."

When Louise returned home, she got a phone call from Dad. "You're only concerned about money! If she wants to stay here, she can stay as long as she wants because it is none of your business," he hollered at her as he slammed the phone down in her ear. Louise was rather wounded by that response.

I was well aware of people taking advantage of the elderly while pretending to be their friend. Elder abuse is common, it is insidious, and it is evil. As a nurse, I had seen and heard of many instances and felt that Dad and Vicky needed to be protected. However, they did not want our help and continued to push our concerns to the bottom of their priority list.

I was still attending the Alliance Church, seeking to further develop my personal relationship with my Lord and Saviour, Jesus Christ. I knew I could only be accountable for myself, what I did, and what I thought. I could not be responsible for others. I had to be careful how I handled these challenges, and often leaned on Jesus for help. In Matthew 5: 44, Jesus says, "But I say to you, Love your enemies, bless them that curse you, and pray for those who despitefully use you and persecute you."

Many years ago, when I had applied this principle to my nursing supervisor, Diane, in Cold Lake, who was always on my case, it worked, but it was a nine-month dedication. After that, I actually felt an overwhelming love for her. I was hurting now, though, and was not sure I had the energy to do that again.

By 1999, my children had left Smithers. Micah had left, and Louise's boys, Anthony and Franklin, had left. They had gone off to their various colleges and universities to build careers for themselves. When the year 2000 came around, Melody decided that she was going to go back to Victoria to get her master's degree in nursing. She planned on taking five years off of work to complete the degree. Dad needed major bypass surgery on his heart, and Vicky was frequently bent on hands and knees on the floor, coughing so hard that she would begin to choke. It was time for them to move out of Smithers, so they decided to follow Melody to Victoria. Dad bought a house, and Melody lived with Dad and Vicky, while she completed her master's. Louise had already moved to Dease Lake, and was preparing to move to Nunavut to work, so I was left in Smithers on my own.

Dad received his quadruple bypass surgery soon after they moved to Victoria, and Vicky's constant coughing mysteriously stopped. I still kept in touch with Dudley, as he was also left behind. Dudley wanted to move to Victoria to be with Melody during the summer of 2000, and he was rapidly making plans. I had talked to Melody several times, and she seemed to be happy, and it appeared like she was moving away from her relationship with Dudley. She began to call him Don, which was his real name, and she kept encouraging him to better himself. I said to Melody one day, "Well, you can call him Don if you want to, but he will always be Dudley to me."

I felt uncomfortable with his desire to move to Victoria, as his only reason was Melody, and in my opinion that was not reason enough to leave his established life and family. Dudley was a big man in a little town. He was well-known and popular in Smithers. If he moved to Victoria, he would be a little man in a big town where nobody knew him, and he might have great difficulty getting work, as well as re-establishing himself. I was so happy when he decided against moving.

The rest of that summer and into the fall, I continued working. I had been orientated to the emergency department and enjoyed the new challenges that came with it. I began to take some courses to increase my knowledge and ability as an ER nurse. There were four of us doing it— Wayne, myself, Julie-Anne, and Maryanne. The provincial government had offered some funding for training of ER nurses, as there was a need that far exceeded the demand. I jumped at the chance. I had been working as an RN for sixteen years and was ready for a new challenge.

It kept me busy, which was good because I was quite lonesome and began to desire male companionship. I think too that deep down I wanted to get married again. I had been single since 1993, and I knew in my heart that I did not do well alone. My friend Carol, who had recently married, said, "You will meet someone one day, Loraine. It will be somebody that you have already met, but perhaps didn't take notice of before. That is what happened to me."

Fortunately, I had my job and my courses to occupy my time. I did not have my dogs anymore, but I still liked to go to the dog sled races that occurred every February at Tyee Lake. I went out there just to watch. I had gotten to know a few racers, and even one racer that was a woman. I was impressed because it was something that had always intrigued me. While I was out there watching, I could feel someone's eyes on me. Funny how you can sense that—you don't even have to see it; you just know. I turned around and looked, and there was a rather nice-looking gentleman staring at me. I was a bit unnerved. He looked a bit familiar, but I couldn't place him. I shrugged and found somewhere to disappear from his gaze.

The ER courses that we were taking were out of BCIT in Burnaby. We had to complete several modules by correspondence, and then for two months we had to go to Vancouver for the practicum and work in one of the emergency departments on the Lower Mainland. It was an arduous task that required much time and energy. I was glad I had it to do, as I would have been unbearably lonely otherwise.

I began to pray for a husband. "Lord, I know in your word you say that if you divorce, you should never marry again, but Lord, you know as well as I do that I don't do well alone. Please, Lord, help me to find a husband. I don't even want to marry a born-again Christian man, Lord. Father God, you know that I have not had much luck in that area. Please, help me to find a kind, and gentle man who will love me unconditionally, and one who at least believes that Jesus is God's one and only son, and that He did die on the cross for all of humanity's sin, in Jesus' name, amen." It was an odd prayer, but I prayed it anyway.

CHAPTER 24

IN THE LATE SPRING of 2001, my mom decided to visit. My mom was always up for a bit of adventure, so we drove to Dease Lake to visit my sister. I never tired of that drive up Highway 37. It was so remote, and there were rarely any other vehicles on the road. I could always be guaranteed to see lots of wildlife. As we pulled into Bell II to gas up, I spotted a green forestry truck. When he climbed out of his truck, I recognized him. He was the one I'd caught staring at me at the dog races!

I said to my mom, "I'm going to go and introduce myself to him." Out I climbed. He was on one side of the pumps and I was on the other side.

"Hi there, I'm Loraine—and you are?"

"Bruce," he said as he reached out to shake my hand.

"You must be a forester."

"Yeah, I am just coming back from Dease Lake. Had to do some work up there," he said.

"This is my mom, Dale," I said as my mom climbed out of my little truck, wanting to see what was going on. He reached out and shook her hand, too. *Nice man,* I thought.

"We're just heading up to Dease Lake. My sister lives up there, so we thought that we'd go and visit."

"Well enjoy your trip," he said as he finished filling up with gas and walked inside to pay for it.

"Thanks." I began filling up my truck. As he drove off, I waved, and he waved back. "I'm glad I introduced myself," I said to Mom. "I've seen him around Smithers several times now, and wondered who he was."

We had a good visit with my sister, and when we got back to Smithers, my mom flew back to Victoria. I continued working on my courses, and didn't think about the encounter with Bruce for some time. Toward the end of May, I was doing an assignment that required me to create a survey. It was a fun project that everyone who was helping me seemed to be quite excited about. I was working in maternity one afternoon, and was walking down the stairs and who did I see, but Bruce. "Hi, what are you doing here?" I said with curiosity.

"I have a friend here who just had a baby and I'm coming up to visit her."

"Who?" I asked, since I knew all of the patients.

"Jennifer, she works with me at the forestry office."

My mind started churning. *How can I meet this guy? I know. I'll ask him if he could take my survey to the forestry office and get his colleagues to fill it out. I have it right there with me at work. It'll be easy."* I ran down the stairs to emergency to do break relief, and thought, *As soon as I get back up there, I'll find him and ask."* So I did. He seemed glad to take it, and said that he'd bring it back later that very day, completed. I was impressed!

Okay, great! We'll see if he actually brings it back.

He did, as soon as his workday was finished. Unfortunately, when he came back, I was on my supper break so didn't get to see him.

Since I knew his name, I looked his number up in the phone book and gave him a call to invite him for coffee. He seemed eager to join me. We set up a time and day. It was an interesting date. We had an enjoyable time, talking and getting to know each other. He was from Nova Scotia, from a family of ten children—nine boys and one girl. He had lived in Smithers since the late 1980s and seemed to like it. I got the impression that he never wanted to move away. I liked that because after Dad and Vicky and everyone left, I promised myself that if I married, I wasn't going to marry anyone who wanted to live somewhere else, because I didn't ever want to move from Smithers. We hit it off, and a few days later, he called me.

Throughout that summer and fall of 2001, we spent time together walking and talking, and visiting and barbequing. When late fall came, it was time for me to go down to Vancouver to do my emergency practicum. I would be gone for two months. I asked Bruce if he might be able to come down and spend a few days with me. His answer was, "I probably could." So, we made arrangements. Julie-Anne and Maryanne, and I suspect Wayne also, snuck into my room when I was not there and decorated it with rose petals and candles in an attempt to change the ambience from practical to romantic. I was kind of embarrassed, but appreciated their effort. My room looked quite lovely when they were done with it. Bruce and I had a good visit, and I was looking forward to getting home for Christmas.

Bruce invited me to accompany him to his niece Cheryl's wedding in May. I was happy to go. I would meet some of his family members, and my son, Mitch, was living in Coquitlam so we would be able to stay with him. Bruce's mom was coming from Nova Scotia, and his brother and sister-in-law were to come from Ottawa. I was looking forward to it. Both Cheryl and her new husband were university students, studying to become physicians. A planned lobster feast was to take place, a couple of days later, at Bruce's sister's place in Courtney. Bruce's sister and her husband lived on a rural acreage. It was easier to get to know Bruce's family members there because it was less formal. The weekend was wonderful, and getting to know Bruce's family helped me to know him better. He was a kind and gentle man from a good family who were raised as devout Catholics. He did believe in Jesus, and he did believe that Jesus is God's one and only son.

2002 was a good year for Bruce and I. In June I got a phone call from my son Cordell. "Hi, Mom. not sure if this is good news or bad news."

My heart sunk.

"I had a bit too good of a time on my birthday in March, and uh, you are going to be a grandmother."

"I told you guys to watch where you put that thing, and I told you that if you ever got a girl pregnant that you had better plan on marrying her. So, now you have to get married and you don't even know her. A one night stand! You ought to know better than that! What is wrong with you anyway? Maybe she should just get an abortion!" I was furious!

"Uh, Mom, uh settle down! We aren't going to do that," he said. "We're going to live together, and have this kid together, and then if it works out, we will get married. I might not be marrying her right away, Mom, but I am not abandoning her and the baby. She is a nice girl."

I slammed the phone down hard. I was just too angry to talk anymore, so I went for a brisk walk. I was devastated! Yeah, I wanted to be a grandma, but not this way. I wanted my boys to get married to nice Christian girls, start going to church again, and get their relationships with the Lord back in order.

"God! How could you let this happen?" I asked. "Trust in the Lord with all thine heart; and lean not on thine own understanding. In all thy ways acknowledge him, and he shall direct thy paths" (Prov. 3:5–6, KJV) kept going through my mind. As I walked, I relaxed more, and my anger began to dissipate. There was nothing I could do about it. It was not my decision, nor was it in my control. I had to let it go. Maybe it would be okay. Maybe they would have a cute little girl. Maybe it would even be fun.

I kept close contact with Cordell and Carol-Anne throughout her pregnancy. Cordell was twenty-four, and Carol-Anne was only nineteen. Her parents lived in Bonnyville, reasonably close to Cold Lake, but she had left home and was working. Cordell was working in the oil field, so was gainfully and steadily employed. *Perhaps it would turn out all right,* I thought. *Cordell is pretty responsible, and my friend Debbie was only nineteen when her first child was born, and she was a good mom.*

My granddaughter Jade was born on December 10, 2002. Cordell was present at the birth, and being overcome with emotion began to cry. He bonded strongly with his daughter, and I was happy that everything went alright. Jade was so cute! She looked like Cordell. She had dimples in her cheeks. But then I noticed that she had no choice; Carol-Anne had dimples in her cheeks too. *Perhaps she looks like Carol-Anne too,* I thought to myself. I fell in love with her from the first baby photo they sent me.

* * *

IN JANUARY 2003, BRUCE'S running days came to an abrupt end. He slipped on the ice, and had a bad fall, injuring his right knee. He was taken to emergency because it had swelled up quickly causing excruciating pain. After that, every time he put any weight on his right leg, his knee would swell – bringing about the need for another trip to emergency so he could get it drained.

Because of the seriousness of Bruce's crippling knee, his essential surgery for a knee replacement was booked for late in May in Prince Rupert, B.C.

I accompanied him and stayed for his duration in hospital. As a nurse, I always knew that patients do better when they have a family member or friend to remain at their side through their hospital journey. The surgery went well, but I knew he would need lots of help for a while, so offered to let him to stay with me at my place. He was happy to do that.

WITH MY JOB AT the hospital in Smithers, I was quite involved with the Nurses Union. My dad had always been a union advocate, so I naturally fell into place when the need arose. I was the first vice-chair for the British Columbia Nurses Union in Northwestern British Columbia for four years. It required me to travel to Vancouver a few times a year to attend meetings. At the end of June 2003, I had to go to Vancouver. I was staying at a lovely hotel down by Stanley Park, and one night I was awakened with pain in my abdomen. I had experienced pain there before, but this was different. This was unbearably excruciating, and it wouldn't go away. I didn't want to bother going up the emergency department at St. Paul's Hospital because I didn't know how I would get there, and I knew the waiting time would be long.

I was too embarrassed to call an ambulance, so I prayed, "Lord, I can't stand this pain in my stomach any more, and I don't want to go to Emerg. Lord, in Jesus' name, please make the pain go away, and I promise that I will get it seen to when I get back home to Smithers." I endured for another hour, and it began to fade. "Thank you, Lord, that you are a God who answers prayer. Thank you, thank you, thank you, in Jesus' name, amen." It didn't come back, and when I got back to Smithers, I forgot about it and didn't get it seen to.

Later on that month, I began to feel ill. I had some severe abdominal pain off and on, but never as bad as it had been when I was in Vancouver. I continued to work my shifts, even though I wasn't one hundred percent up to par. Bruce had stayed with me for a couple of weeks, but had returned home and was able to manage on his own.

One night shift at about eleven o'clock, I became too ill to work and went home. I didn't mind, because my mom was coming to visit the following day and I felt I just needed a good sleep. I thought that because of the stress of Bruce and caring for him, I was just worn down.

My mom arrived the following evening, and I was ever so glad to see her. "My you do look pale and drawn," she observed.

"I think I'm just tired from my ordeal with Bruce. I'm glad he's well enough to go to his own home and care for himself," I said. "I think I just need some sleep." I was on days off, and we had a good visit for a couple of days, but I just didn't feel well.

"I think you should go to the doctor," my mom said with authority.

"I am okay," I said.

"You are not okay, Loraine," she insisted. "You are not your usual self."

"All right." I made an appointment to see my family doctor. When I saw him, he agreed with my mom and did some tests. My white blood cell count was quite elevated. He called me back into the office. "I'm going to refer you to Dr. Evans. He'll be here tomorrow, and I've scheduled an appointment for you to see him."

Dr. Evans was the general surgeon from Terrace. He admitted me into the hospital and put me on antibiotics by intravenous. He thought I had a huge infection somewhere. By this time, I needed regular Demerol shots to control my pain. After a couple of days, I was not improving, and the Demerol was not helping me as much.

Dr. Evans came in to see me. "I'm going to send you to Terrace by ambulance. I'm going to do some exploratory surgery on your abdomen, because I need to see what is going on. It could be that you have peritonitis due to a leak in your bowel because of diverticulitis, but I'm not sure." I was loaded on to the ambulance and transferred to Terrace. They wanted to do surgery right away. When I looked at the consent form, it said that I might need to have a colostomy, and I had to sign that consent form.

"A colostomy! No! No! No! I couldn't stand it! I hate shit! I hate the smell of it! I can't do this," I told the doctor.

"That's only a possibility that may come up during the procedure," he said patiently. "If I do have to do one, the chances are that it would only be temporary and it is easily reversed after a few months. Hopefully, we don't have to, but I need you to consent to it just in case."

I was horrified. "Please, Lord, you know how I feel about this, and I know I am too vain, and vanity is pride, and pride is a sin, Lord, but I just couldn't … I just couldn't bear it. Please, Lord, don't let that happen, in Jesus' name, amen." I knew it said somewhere in the Bible that God would not put more on us than we could bear, so remembering that gave me faith to believe, and I signed the consent and went down to the operating room.

"Loraine, Loraine," I heard through the fog. "Wake up, wake up, your surgery is over."

Oh, go away and let me sleep, I thought. *Colostomy! Colostomy! Did they give me a colostomy?* I wondered as I felt my lower abdomen. It didn't feel like it. I brushed my hand across my stomach. *I can't feel any colostomy!*

"Do I have a colostomy?" I asked whoever it was that was waking me up.

"No, there is no colostomy, Loraine. It was not necessary. The doctor will be down to talk to you shortly."

"When we opened you up, there was lots of green stuff oozing out. We removed your uterus because it was an odd shape and we have now sent it to pathology to get it checked out." I stayed in the hospital at Terrace for a couple more days, and then I was transferred back to the hospital in Smithers. My recovery was uneventful, and my mom stayed on to care for me until I was able to care for myself. I called my mom about ten days after she went home, to see if she had recovered from the ordeal.

She said, "No, it seems to be taking forever!" My mom was seventy-five. I was glad she had stayed because I needed someone there, and Bruce hadn't recovered enough to care for both of us, but I felt bad because it was so hard on her. I was to be off work for a total of three months. When September came along, Bruce asked me if I wanted to go to Nova Scotia and meet the rest of his family.

We planned the trip to be three weeks. I wanted to go to Nova Scotia when the leaves were at the height of their fall colours. Bruce wanted to see two of his brothers in Ottawa first, and then continue on to Halifax, where we could rent a car and drive to the homes of his other brothers. I was looking forward to the trip. We flew from Vancouver in late September, and landed in Ottawa. Bruce's brother Lorne met us at the airport and took us home with him. We were treated to a small trip into Quebec where they had a cabin by a lake. It was beautiful there! The fall colours were just beginning to show, yet it was still warm enough to enjoy the outdoors. I felt like I was on my honeymoon. We visited with his other brother Peter and his wife, and flew on through to Halifax.

My mother had arrived in Halifax in 1948 from England as a young bright-eyed twenty-one-year-old woman. Louise had told me that they had put those names on a plaque and asked me to go find my mom's name. I did, but it felt weird. It made me think of my mother again, and her sense of adventure, and the bravery it must have taken her to hop aboard that boat, and sail across the Atlantic, not knowing what was on the other side. She wasn't even a war bride, like so many others who came across with future husbands waiting for them. She came all alone. To this very day, I admire my mother and thank God for her. We went from Nova Scotia to New Brunswick and over to Prince Edward Island, as there was a brother and his family that lived in Summerside. After our visit with relatives, we took off on our own to Cape Breton. The scenery was lovely and the leaves were getting quite colourful. You could tell fall was arriving quickly from the frosty bite in the air. We enjoyed the time together, and when we arrived back home to Smithers, it was time for us both to go back to work.

CHAPTER 25

On December 9, 2003, I went to Grande Prairie, accompanied by Jeff. It was my granddaughter's first birthday on December 10, and any grandmother in their right mind would not even think of missing that milestone in her grandchild's life. Jade was so cute and charming, wrapping everyone around her little finger. Jeff, Carol-Anne, Jade, and I went shopping while Mitch and Cordell were at work in Grande Prairie. All the salesladies just oohed and awed as they gushed over Jade's cuteness. She just smiled, showed her dimples and her two teeth, and chattered away in baby talk. She was one special little girl. Jade was the first great-grandchild for both sets of grandparents, so she was quite a novelty.

Her actual party was a weird, emotional time for me. Dave and I had been divorced since 1981, and here we were, all together again as a family. Jeff and I stayed with Dave. He was hospitable and kind, but again, it was weird, because we were together as a family should be, but we weren't. This hadn't happened for over twenty-five years, and I was planning to be married to the love of my life—Bruce. Despite the emotional turmoil, I was glad we were staying there. We had fun and laughed a lot as we talked about old times and re-related old stories to one another. When Dave and I split up so many years ago, I'd made a vow that I would never say anything negative about the boys' dad, and I made a point of respecting him when we were thrown together for family tragedy or other occasion. I had always loved his family. His mom and dad were kind to me, and I had enjoyed the company of his brother and sister, and his grandparents.

Dave had also been married a second time, and divorced. He never had any other children, which I was happy about, because I knew how much pain and jealousy could worm their way into the lives of those left behind. I had experienced it with my parents when my dad found his new family, where his true heart and life was. There were times when I had felt totally abandoned and unloved by him. I did not want my children to experience those feelings. They were too painful, and I had been wrestling with them since my dad re-married.

My only hope was my personal relationship with Jesus. I knew that I was God's daughter, and He would never leave me or forsake me. I knew that my needs would be met by my heavenly Father, not my earthly father.

When I came back from Grande Prairie, we were right into the Christmas season, and I wasn't excited about it at all. My enthusiasm for Christmas, marriage, a new place to live, going out to the hospital Christmas party, or anything just was not there. Our wedding date was set for June 26, 2004, and I was beginning to have pre-marital jitters. I wasn't sure what to do or to think. Bruce kept telling me he loved me, but sometimes I was not convinced. I knew that I could not go through another divorce. I would rather be single forever.

EXCERPT FROM MY JOURNAL, DECEMBER 30, 2003

We had a good few days together. We walked, skied, and I went snowshoeing on Sunday with the backpackers. Yesterday we cross-country skied for 7.5 km. Bruce did really well. He was even faster than me. I was happy because now we knew that he could do it. We discussed our fears regarding marriage, and I shared my concerns with him. I told him my alone time was important to me, and that I must be free to hike Cape Scott with my friend Cleone, or even fly over to Europe with my sister if I chose to. He admitted that he was nervous about getting married because he was not comfortable sharing half of his assets with me. I understood his concern about losing everything that he took so long to acquire. His worry was that if I died, and he had to pay my children out for half of the house, it would be devastating for him financially. We even discussed divorce, and how devastating it would be for both of us. We decided that divorce was not an option.

BRUCE AND I WERE married on June 26, 2004. My dad and Vicky both came, as well as Melody. My mother came, and even my cousin Ken and his wife Sandy showed up. There were a total of about 35 guests, including Bruce's sister Margaret-Anne and her husband George, and Bruce's brother Rand, and his wife Emily. Louise was my attendant and Bruce's attendant was his best friend Brian. We chose to be married by the marriage commissioner because Bruce, being raised Catholic, was unable to marry me in a Catholic church due to my previous divorces, and I couldn't be bothered checking out all of the local churches to see who would actually be willing to marry us.

We hired The Old Time Fiddlers for a band because I always liked dancing to fiddle music. Both Jeff and Mitch were talented musicians, so they played a few tunes. Cordell, Carol-Anne, and Jade also came. Jade was dressed up as a little flower girl with a purple, flowered dress and a basket full of rose petals. She stole everybody's heart. It was great fun.

When the call for speeches came, my son Jeff gave a short speech wishing us happiness, and he said, "I hope Bruce knows how to handle my mom." Everyone got a good chuckle about that, and we all went out to the Logpile Lodge for the reception. That time of year in Smithers was the peak season for flowers, and there were flowers everywhere! We spent our wedding night in our house, and then headed off to the Queen Charlotte Islands (now Haida Gwaii) for our honeymoon.

We went on another trip to Grande Prairie at the end of August. Cordell and Carol-Anne decided that they had lived together for long enough, so thought they should get married. I was happy that Bruce consented to go with me, even though it might be awkward. He and my ex-husband and ex-in-laws would meet each other. I was nervous and torn, but in the end I was glad he came. He got along very well with Dave, and even Dave's parents and siblings.

My delightfully dysfunctional family, I thought, realizing how large my delightfully dysfunctional family really was. It included more than one group of family members. *At least we're not fighting or anything. This is a good visit.* It was a fun time, and Cordell and Carol-Anne got married in their backyard by a marriage commissioner just like Bruce and I. We stayed for a few days and then returned home.

EXCERPT FROM MY JOURNAL, FEBRUARY 1, 2005.

I got married to Bruce, the love of my life on June 26, 2004. It has been seven months now and the longer we are married, the more certain I am that it was the right thing to do. He is a good husband, kind and considerate, always putting my needs before his own. He tells me he loves me every day, and I know he means it. He appreciates me, and my kids quite like him. He is even quite fond of Jade, my granddaughter, and fits well into my life.

LIFE IS FULL OF interruptions. In October 2006, I took some time off work, basically to relax, and because I had holidays coming to me that I needed to use. Nursing is a profession that drains you physically, psychologically, and emotionally, because you always see people at their worst. Sometimes it is heartbreaking and sometimes it is maddening. The area that I worked in continually since 2001 was emergency, so I was constantly dealing with life and death, as well as the results of criminal activity. It was stressful, and at times overwhelming, and many times I was tempted to completely lose faith in humanity, and sometimes even God.

One morning, I woke up and my left foot and leg up to my knee was swollen and painful. I was having difficulty walking, and I didn't know what was going on. There was nothing that I could think of that had caused it. I rested for a day, and it eased up a bit, but as soon as I put weight on it and tried to walk around, it would swell up again. I knew something was wrong so made an appointment to see the doctor. We were planning a trip to go biking around Ireland in May 2007, and I didn't want anything to stand in the way of that.

My doctor said, "I think it's okay, and there's nothing wrong with your foot and leg that I can see, but I think you should take a couple of weeks off work and give it a good rest. I'll fill out the form for your workplace."

I rested for two weeks, and the swelling and pain went down. I thought I was healed, but as soon as I returned to work and was on my feet, the pain and swelling came back. "What is this Lord?" I asked, "Why is this happening to me? What is wrong?" I received no answer. I thought that if I ignored it, it would go away, so I continued to go to work.

Video cameras had been installed in all of the departments at the hospital for safety reasons. Anna, one of my colleagues happened to look at the camera one shift when I was working in maternity. Even though I was trying to hide my pain, she caught sight of me on the camera, and noticed me trying not to cry, while rubbing my leg and foot. I spotted her walking toward me, and quickly wiped the tears from my eyes.

"What is going on Loraine?"

I had to tell her.

"You had better go and see the doctor again. Obviously, there is something seriously wrong with that leg and foot."

I knew she was right, and I knew I was in denial. I made it through the shift and made an appointment. I was sent for a bone scan and x-rays. When the results came back, I was sent to an orthopaedic surgeon. I had arthritis in my left foot, and two of the toe bones were too long—½ centimetre was taken out of one bone, and ¼ centimetre from the other bone.

I was in a cast for eight weeks, unable to put any weight on my foot. We cancelled our trip to Ireland in May, and thought that perhaps we'd be able to go later in the summer. It was a bike tour, so I wouldn't be walking.

Throughout the spring and summer of 2007, while Bruce was at work and I was at home all day, I decided to spend more time in prayer and reading the Bible. "Why did you allow this to happen to me, Lord?" I wondered. "You know Lord, people down here say all the time, 'If your God is such a loving and merciful God, how come he allows all the terrible things to happen here on earth?' It is a difficult question for us to answer, and it is a convenient excuse for people to deny your existence." I prayed. I sat there in silence for a while. I have frequently been told by Christians to "listen to God, just shut up and listen," so I did.

I started to think. *I know I love the sporting activities that I do. I love skiing and hiking and the, rushes that I have experienced—sometimes I feel like that is what I live for. Are my sporting activities my true god? Is that why you allowed this to happen to me, Lord? Is it because you want me all to yourself? The Bible does say you are a jealous God. I think that is in the Old Testament, though. I will have to look it up. Now I am crippled up and am actually taking time to pray, and read your word, and just try to spend time with you, basically because I have nothing else I can do. That is pretty bad, isn't it Lord? I don't think I realized it. Please forgive me, in Jesus' name. Lord, please heal my foot and leg because I don't think I could stand being totally crippled. I really do want to bike around Ireland. I have wanted to do that for years. I promise I will keep this revelation in mind, Lord, and I will make sure you are first and foremost in my life. Thank you, Lord, in Jesus' name, Amen.*

I thought I would focus on the positive aspects of my life. Cordell and Carol-Anne had informed me that they were pregnant again, and the baby would be due in May. I was excited about that, and I even think Bruce appreciated it. He really liked Jade, and thought it would be nice to have another grandchild. Little David was born on May 5, 2007, and Bruce and I flew to Ireland on July 17, 2007. It seemed to be a very long flight, and neither of us slept much because, as Bruce said, "There is just no room." I found the flight difficult because both my feet were very swollen and sore.

I never did see why people got so excited about travelling. Sitting on a squashed plane for so many hours, and being uncomfortable, and paying dearly for it, was not my cup of tea. I just wanted to get there.

Mitch had suggested that we stay at the Picadilly Backpackers Hostel, because he had stayed there when he had gone to London. He said he had a great time. Well, he was young, and Bruce and I were old. Paying extra for sheets and towels, and sharing bathrooms, and living with young, drunk partiers running around all night knocking on our bedroom door was not our cup of tea—and on top of that, it was expensive.

For a couple of dollars more per night, we found the Thistle Picadilly Hotel. It was in a noisy area, but we didn't hear the noise because the walls were about a foot thick. Once the windows were closed, and the shutters pulled down, we were shrouded in silence. It was great! We even had our own bathroom! We stayed there until we flew from London to Dublin to start our bike tour.

Our flight to Dublin was unremarkable, and we were both happy to be in Ireland. There were still many people everywhere you looked, but it seemed to be a bit more relaxed, and people had a bit more time to be friendly. We stayed for four nights at the Trinity College in Dublin, did a bit of exploring around the city and then moved on to the first leg of our bike tour—*Muine Bheag* (Bagenalstown).

I was able to complete the bike tour that we planned. We biked forty to sixty kilometres a day and it was a great cycling trip. All of the bed and breakfasts that we stayed at were unique, some old and some new, but everyone was kind and helpful, and we saw many of the rural areas of Ireland. When we got back, we both had to go back to work. I was unable to go back to my original job yet, but the local community college in Smithers was happy to hire me as an instructor for the Home Support/ Resident Care Program being offered there. It was a position that I was quite capable of teaching because I did not have to be on my feet, and I was quite familiar with what the Home Support students needed to learn.

CHAPTER 26

CORDELL, CAROL-ANNE AND THE children joined us for Christmas 2007. Jade was five, and David was seven months. One evening we were sitting around discussing the state of the economy in Alberta, and the fact that it appeared that Alberta was about to "bust" again. Cordell and Mitch had put together a small renovation business, and between the two of them and their combined talents, they had a lucrative little enterprise going. I suggested, "Why don't you think about moving to Smithers, and start doing renovations here, locally. I bet you would be kept quite busy."

"I don't know, Mom," Cordell said. "We will just have to see how things go."

"Well, I bet houses are a lot cheaper here than there," I suggested. Dave had helped Cordell and Carol-Anne buy a house in Grande Prairie. "Perhaps you could sell your house in Grande Prairie, make a bit of a profit, and buy one here? Anyway, it's an option. Just think about it." I selfishly thought about how wonderful it would be, to have my son and my grandchildren close by. They decided that they would continue to monitor the situation.

The Albertan economy deteriorated further. Cordell and Mitch were unable to continue with their business, so Cordell got behind in his house payments. His only choice was to sell his house, so they put it on the market and it sold immediately. They moved in with Bruce and I, so we had a houseful of children and grandchildren. Carol-Anne got a job right away at the local bakery and deli, but Cordell did not. He had contacted a local construction company in Smithers, prior to moving, and thought that they'd offered him a job. Sadly, when he arrived, he'd either misinterpreted their offer or they'd found somebody else. He got hired on by another construction company, but they only called when they needed him. It was tough for Cordell, but he never really had a problem finding a job, and his optimistic attitude kept him looking. With Carol-Anne working, they managed, but they needed their own place to live. After much searching, they were able to find a cute little bungalow near the elementary school. Bruce and I helped them with the down payment, and we were happy to have the house back to ourselves. Work continued to be erratic for both of them, and they continually struggled with finances.

Surprisingly, in the early summer, I got a phone call from my dad. "Hi there, Lorainy," he said. "I think I am going to drive up there to Smithers and visit you. I want to see that little girl [Jade]." My dad always enjoyed little girls, so I thought it was a good idea.

I was a bit concerned about him driving all the way to Smithers from Victoria, but he assured me, "I'll be fine. I'll take my time and stop along the way if I get tired. I'll take a couple of days to drive so I can rest when I feel like it." Bruce and I decided that we would let Dad have our bedroom with the bathroom so he could have somewhere to escape when he needed a rest. Cordell and Carol-Anne were in their own house by the school, so I would plan a big family dinner. Sometimes our dinners were more fun than others, but that generally depended on my dad, and how nasty he was feeling when he had a few too many shots of whisky. He arrived safely a couple of days later, and since all of my sons were in Smithers, they all came over.

We managed to get through dinner without fighting, and then my dad started to lay into me about what a failure I was as a mother, and how my kids didn't have very good jobs, and it was my fault. He always got nasty when he drank too much whisky. Me, not helping matters, always fought back, and my dad didn't appreciate that. I was mad! I hated it when he started saying things like that. Yes, my kids had gone through tough times, but they had always gotten through it all.

When my dad got angry, he got really angry. He yelled lots, and sometimes I was afraid that he was so angry he would get a stroke.

Dad insisted, "I am going to go home!"

Mitch, the peacemaker, stepped in. "Come on, Grampa. You can't drive home now. It's too late. Come with me and let's go for a walk so you can calm down." Mitch took Dad by the arm and led him outside.

Nice end to our family dinner, I thought. I calmed down, and so did my dad. He stayed the night and then left for home the next morning. I was happy to see him come, and happy to see him go.

Cordell and Carol-Anne continued to struggle in Smithers. Bruce and I were paying some of their bills, as their work was erratic. They refused to apply for welfare, and Cordell was unable to collect unemployment insurance because he had recently owned his own business. They were unable to go anywhere or do anything, and I think sometimes they didn't even have enough to eat. I suspected they both were suffering from depression. They both admit now that it was a very dark time for them.

To add insult to injury, Carol-Anne's dad died suddenly in 2009. He was only fifty and had no known health issues. Carol-Anne and her father were extremely close, and he and Cordell had become good friends. Both Cordell and Carol-Anne were devastated to the point of not being able to function. I tried to convince them to get some help, like counselling or something, but they declined, thinking that they didn't need it. In 2010, they decided to move back to Alberta. Their house was in Cordell's and my name, so I kept the house and offered it to my other son, Jeff. He readily accepted and moved in as soon as he could. All he had to do was make the payments.

All of my children loved animals, and Jeff began to gain interest in a television show that featured the training of dogs. He decided to get one for a pet, and use what he had learned from the show to train Capone, his new puppy. Capone was going to grow up to be a big dog, and I believe he had some pit bull in him, but he was active and fun, and Jeff's methods of training him seemed to work. He was a good dog, but sometimes Jeff had to go out of town for work, and it was always a challenge for him to find someone to care for Capone while he was away. I was discussing this with my hairdresser, Tracy, one day as she was giving me a trim. She said, "My roommate and I board dogs. You could tell Jeff, and we could care for Capone while he is away."

"How much do you charge?"

"It's only $10 per night. We care for lots of dogs and they just stay with us in the house. I also have a big, fenced yard so they can run around outside."

"Well, can I have a phone number? I'll tell Jeff, and he can give you a call."

"Sure," she said as she pulled out a piece of paper and a pen. I gave the number to Jeff, and Tracy and Jessy's house became Capone's second home.

* * *

CORDELL WAS SUCCESSFUL IN gaining full-time employment in the oil field, in Cold Lake. They moved into the house that his childhood best friend Ryan's parents owned, renting it for a couple of years until they were able to buy it. Both Cordell and Carol-Anne were still struggling greatly from the effect of her dad's death. Accepting help was still not an option for either of them. Cordell busied himself with work, leaving most of the responsibility of the family to Carol-Anne. She started to drink excessively, and so did Cordell when he was home.

Things came to a head in January 2012 when Carol-Anne needed to go to rehab. Dave, the boy's dad, covered the cost of the rehab, and I drove to Cold Lake. Cordell had to work and David was only five, not yet in school, and Jade was ten. It was a difficult time for all. I remember driving through the winter blizzards and ice-covered roads. Between Grande Prairie and Cold Lake the road was solid ice, and it was about minus thirty degrees outside. There was barely any traffic on the road. I prayed, "Lord, please, in Jesus' name get me to Cordell's safe and sound. Help me,

Lord, to negotiate these roads safely and surround me and my car with your shield of protection. Thank you, Lord, in Jesus' name, Amen."

That simple prayer gave me the courage to continue. I am sure I would not have otherwise. I had that sense of peace in my heart. I knew it was God's will for me to stay with Cordell to look after the children. I was there for three weeks, caring for the children and keeping the house in order, until Cordell was able to hire someone to come in and look after them. When Carol-Anne came back from rehab she was able to manage the responsibility of caring for her family for a while, but she wasn't cured of her alcoholism. It was as if rehab hadn't been long enough, and many of her issues remained unresolved.

She went to rehab again for another six or eight weeks. Again,when she returned home. Things were okay for a while, but then the drinking and ability to function responsibly just was not there. Cordell realized what a toll it was taking on his children and he asked her to leave. She did, and Cordell became a single father. That summer, Jade and David came to stay with Bruce and I to give Cordell an opportunity to just focus on his own life and his work so he could adjust to his new life. I remember David as a very angry little boy. He was so cute. He looked so much like Cordell when he was that age. My most vivid memory was of him standing there, defiantly yelling at Bruce, "You aren't the boss of me!" Jade was suffering, too. She wasn't yet, eleven, and she had often had to be the one to care for David.

Both Jade and David were the continual objects of my prayers. Jade was concerning because she was a pre-teen, and I could tell that she was already beginning to mature physically. I thought, *She's too young—way too young.* She was worried about the way she looked, and dressed herself a bit too mature for her age. God had chosen not to give me a daughter, and I could now understand why. I was thankful for that because I felt that to raise a daughter was much more difficult than to raise a son.

David had been kept busy, and been happy to play with the neighbour-hood children. He used up lots of energy during the day, and went to bed quite early in the evening. Jade was a bit more challenging. She was never ready to go to bed and always wanted to stay up late with Bruce and I. I was aching for some time just to spend alone with my husband. Jade loved Bruce, and I could tell she had him wrapped around her little finger. It was an interesting summer, and with close monitoring of the children, it went by without incident.

Closer to the fall, Bruce and I discussed the possibility of keeping the children, as things at home had not yet levelled out. I felt unsure, but Bruce said that it might be a good idea, and that we should talk to Cordell and Carol-Anne about the idea. We did. Their decision was, "We thought we would let the children decide, and they said they want to stay here with us."

"Let the children decide? Great!" I said to Cordell. "And you and Carol-Anne think that a ten year old and a six year old are capable of fig-uring out what is best for them?" I exclaimed. I thought about God and what he wanted. *Well, Lord, you did choose Cordell and Carol-Anne to be the parents of both Jade and David. You didn't choose us. Perhaps it is not your will that we take them.* I prayed. I had to trust in the Lord. It was difficult, but I had no choice.

Both Cordell and Carol-Anne continued to struggle, even after their separation. The children remained with Cordell as their legal guardian. Thankfully, both of them were in school, and Cordell was home every night. Jade was old enough to ensure that both her and David got on the bus. Their day at school was a long one, so they were only left alone for a short period of time when they got home. Sometimes Carol-Anne would be there for them, and sometimes they had to manage on their own until Cordell came home from work.

I prayed for them daily. They were always in my mind and heart, and I reminded myself of the many testimonies that I had heard in various church services about the effectiveness of a grandmother's prayers. I clung to those thoughts in desperation, and I continually had to "Trust in the Lord with all thine heart; and lean not on thine own understanding" (Prov. 3: 5, KJV). It was a time when I remember thinking, *When did my son start to suffer like this?*

I realized that it began when he decided to turn his back on God and his own personal relationship with Jesus Christ. He seemed to have to deal with one crisis after another. My heart and many prayers went out to him, but I knew that God gave us human beings a will of our own, and each person makes their own choices. All I could do was to encourage him to look through all of the Christian people that he felt failed him, straight into the eyes of Jesus Christ. "They are only humans," I would say. Jesus was and is the only perfect being ever to be on this earth.

CHAPTER 27

WHEN DAD AND VICKY made out their wills, they both opted to have Melody as their power of attorney, and she and David, my brother, as co-executors. They were getting on in years, still doing well, but getting older. Louise and I rarely broached the subject of wills and death because any time we had ever mentioned it in the past, we were immediately shut down with statements such as, "Oh, you only care about an inheritance. No! Why should we tell you anything? Everything is in order." It was difficult for us, because, according to modern society, it was prudent to discuss those types of things with the family. We were Dad's DNA children, after all.

I could tell Dad and Vicky were struggling, and I was trying to assess whether they needed any help with anything. I was often concerned that they might be taken advantage of by the many people whom they barely knew who still seemed to frequent their home continually. Dad rarely called me, Melody never called, and of course Vicky never called. When Dad called, he was always talking about how wonderful Bethany and Micah were doing, and what Melody was doing, but rarely, if ever, asked me about his own DNA grandchildren. Unfortunately, there were times that I felt quite angry. Now family dinners consisted of Dad's new family and their friends, as well as Gudrun, her daughters and their latest dates, and Gudrun's Japanese students. Bruce and I were never invited to join them; neither were my children.

My mother would phone, and sometimes ask about my children and grandchildren, and I felt that at least she cared a bit. My mother was beginning to show signs of dementia, though, and she would forget many things, occasionally become disorientated, and ask the same question over and over again. She had moved to the Oak Bay Lodge in Victoria, into the assisted living quarters, which made me feel a bit more comfortable. At least someone would be around to keep an eye on her.

When I went to Victoria, I would visit both Dad and Mom. Dad would always say to me, "Don't worry about me; you just take care of your mother." My mother was accepting of both Louise's and my help, and she was open with us regarding her wishes for death, money, power of attorney, and executor of her estate. I guess her children were all she had. Dad had his new family to care for him. When 2010 came along, I began to receive phone calls from the Oak Bay Lodge regarding my mother. She would say she was going out shopping when, in fact, she would not go past the parking lot. She assured Louise and I that she was fine, and fabricated stories about what she did on a daily basis. The final phone call came, when Mom left a cloth over the lamp, to shade the light a bit, and the cloth caught on fire, causing smoke to invade her room.

I was the long term care case manager in Smithers at that time, and I knew my mom needed 24-hour care. At Oak Bay Lodge, they said that they could accommodate her, but she would have to share a room. I knew that would not go over very well with my mom. She was a very private person and did not appreciate people. In her later years, she had very little human interaction. I talked with my manager, and got Mom on the waiting list for the Bulkley Lodge in Smithers. When she got accepted, and a space became available, it was the end of December. Louise cleared out Mom's room at Oak Bay and organized for all of her belongings to be shipped to Smithers. It was rather expensive, but Mom had some savings, and I was her power of attorney, so I just used her money to move her.

There was a Norwalk virus invasion at the Bulkley Lodge, so it was shut down for about two weeks. When Mom came to Smithers, she had to stay with Bruce and I until the virus had exhausted itself. She was quite confused. She was up at night, trying to figure out where she was. Bruce, being an early riser, was up having coffee one morning.

"Who are you?" my mom asked him. "How did I get to this godforsaken place?"

Bruce woke me up. I sat patiently with my mother and orientated her to her surroundings. It was a difficult time for both Bruce and I, and I had a new respect for those adult children who had to care for their ageing parents. I think it was the only time that I was glad that Dad had found a new family. How would I care for the both of them if I had to? They had been divorced for years, and lived totally separate lives. I thanked God for Dad's new family, and began to pray for them, even more frequently. I was happy that Melody was in a position to look after dad's needs, because I could not, and was happy he was being monitored.

I knew that sometimes in the past, I had experienced anger, and rejection, and even abandonment by my dad. It had appeared, more than once, that all of his resources, financially and otherwise, had gone to his new family. My sister and I, and our children, had gone through difficult times, and could have used some financial help, but when we asked, we were generally denied. I felt, "Yeah, dad and Vicky and his new family are all living high on the hog, and his own DNA children and grandchildren are starving to death, and he doesn't give a shit!" It wouldn't have been so bad if he hadn't always ragged on us about mismanagement of the funds we had, and bragged about his new family and how wonderful they were all doing. He had no idea what we spent our money on, or what our expenses were. Louise and I rarely drank alcohol, and we never smoked, and we had already done enough travelling.

We didn't have the resources for those things. I knew I had to address those feelings, and the only way to do it was to apply God's word to my life. "But I say unto you, Love your enemies, bless them that curse you, do good to them that hate you, and pray for them which despitefully use you, and persecute you." Matthew 5:44 (KJV)

Soon after Mom moved into Bulkley Lodge, I resigned from my position as long term care case manager. I wanted to spend time with my mom, and take her out on short walks or to see the local concerts and plays. She would occasionally come to church with me, particularly at Christmas and Easter. She loved our home, and our dog, Oscar, and the cat, Abby. I had always loved gardening, as did my mom, so she enjoyed seeing the flowers and eating the fresh vegetables that I had grown. It gave her an opportunity to spend some time with Jeff, who was also living in Smithers. When Cordell came to visit with Jade and David my mom was able to develop a bit of a relationship with her great-grandchildren. Louise would come to Smithers to visit two or three times a year, and my brother David came twice a year. Until my mother moved, my brother had not once come to visit me. I would take a trip to Victoria when he came down to see our parents so I could see him. I made a point of doing that at least once a year.

* * *

VICKY HAD HER FIRST stroke around 2009. She recovered somewhat from it, but a second stroke soon after, left her blind and dependent. Dad ended up having to be her caregiver. He said to me, "I can forgive her for her first stroke, but I will never forgive her for that second stroke. She was doing too much and I told her, but she wouldn't listen." He was elderly himself, struggling to care for his own needs, and Vicky was dependent on him for everything. He had to do all of the required cooking, as well as the cleaning the house, and he had to help her with all of her personal care. He even did the shopping for both of them. She had always been a good cook, and loved to eat, and many times asked Dad run out to the store to buy her something that she craved at the moment. Dad did an admirable job at the beginning, but it became more and more difficult for him to keep up to her demands. I could see the wear and tear on him.

Again, both Louise and I tried to "interfere," as we were told by Dad, but we were powerless to do anything about it. We tried to talk to Melody with little success, as she was busy with her own life. The phrase, "Oh, you're only offering because you want to get your hands on my money" was commonly heard by both Louise and I from our dad.

My brother David continued to reassure us. "It's all fine. Don't worry about it. Take it easy." But this only assured us that he didn't have a clue, and was sticking his head in the sand like an ostrich. As time went on for Dad, he realized that he needed some help, so he hired Gudrun to do his housecleaning for him. That in itself was a godsend. I had noticed that his ability to clean was declining, and when I came to visit, and tried to clean such things as his fridge or stove, he would not let me do it. I had always kept an extremely clean house, and it was difficult for me to stay with him because his house was so filthy. I remember putting peanut butter on some toast that I made for myself one morning and there was rat poop in the peanut butter.

There were times that I believed that Dad was abusive, physically, of Vicky, and I hated it. He had never been physically abusive before. She would show up with unaccounted for bruises, and I noticed that in his interactions with her, he was quite frustrated. When she took an unexpected fall down the stairs, that was enough! I called Melody and shared my concerns with her. It was her mother, after all. Melody told me that she had already done the legwork to get Vicky into Luther Court, a facility for the elderly, owned by the Lutheran Church, when they needed help for their daily needs. She said that she was just waiting for there to be an available place for her.

I was ever so thankful. I prayed, "Lord, you know what is actually going on there, I don't, but please, Father God, in Jesus' name, cause a room to become available at Luther Court for Vicky to move in to soon. Amen."

When Vicky was finally offered a room at Luther Court, my dad said, "I cared for her for four years, and it broke me, and traumatized me. Twenty-four hours a day I was at her beck and call, and even when I tried to get up at five o'clock in the morning to get some time to myself, I would just be sitting down to drink my coffee and read my newspaper when she would holler out, 'Steve, I would like to get up now, is the coffee ready?'" Dad admitted that he had some pretty angry feelings at those times.

I think that all of the members of my delightfully dysfunctional family were relieved when Vicky was admitted into Luther Court. She was given a room in the independent living quarters, which meant that she could come and go as she pleased, but there was help available for her if she needed it.

* * *

BETHANY HAD SUCCESSFULLY GRADUATED from university with the completion of her master's degree in humanities. After graduation, she was able to secure a position with the federal government of Canada. My dad was so proud of her accomplishment that he talked about it all the time. He even had her graduation photograph placed strategically in his house so everyone could see it. After working in Ottawa for a year or two, she became pregnant. She stayed in Ottawa until she had her baby, and then moved back to Victoria and lived in the house with Dad. Bethany had always been considered a family-orientated person, so everybody thought that as a single mother, she would be better off living as close to family as possible. With today's computer technology, she was able to live in Victoria, keep her job in Ottawa, and work from home. My dad, who always loved children, fell in love with Kayyem. When the baby was five months old, Bethany met Dave through a dating site on the internet. Many people were using internet dating sites to meet boyfriends, girlfriends, partners and lovers. Sometimes it worked out well, and sometimes it did not.

CHAPTER 28

MY MOTHER WAS BEGINNING to require more and more care. She still liked to "hike," but a hike for her was about 500 metres. I took her up into the alpine of Hudson's Bay Mountain where the ski hill was, as often as I could; however, it became difficult for her to do things such as go to the bathroom. Access to the outhouses required one to climb long, steep stairs, because they were built to be used when there was deep snow in the winter. Mom began to have difficulty getting down, and then up again. I knew that I would wish for someone to take me up there if I was in her situation, so continued to escort her to the alpine meadows as often as she wanted to go. She was also beginning to have falls. She had one fall at Bulkley Lodge, where she broke her wrist. I began to suspect she was continually having pain—everywhere.

I knew that she had been diagnosed with bladder cancer when she was in her sixties, and she took treatment at the time, but when she moved into Bulkley Lodge, she did not even want to go to the doctor or the dentist. "It is too much bother," she would say. "Have you heard from Louise lately?"

"Yes, Mom," I would answer. "I just talked to her on the phone yesterday."

"Oh, that's nice, dear," she would say. Then there would be complete silence from her for about two minutes.

"Have you heard from Louise lately?" my mom would ask again.

"Yes, Mom. I talked to her just yesterday, and she's doing fine."

"Oh, that's nice, dear," she would repeat, then there would be complete silence for a couple of minutes. We would carry on this conversation until I was able to distract her or try to change the subject. I knew she was going downhill, and I continued to pray for wisdom and guidance for how to deal with her, as well as my own frustrations.

It had been almost five years that she had been in Smithers. None of us had expected her to live for that long, and it was beginning to take its toll. I continued to share the gospel with her as much as I could, and I would take her to church with me if I could convince her to come, but Louise told me that Mom had lost her faith in God during the second world war.

In February, my mother took a bad fall, breaking her hip. She was transferred to Prince Rupert for the surgery to repair it. I knew she was in lots of pain, and I suspected that there were more breaks than just her hip. I phoned Louise, and told her, and also phoned my brother, David. I asked them if they wanted to come to Prince Rupert to see Mom. Both of them wanted to be there, so I organized the accommodations for us all, and left their flight arrangements up to them. I was glad that they both were going to be there.

When she was having her surgery, the doctor noticed that there was something wrong with her bones. He phoned me up. "There's something not right with your mother's bones, Loraine. I could not fix her hip. I could just temporarily pin it. Her bones are so fragile they are just falling apart; it's almost like they are mush!" he told me.

My first suspicion was that the bladder cancer had gone into her bones. I wondered how many actual breaks she had. When the Lodge had sent her up to the hospital for x-rays, they said that it wasn't worth it because it caused her so much pain to move her around like they needed to for the x-rays. My mother's attitude was to keep a stiff upper lip, which I believe is an old English cliché. My mom had rarely complained about pain, but I realized how much she must have suffered in silence.

She was transported back to Bulkley Lodge by ambulance to recover. My mother refused to eat or drink, except that she would take an occasional sip of tea. She lived for 27 days.

A week or so before she died, while I was sitting by her bedside, reading the Bible, I shared the message of salvation with her, explaining what it meant to ask Jesus into your heart. I said, "It is like a gift, Mom," as I took a pen from my purse. "The Bible says in (Ephesians 2:8–9,KJV) "For by grace are ye saved through faith; and that not of yourselves: it is a gift of God: Not of works, lest any man should boast."

"See, Mom," I said. "I can give you this pen as a gift, and it is your choice whether you accept it or not. That is salvation, Mom. Take the gift or refuse the gift. What do you want to do?"

"Take the gift," she said. I prayed with her to ask God to forgive her sins and to ask Jesus to come into her heart and live his life through her.

The following week, I received a call from Haley, a nurse at Bulkley Lodge. "Loraine, I'm calling about your mom. I don't think she'll last very long, so if you want to see her, I would suggest that you come up now."

I wasn't that surprised. I had been seeing her every day, and had seen the constant pain and the steady decline. It was still hard to wrap my head around it, though.

"What's happening with her?" I asked Haley.

"She has mottling on her legs, and she states she is feeling cold. She is not moving much, but she is awake at this time."

"Okay, I'll be right up," I told Haley.

It was March 12, 2016. I sat with Mom at her bedside, reading the Bible to her. She did not want to talk. I knew the end was near. All of a sudden, she looked up at the wall behind me, a big smile came over her face for a second or two, she turned her head to the side, and I knew she had gone. I did not look behind me. Was it because I was too scared of what I would see or was I too scared about what I wouldn't see? To this day, I regret not looking. I ran to the window to open it and let her spirit free.

I sat there for a few minutes thinking of my mother and what she was to me. She taught me how to clean, sew, and use basic cooking skills. She taught me about men, and told me that if a man ever needed to borrow money off me, he wasn't worth his salt. She had advised me to find a man, when I was looking for a boyfriend or husband, to search for someone who had things in common with me. A man who enjoyed doing the same things that I enjoyed doing. She told me not to marry a man of a different culture or colour, because she knew that it would cause problems in our relationship. She advised me to get a proper education so I could always be assured of finding a decent job, and I would never have to rely on a man to support me. She shared with me some of the things that women endured in their marriages, just so they could have a roof over their head and food to eat. She did not ever want me to be in that situation. My mother was a brave and unique lady. I thanked God that he chose her for my mother. I sat there for about ten minutes before I went and summoned the nurse to declare my mother's death. Mom was 88 years old.

Bruce was very kind and understanding, and he looked after David for the rest of the evening, leaving me alone to mourn and ponder. I phoned Louise, and my brother David, informing them of her demise. Louise offered to phone the few friends that my mother still had in Victoria.

Mom's cremation was arranged within the week, which was a godsend because Bruce, David, and I had previously arranged a trip to Victoria to visit with my dad and his new family, for the spring break from school. Also, Louise was the executor of Mom's estate, and she knew what Mom's wishes for burial were, so she arranged for a plot in the Royal Oak Burial Park. We went out there together to bury Mom's ashes. We chose a spot that was at the bottom of a game trail, at the end of the cemetery. And every time we go out there to see her, we talk about the fact that she would like to be taking a hike up that game trail, just to explore and see what she could see.

CHAPTER 29

In March 2016, Bruce, David, me, and Mom's ashes drove to Prince Rupert to board the ferry and sail from Prince Rupert to Port Hardy. Cordell was not coping well with being a single father. Bruce and I felt that perhaps it would be helpful if David came to live with us, so in January we had him enrolled in school in Smithers. We were happy to have him. The ferry trip to Port Hardy was an eighteen-hour sail overnight, so we got a berth with four bunks in it. David was absolutely thrilled! He had always been intrigued by the ocean and loved to fish.

Bruce and I had taken this trip before, but it was David's first trip on a ferry, and his first sighting of the ocean. His big dream was to see a whale. The humpbacks and orcas would be migrating, so his chances of spotting at least one whale were pretty good. He loved it! He was always outgoing and friendly, and managed to make a few friends, so he had a great time playing games and watching movies with the other children. When we all went to bed in our bunks, he slept soundly and didn't even notice the middle of the night stop at Bella Bella; about half of the passengers were going to Bella Bella and the other half were going to Port Hardy. The boat seemed empty when we got up, and David was unable to find the friends he'd played with the day before.

David and I went out on deck to see if we could spot any whales. It was cold and windy but relatively clear. As we searched the water, I said to David, "Look for blows, Honey. See if you can spot some waterspouts. That means there is a whale over where you see the spout."

All of a sudden, "Look! Look! Grandma – over there!" he exclaimed as he pointed to show me where.

"There are three whales over there!" I hollered.

He was so excited! Spotting whales kept him occupied until we reached Port Hardy. The road trip to Victoria was about a six-hour drive. Bruce planned to stay in Victoria for one night, then hitch a ride back to Courtney with Melody the following day, to stay with Margaret-Anne and George. He and Margaret-Anne would then take the ferry over to Vancouver for Easter, to spend some time with Bruce's niece. That would leave me with David and the truck.

When we got to Dad's, Bruce and he, had a good visit. I think Dad just enjoyed having another guy to talk to for a change. Bethany and her ten-month-old baby, were still living with Dad. I could sense how attached Dad was to that baby.

That evening, though, I was trying to talk to Dad about Mom's death, and tried to share with him, some of the things that I had learned from Mom.

He suddenly got very angry. "Your mom didn't teach you anything! She didn't even love you because she couldn't love anybody!" Then he continued to say such horrible things about my mother that I am unable to repeat them.

I was so stunned! I couldn't believe what he was saying. Mom had just died ten days before that! How could he even think of anything like that? I remember thinking, *Has he gone bonkers? He must be suffering from dementia.* I walked away, nursing my wounds and fighting the tears running down my face. I went downstairs where David was sleeping, and sat, enjoying being alone.

The next day, Bethany was going to cook dinner, and Dave, her boyfriend was going to come over and join us. I was looking forward to meeting him. Vicky would be there, and she was looking forward to meeting little David for the first time. Dinner was delicious, but that evening after Vicky had gone back to Luther Court, Bethany, Dave, David, and I were still there, and Dad was sitting in his chair holding the baby.

Dave was half in the kitchen puttering around and half in the living room visiting. David was playing on the floor with a few toys and books.

We were just sitting around chatting when all of a sudden Dad yelled at David, "Get the hell out of here and get downstairs. I am trying to get this kid to sleep!"

David jumped up, looking at me in surprise and confusion, and took off running down the stairs.

Bethany stood up, and I thought she was going to say something, but she didn't. She just sat down again, looking bewildered.

I followed David downstairs and put my arms around his shoulders. He was sitting there all alone and upset, trying not to cry. "What did I do to make him so mad, Grandma?" he asked me innocently.

"Nothing, Honey, nothing," I assured him. "Sometimes Dad gets really cranky for whatever reason. I don't know. Don't worry about it, though. It's time for you to go to bed anyway. You go and get your pyjamas on and brush your teeth."

I sat there for a while. *I think we had better leave tomorrow. Obviously, Dad isn't interested in meeting or getting to know his own DNA great-grandson.*

I went upstairs to say my goodnights.

Dave, Bethany's boyfriend, knew something was not quite right. He asked, "What happened?"

"Oh, Dad just got mad at little David," I told him. "This is the first time Dad has ever met David, and he is almost nine years old, and he tells him to get the hell out of here."

Dave looked a bit surprised. "He's never met him and he's almost nine?"

"Yep! Well, you guys have a good evening. I am going to bed" I said.

The next morning, I got up, vacuumed the stairs and the basement where David and I were staying, and we left. I did not want to subject David to any more unkindness.

We headed over to Sooke, where we had organized a bed and breakfast to stay in. We planned to explore Port Renfrew, and Sooke Potholes Provincial Park, where David could find starfish and other exciting ocean creatures. It was a great time for David and I. I was always pointing to

God, and His creation when I showed David interesting things. I shared the gospel message with him every opportunity that I got. There was a little village call Shirley, just outside of Sooke, and every time we would drive by it I would say, "Surely goodness and mercy shall follow me all of the days of my life and I shall dwell in the house of the Lord forever," from Psalm 23.

David got tired of me saying that. "Grandma!" he would plead. "Please don't say that every time!"

David asked Jesus to come into his heart on that trip. It was so cute. He and I prayed together. "God, please forgive my sins, and Jesus, please come into my heart and live in me. I love you. God. Thank you for my grandma, and thank you that we are here, by the ocean, in Jesus' name, amen." He was so excited about his new friend Jesus that all he wanted to do was pray and hear Bible stories.

"Grandma, lets' pray for my dad," he said.

"Okay, Honey," I would say, and we would pray together.

"Grandma lets pray for my mom." So we would. It seemed like we were praying for everybody. Actually, it got kind of tiring for me because it was so constant. Still, I patiently endured and was looking forward to going back to Smithers so I could take David to Sunday school and encourage his new-found relationship with Jesus.

We drove back to Courtney to meet Bruce at his sister's place, and the plan was to stay there for a couple of days then continue on to Maurelle Island to spend some time with my long-time friends, Rob and Laurie. I thought that would be the ultimate adventure for David. Rob and Laurie had lived there for years, and when I was a young single mother I used to bring my boys there. It was different and exciting for them because they could fish, run around, play with all the animals that were there, and go swimming. It was one of their favourite destinations. Maurelle Island would be our last stop before catching the ferry back to Prince Rupert and heading home to Smithers.

* * *

BY THE END OF June, I was tired and felt that I had been through a lot, with my mom dying, and my dad's reaction to David, and the responsibility of having David until the end of the school year.

I said to Bruce, "I want to run away. I want to go to Atlin, with my canoe and my tent and camping gear, and take some time for myself, do a bit of fishing. I feel like I need to spend some time with just me and God."

"When do you want to go?" he asked.

"Right now?" I had been reminiscing, remembering the times when I would jump in my car and drive, turn my Christian music up to full blast, and listen to my teaching tapes. It would be just me and God, and I could sense His very presence during those times. I would spend time in prayer and reading and studying the Bible, and I just felt that I really needed it.

I loved the wilderness of northern British Columbia. I knew it was created by God, and when I entered it, there were no distractions. I loved to ponder the intricacy of his artistry and was always amazed. "Our God is an awesome God," is one of my favourite songs, because I believe every word of it. Bruce was in agreement, so I made arrangements to stay in a somewhat remote cabin at Atlin, and I would camp on the way up and on the way back.

It seemed like Bruce was unwell. He had a pretty good case of bronchitis, but was already on antibiotics and puffers. He had suffered from the same thing, off and on, since he had retired in 2015. I was a bit concerned, but not really, as I thought that perhaps me being away would give him an opportunity to rest and do what he wanted to do.

Closer to the time I was going to leave, we talked. "Are you sure it is okay if I go? Are you sure you will be alright? Are you getting any better? How do you feel?"

"Go," he said. "I'm sure I'll be fine. I have friends and neighbours close by if I need any help." The next morning I jumped into my previously packed car and hit the road on Highway 16 and on up to Highway 37. I put my "Worship Hymn – Volume 1" into the CD player. I listened, and focused my thoughts and mind on God, His creation, and His love for me. I thought about how He loved me so much He sent His only son Jesus to die on the cross for not only my sins, but every other human being's sins. I felt alive! I felt whole! I felt free! Praise the Lord!

I prayed, "Lord please, in Jesus' name, let me see lots of wildlife. You know how much I love to look at it, Lord. I think of it as a gift, from you to me thank you that you are a God who answers prayer, in Jesus' name, amen." I saw a fox, and a bear, and a bit farther down the road, I saw this thing, cross the road in front of me. It was two shades of brown, and odd-looking, then I recognized the unmistakable lope of a wolverine! I was so excited! I had never seen a wolverine before. They are elusive, and rarely seen in the wild. I felt privileged, blessed, and thanked God for my answered prayer.

I drove for six hours that day so I could camp at Kinniskan Lake. When I arrived, it was raining a bit. I sat in my car, and said, "God, why is it raining? I prayed that it wouldn't rain, and you always answer my prayers." *Well, perhaps I should just take a step of faith and put up my tent.* I wasn't that concerned. I got my tent set up, a bit of supper under my belt, and was getting the fire going when it began to rain a bit harder. I didn't care. I put up my umbrella, poured myself a shot of whisky to warm me up, then I sat by the fire, soaking in the warmth and the peace surrounding me.

EXCERPT FROM MY JOURNAL, JULY 16, 2016

Then he showed up. He had a small car and parked in the campsite right beside me. Shit! I wanted the place to myself!

What? What the heck is he doing? *I thought. He was walking boldly and confidently toward me and I did not want company. Bob actually turned out to be an interesting fellow—had all sorts of adventures and enjoyed sharing them. I was intrigued. He stayed about an hour and we just chatted, sharing our various adventures, and then he left. I finished my whisky and built up my fire. I could hear the camp attendant's truck and I knew she would be coming around to get me registered and collect my camping fees.*

LATER THAT NIGHT, THE rain stopped, so I was able just to sit at the fireside and ponder. I loved the peace and quiet, the few bird sounds as they were all settling into bed, and the soft swish of the waves as they rolled gently up on the beach.

I was thoroughly enjoying myself, and then Bob came walking over to my campfire and sat himself down on my splitting log as if he planned on staying for a while. *Why don't you go and build your own fire and sit around it, and leave me alone?* I just wanted to relax, not indulge in the burden of conversation with anyone. I had to be polite, though, so I didn't say anything to him. I just took a breath. *Okay, Loraine, show some hospitality. You will have lots of time to spend alone, so take advantage of this company.*

We sat around the fire, and he told me a bit more about himself and his family, and what his plans for his trip were. He was also on his way to Atlin, but he wanted to continue up into the Yukon, and hike into the Tombstones of Kluane National Park, and he was thinking about taking a side trip to Spatzizi. He stayed at my camp until about midnight, then told me, "I have to get up about 5:00 or 6:00 in the morning, so I will be gone by the time you get up." He came over and gave me an impulsive hug, and said, "Goodnight."

Why did you send this guy to me, Lord? What do you want me to do? I did enjoy his company, though, so thank you for sending him.

I had been listening to a CD by Bill Fay called "Sharing Jesus without Fear." I had always thought of myself as some kind of evangelist, and I had shared the gospel message of salvation before, but I had not said one word about it to Bob. *I'm sorry that I did not share Jesus' with him, Lord. If I run into him again, Lord, I promise that I will share the message of salvation with him.* I really didn't think that I would run into him again. There was lots of empty country up North. I left for Atlin the next day, as I still had a long way to go. It was an uneventful drive, but by the time I got to Boreal Lakes, I was tired and didn't want to drive any farther, so decided to make camp, again, for the night.

Boreal Lakes was well named, and as I set up my camp, I remembered the trip that my mother, my son, and I had made several years ago when

Cordell and I wanted to hike the Chilkoot Trail. We had stopped there and camped. I woke my mom and son up about 2:00 in the morning because the northern lights were flashing all over the place. The greens and yellows, and short shows of red and purple were predominant over the whole sky. It was a sight to behold! I was hoping that they would show themselves again that night—but they didn't.

When I arrived in Atlin, I had to stop and get a few things at the general store. I had been told by someone that the bakery they had was very good, so I wanted to pick up a loaf of bread. I looked out the front window, after paying for my bread, and there was Bob, sitting on the bench, munching on a cinnamon bun.

"Shit," I said to myself as I looked around for a back door to escape before he saw me. There was none. I had made a promise to God—now I had to keep it, but was completely taken off guard and unprepared.

As I walked out of the door with my loaf of bread, hoping he wouldn't see me, he caught my eye. I said, "Fancy meeting you here. Did you go to Spatzizi?"

"No, I got to Tatogga Lake and there was no one around, and I started to think about what you had told me about the lack of wildlife up there, so decided not to go," he told me.

"Where are you staying?" I asked.

"Pine Creek Campsite," he said.

I stood there thinking. I can't share the gospel with him here. There are others around. It's a busy place. He's not staying that far from me. I'll invite him up to my cabin. We conversed for a bit longer, but I didn't say a word about Christ or the gospel of salvation. "Well, I'm staying at Sentinel Mountain Cabin for a few days until I head back home. If you want to stop by my place, please feel free to, but I must go now and get settled into my quarters. See you later," I said, not really expecting to see him later, but knowing in my heart that I would anyway.

I went to my cabin and began reading the Bible—going over the salvation scriptures. I would share Jesus with him. I would be prepared if he did come to my place. I had given God a promise, and I knew I must keep it.

EXCERPT FROM MY JOURNAL OF JULY 19, 2016

I was on my patio admiring the view and reading my Bible.

"Hello," I heard.

Shit, *I thought.* Lord please help me with this and thank you for giving me another chance. *I prayed.* "I'm on my patio," *I responded as I saw him walking toward me.* "Come and sit, I might have an extra cider for you if you want."

He came and grabbed a chair and sat down in the shade beneath the tree growing through the patio floor.

I brought him the cider, and we discussed his campsite, and he told me about the two young guys he had met.

It was now or never. "So," *I said, using the information of the CD by William Faye.* "Do you have any type of spiritual belief?"

"I don't want to discuss religion," he stated rather firmly.

Oh dear, this answer is not on the CD. *I prayed,* Please Lord, help me to be sensitive to the Holy Spirit. *"Well I was just wondering with all of this wandering that you are doing, are you searching for something?"*

"I don't want to talk about it, you know with all the stuff that church people do, you know like molesting children and that, I don't know how they can do that," he stated.

"Well in Romans 3:23 it states that, 'All have sinned and come short of the glory of God,'" I told him. "I am just a sinner saved by grace. Grace because I asked Jesus to forgive my sins and come in to my heart on July 2, 1984." I continued. My mind kept telling me, "share your testimony, share your testimony." *I thought that perhaps that is what the Holy Spirit was telling me to do. So, that is what I did.*

He said, "Well I better get on with my canoe trip. It was nice meeting you and nice talking to you."

"Don't you want to finish your cider?" I asked him with a smile, trying not to laugh. He was in such a hurry to get out of there that he practically fell down the stairs. I was chuckling to myself, but quite disappointed until I remembered that in the CD Bill Faye had said that "a non-believer must hear the gospel 7.6 times before they believe it. How do you know that you aren't the .6th?" They

aren't rejecting you, they are rejecting God and his word." Anyway it did make me feel better.

THE REST OF MY trip was both relaxing and peaceful. I had made a point of reading the Bible and listening to my different CDs regarding God's word. Atlin was a beautiful place, and I felt like I was in heaven. I went canoeing on a couple of lakes, caught two fish, and met and talked to several different people. On July 21, 2016, I started the three-day trip home. I felt I'd left my husband long enough. I was rejuvenated, and ready to face life again.

As I got into my car and started driving down the highway, I was listening to music and praising the Lord. "It was an awesome trip, Lord—absolutely amazing—too amazing! Lord, is this the calm before the storm? Are you preparing me for something?" I just had an uncomfortable feeling. *No, I am not going to let anything wreck this trip. I will focus on the good times with my Lord, and I will phone Bruce when I can.*

I continued driving, but my car sure seemed to be noisy. "Was it this noisy before?" I asked myself. I couldn't remember. It was running okay, but it just seemed noisy.

I continued driving. It got noisier and noisier. I realized that my muffler was probably ready to fall off. I could smell gas fumes as well and remembered my work colleague, Mary, who passed out due to gas fumes in her vehicle and got into a severe car accident. I didn't want to take any chances. There was a place several kilometres down the road called Rancheria. It was basically a truck stop, but I thought I could get someone there to help me. I pulled in and asked if someone could look at my muffler.

A handy fellow who knew lots about cars came to take a look. "Yeah! Your muffler isn't off yet but could fall off any time. I might be able to tie it up and get it to stay on until you get to Smithers, but I can't do it tonight. I can do it tomorrow morning, so if you want me to you will have to stay the night."

I agreed to stay. It was a bit of a rundown motel, but it looked like it was getting stormy out again, and I thought I might be happy to have a proper roof over my head for the night. The room smelled like diesel fuel, and the patio door was broken. The owner of the motel seemed to be following me around, and letting me know interesting things like, "Did you know that one bull moose can fertilize at least eighteen cows?" I ignored him and showed him how the toilet wouldn't flush properly.

The next day I got up and had my usual coffee and muffin while the handy fellow fixed my vehicle. As soon as he was done, I got in and drove away. I wanted to get to Kinniskan Lake. I was ready to go home, and wanted to speak to my husband, and knew I could contact him there as there was cellphone coverage.

I arrived at Kinniskan Lake that evening without incident. My muffler continued to be noisy, but I knew it was securely fastened so wasn't worried about it falling off. I set up my campsite. Margaret, the park attendant, came around to collect the fees while I was sitting at my fire. I was past the desire to be alone, so was thankful for her company. We sat there and chatted. I told her about my trip, and she talked about what had happened at the campsite during the last couple of weeks. It was an enjoyable evening. I was tired after the long drive, so was happy to climb into my sleeping bag.

CHAPTER 30

THE NEXT MORNING, WHILE I was sitting by my fire, drinking my coffee and admiring the lake, I saw Margaret coming to my campsite with a piece of paper in her hand and a solemn expression on her face. I knew it was bad news.

Bruce was in the hospital. The message was unclear, and I could not determine whether he was in the hospital in Smithers or Terrace. I needed to leave at once! Margaret kindly offered to help me break camp. We got packed up pretty quick and I was on my way again.

When I got to Bell II, I borrowed the phone to call the hospital in Terrace. They informed me Bruce was in Smithers. I had noticed that there was an unfamiliar phone number on the paper, so when I got to Meziadin Junction, I borrowed the phone at a gas station there and called that number. Bonnie, the wife of Bruce's very good friend Brian, answered. When she handed the phone over to Brian, he told me that he had contacted his work colleague Klause in Dease Lake. Klause had put a bulletin out all through the North, alerting the RCMP and the park attendants at every campsite along Highway 37. It took a mere 24 hours to reach me.

Bruce was having great difficulty breathing, and he was to be medevacked out to St. Paul's Hospital in Vancouver at 3:00 p.m. that day. I thanked Brian, jumped in my car, and sped down the road. I needed to see Bruce before he was sent out.

I arrived at the hospital in Smithers at 3:18. Bruce was still there, but he looked terrible, and in spite of the oxygen he was receiving, he was having great difficulty breathing. He was so short of breath he couldn't say more than a couple of words at a time. He managed to stabilize a bit after I got there, so they postponed the trip to St. Paul's until the next day, Sunday.

I was upset, scared, and didn't know what to do. They didn't know what was wrong with him at Bulkley Valley District Hospital. I was glad that Dr. Haskins was on, because I knew him from work, and he was known to be a thorough and caring doctor. I called my children and let them know the situation.

Mitch was planning on coming to Smithers later in July anyway, so he asked me, "Do you want me to come now, Mom?"

"Yes, yes, please do, you could come and look after the house, and care for the animals," I told him. I wanted to be free to fly to Vancouver to be with my husband.

EXCERPT FROM MY JOURNAL, JULY 24, 2016

Bruce is so sick! His breathing is so laboured he is sweating with the effort. I have never seen him so sick! The ambulance is supposed to come and pick him up at 1:00 p.m. and take him out to the airport to meet the medical plane.

Bruce knew he was ill and so did I. "You know - that I have - left - everything - to you - if I don't make it," he told me taking a breath between each word.

"I know," I said. My poor sweet darling, I thought. My heart was breaking! It was so hard to watch him suffer so.

"I love you," he said breathlessly.

"I love you too, darling," I said as I kissed him on the head. The ambulance attendants wheeled him away. I was shaking so bad, I couldn't text or talk, but I knew I needed to call Margaret-Anne, his sister.

I WENT HOME AND was happy to see that Mitch was there. When I sat down, he noticed I was shaking uncontrollably and poured me a shot of whisky. I drank it slowly and settled somewhat. I phoned my friend

Leona, in Calgary, and told her of the situation. I could not even pray, so I asked her to pray for Bruce. She did better than that! She called her church in Calgary, and they put out a prayer chain. I did not want him to die. I could not imagine life without him. I phoned Bruce later that evening. He was in emerg at St. Paul's, but he was hoping to go to the ward soon. I was to fly out at 9:45 a.m. the next day. I went to bed and took a sleeping aid, as I knew I would not sleep otherwise.

EXCERPT FROM MY JOURNAL OF JULY 25, 2016

At 4:15 a.m. I was awakened by the phone ringing beside my bed. It was a call from St. Paul's Hospital. They said Bruce had taken a downturn at 3:00 a.m. or thereabouts, and he had been moved up to intensive care. He had stopped breathing and his heart had stopped, but they got it going again with CPR. They put him on the respirator, which was now doing his breathing for him. I was thankful that he was at St. Paul's and they had the ability to do that. If he had still been in Smithers, he would have died.

I GOT ON THE plane, and after an uneventful flight to Vancouver, I hopped on the Canada Line, where Louise was to meet me at the Roundhouse. I wanted to go straight up to the hospital, but Louise encouraged me to go to her place, drop my bag and have a cup of tea before I ventured up there.

Bruce was in isolation, his face was red and puffy, and he looked awful. "My poor, poor darling," I cried. I couldn't hug him or even get near him because of all of the monitors and tubes he was hooked up to. It was heart wrenching—almost unbearable—but not quite. I knew God's word said that we would not be given any burden that is more than we can bear. I remembered, "Cast thy burden upon the Lord, and he shall sustain thee: he shall never suffer the righteous to be moved. (Psalm 5:22, KJV) Also, "Bear ye one another's burdens, and so fulfill the law of Christ. (Galatians 6:2, KJV) I was ever so thankful that God had given me Leona for a friend, and that she had called the church in Calgary and put out a prayer chain for Bruce.

The doctors still didn't know what was wrong with him, so they asked many questions, "Have you been in the tropics lately?"

We had been in Costa Rica, but that was two years ago.

"Was it a resort vacation or was it a vacation in the jungle?"

Actually, we had spent quite a bit of time in the jungle.

"Has Bruce been exposed to any birds or bird droppings—like do you have chickens or something?" They thought that perhaps it was a parasitic or a fungal invasion of his lungs. They did some further tests, including a bronchoscopy, and determined that it was a fungal invasion. It was identified as Aspergillus, which is a fungus that is everywhere in the air, and particularly dense on flood plains.

There had been three little baby ducks abandoned in our pond, and I felt sorry for them, so both Bruce and I began to feed them. The little ducks kept pooping in their food dish, so Bruce was patiently cleaning it out a couple of times a day. Aspergillus is often found in duck poop. Unfortunately for Bruce, he was highly allergic to it.

I was ever so thankful that they had figured it out, now they could treat him. He was on the respirator for five days. When they removed it, Bruce said, "I felt like I was drowning!" How horrible that must have been for him. He was put on several medications and slowly began to recover. Bruce would have to travel to Vancouver several times for re-checks, and I did not want him to go down by himself.

We began to think that moving off the flood plain might be a good idea, and decided that we should not take David back for the following school year. We weren't sure what was going to occur, and felt that it would be more unsettling for him to live with us than at home with his parents. Cordell and Carol-Anne were happy to have David back at home with them, but he was pulled between wanting to stay and wanting to go home.

* * *

In the beginning of November, Bruce was putting up the Christmas lights when he slipped off the ladder and tore his Achilles tendon. He was put in a cast until they could schedule his surgery for repair, which was booked for December 16, 2016. It was difficult for him because it was his right foot, and he could not drive. He rarely complained, and when he went down to Vancouver for the surgery, I accompanied him. The prednisone that he had been put on for the inflammation due to the fungal infection, was a huge contributing factor to the rupture of his Achilles tendon. He had the surgery, was brought back to the Emergency Department of St. Paul's Hospital, and was discharged at 11:00 p.m. that evening, in a cast and needing a wheelchair. I was shocked!

"What?" I asked, "This is major surgery and you want to discharge him at 11:00 at night, are you crazy?"

"We need the bed, and he will be fine. Just take him downstairs. There's a phone down there where you can call a cab directly, and he can be taken back to his hotel," the nurse told me. We found a wheelchair, helped Bruce into it, and I went downstairs and called a cab,

"Yes, we'll be there in about ten minutes," the dispatcher said.

"Okay, the cab will be here shortly. Let's go and wait outside for it." I told Bruce.

He settled into the wheelchair and I pushed him out to the back parking lot. Many cabs were coming and going, but not ours. I phoned the cab company again. The line was busy, so we waited some more. It was cold, minus seven, and we were waiting around, trying to spot our cab. None came for us.

I phoned Yellow Cab again. "Our priority is patients discharged from the hospital. I will make sure somebody comes to get you right away," I was advised by the dispatcher.

No cab came. I tried to wave one down, but they were all obviously busy and were totally ignoring me. It was 1:00 a.m. and both Bruce and I were cold and tired. The back door had been locked, so the only way back into the hospital was to walk all the way around it to the emergency department. I didn't want to push Bruce all that way—he weighed 200 pounds! I said, "No cab is going to come. We'll have to walk back to the Sylvia Hotel. I will push you in the wheelchair." I ensured Bruce was wrapped up well, as it was so cold, and we began the trek. "Thank you, Lord that it is mostly downhill" I prayed. If it had been uphill, I could not have done it.

We got to the hotel about 2:00 in the morning and I was angry! I hated Vancouver and could not understand why it was touted as the best city in the world. There were rats everywhere, homeless people sitting and lying in the streets, smelly garbage bins all over the place, and hordes of people everywhere you looked. You can't even get a cab. The sooner we got out of there, the better, as far as I was concerned.

Bruce never totally recovered from the invasion in his lungs. He was continually coughing up debris, he continued to experience some shortness of breath, and he just never felt well. Things went along reasonably decent until the beginning of February 2017.

Bruce went up to the hospital and saw the doctor on call in emerg. The doctor gave him some puffers, told him he would be fine, and sent him home. That evening he was not feeling very well at all. He went to bed, and I slept in the other room, just so we could both get some sleep.

I was awakened at about 5:15 in the morning. I did not want to get up; I was tired. I thought, *Oh Bruce must be up. He probably is okay because he just went to the doctor.* I kept hearing the disturbance he was making, still not wanting to get up. I thought, *Well, I'd better get up and see what is going on, just in case he's not okay.*

He was bent over the chair, coughing and coughing. "I can't breathe," he said.

I checked his pulse, it was irregular and pounding, as if his heart was working really hard. He was grey—that familiar grey that envelops people who are having a heart attack. My heart sank. *Should I call an ambulance? I would hate to call them if it wasn't necessary.*

He looked horrible as he sank deeper into the chair, struggling to breathe. I called 911.

"Is he conscious?"

"Yes, but he seems a bit out of it," I answered.

"Is he breathing?"

"With great difficulty," I informed them.

"The ambulance will be on its way right away."

"Can you please not turn on the siren as you come through the neighbourhood?" I asked after giving them our address. "Can you just use the lights? I don't want to wake everyone up in the neighbourhood," I said politely.

"Okay, I'll ensure that the ambulance gets that message," he told me.

I monitored Bruce. He seemed to be falling deeper and deeper into somnolence. It was bothersome, and I was glad I had called the ambulance. I knew they would be here shortly.

When they arrived, they put the oxygen on and packed him into the stretcher. "Do you want to ride with us?"

"No, I'll follow behind you in my own vehicle; that way I'll be able to come home when I need to," I told the ambulance attendants.

They drove off, and I put on a pot of coffee. I needed to prepare myself. A few minutes after they left, I could hear the siren wailing. It was a code 3. Bruce must have crashed. I quickly got my coffee down, and got washed and dressed. By the time I got up there, it was a bit after 6:30 a.m.

They had Bruce in the trauma room and were getting him into the bed. "He lost consciousness on the bridge," they told me. They were in the process of contacting the doctor for orders. The shift changed at 7:00 a.m.

I was sitting there in the chair beside Bruce, with nurses and ambulance attendants milling about. All of a sudden, I heard, "What the fuck?" It was Julie-Anne. She was just coming on shift for the day, and she spotted me sitting on the chair with tears running down my face, and turned and looked at Bruce—the reason I was crying.

"Call the lab in here now, and get some blood work done," she barked. "Call in x-ray for a chest x-ray and get the fuckin' doctor in here. Get a line up and somebody find me a catheter." Julie-Anne was one of the nurses who had taken the emergency nursing course with me back in 2001. I was glad she was on because I had confidence in her ability, and everyone listened to her. I felt safer and more comfortable with the situation because she was there.

Dr. Haskins, who had been on call during the night, soon arrived. He knew Bruce from the last time he'd had an incident, so informed everyone that he would stay until he could get Bruce sent out. The jet would be up within a couple of hours to pick up Bruce and take him down to St. Paul's Hospital for a second time. I was trying to text Leona in Calgary. I knew she would again set up a prayer chain for Bruce. I was shaking so bad I couldn't text very well and kept making mistakes.

I tried to call Margaret-Anne but couldn't talk. "Bruce is –" I stuttered.

"Bruce is what?" Margaret-Anne asked in alarm.

"Bruce..." I stuttered again.

"Loraine, what is going on?" Margaret-Anne demanded.

I had to tell her, but I could barely get the words out.

I came back into the trauma room, looked at Bruce, and he seemed to be having a seizure. I said to the doctor, "Is he having a stroke or something? He looks like he is seizing."

I had a heavy heart, filled with dread. "Lord, please don't let him have a stroke—I don't want to have to care for him if he can't care for himself, Lord. Please, in Jesus' name, don't let him have a stroke. I think I might rather that he die, Lord, in Jesus' name, amen." It sounds a bit callous, but I was a registered nurse for 32 years, and I knew that to care for a debilitated husband who needed 24-hour a day care, would do me in. I knew what it entailed, and I did not want to have to do it.

The jet came as planned, and Bruce was sent out to safety. They immediately put him on the respirator. I was comforted to know that he would be in good hands at St. Paul's Hospital, even if I hated Vancouver. I made arrangements again to fly to Vancouver to be with him.

When I phoned my dad to tell him about Bruce's situation, he said, "Well, Lorainy, if Bruce dies, you will be a rich woman."

What the hell is the matter with him? I thought, but didn't say anything. I didn't feel supported or cared for with that remark, and besides which, Bruce was far from being rich.

This time, he was on the respirator for three days, and he did recover. With some new experimental medications, he started to improve, steadily. We decided that we needed to get out of the flood plain, though, because it was making Bruce sick. We did not know where we wanted to move to though—certainly not Vancouver.

CHAPTER 31

IN THE LATE SUMMER of 2017, Dad realized that he needed move into Luther Court where he could get some daily assistance. It was the same care home that Vicky was in, but she needed 24-hour a day, care, and my dad was suitable for the independent living wing of Luther Court. He put his house up for sale, and immediately had an offer for it, so began the moving process.

Louise went over there for a week to help him clear everything out, but ended up calling me because she was overwhelmed and needed some help. I hopped into my Toyota Corolla and drove to Victoria to give her a hand. Dad's house was large, and he and his new family had lived there for 17 years, so there were many possessions that he had to find new homes for.

Bethany and Dave had decided to live together, after their two-year relationship, so Dad went with them to help them choose a good house to buy, that would also be a good investment. Dave's dad helped them with the financing. They were of the generation that would never be able to own a house on Vancouver Island, unless they had lots of help from their families.

The house that Dad had helped Dave and Bethany find became an extension of his house. When family and friends came to visit Dad and Vicky, they would stay with Bethany and Dave. Family dinners happened at Dave and Bethany's house, which was convenient because Dad and Vicky could both attend. When Melody came to Victoria to work her nursing shifts, she stayed with Bethany. It worked out well, and I began to understand why Dad wanted them to have a house. Both Bethany and Dave had good jobs. Dave was a school teacher and had his master's degree in teaching, and Bethany, with her master's degree in humanities, continued working with the federal government.

Bruce and I frequently discussed where and when we would move. We spent hours on the internet, looking at houses in different towns in British Columbia. We thought about just staying in Smithers and moving into town. We checked housing prices—what we could and could not afford.

Bruce said, "If I am going to spend $500 000 on a house, I am not spending it on a house in Smithers. I want to go to Courtney." Bruce had criteria. He wanted to be within twenty minutes of a hospital. That meant a larger centre. He wanted to be closer to his family. Margaret-Anne had been diagnosed with lymphoma, so knowing her days would be numbered, he wanted to be closer to her and her children. Bruce and Margaret-Anne were the only members of his family who lived on the west coast, and he had always been close to her three daughters. My dad was wrestling with his lung cancer, and Vicky was in and out of the hospital, even in her 24 hour a day, care room at Luther Court. Louise had been living in Vancouver for a couple of years, and Melody had been living in Courtney. We decided to move to Courtney.

* * *

BRUCE HAD A DOCTOR'S appointment in October, so we thought we would drive down for his appointment, then go over to the Island and look around to find a place to buy.

EXCERPT FROM MY JOURNAL, OCTOBER 17, 2017

My dad phoned me, and said to me, "I don't want you to come and visit, because you are so jealous of Bethany and Melody and Vicky that it makes me uncomfortable. You are so afraid that you will be left out of the inheritance—that is why you want to come. You abandoned me when your mom left, and left me stuck with an eight-year-old kid."

"Dad I was only fifteen years old. I was just a kid," I explained.

"I will phone Louise and tell her the same thing. Both of you abandoned me and left me all by myself to raise your little brother."

"Dad, Louise was only seventeen, she was also a kid. I don't see it that way. I feel like you abandoned us! I was the one that saved $2 000 – $2 500 per year so I could come and visit you. I had three little kids, and I drove all the way from Manning, Alberta, to Vancouver, when you lived there, so my children could have a relationship with their grandparents. I always wanted a grandma, and you told me she was dead and she wasn't. No Dad, you abandoned us, and found yourself a 'new family.' I could have taken that money that I saved and done something else with it, but I chose to come and visit you," I continued.

"Well you just do that," he told me. "You didn't want to see Melody, Bethany, or even talk to Vicky. You abandoned me so they became my family," My dad retorted.

"I see them all Dad—even recently I went and stayed with Melody and we had a great visit. I occasionally phone Vicky, and I don't have any issues with her except that she is annoying. She was always kind to me—even when you weren't," I said.

"She was kind to your children too," he said.

"Yes, she was Dad, and that is enough," I said pointedly. "I will tell you what. I won't visit, and I won't phone you. When you want to talk to me, you phone. If you want me to come and visit, you ask. I am going to hang up now because I think you are going bonkers," I told him firmly. I was mad!

"Okay, well I will have to figure this all out. Goodbye," he said.

That was the last I heard from him for quite a long time.

A FRIEND OF MARGARET-ANNE'S was a realtor in the Courtney/Comox/Campbell River area, where we decided that we wanted to move. She took us around and showed us several houses that were for sale, and we made offers on two of them. Both offers were outbid by another buyer. It was a seller's market, and many houses listed for sale erupted into a bidding war. They were selling for thousands of dollars over the asking price. I was discouraged and angry. I said, "I am not playing that game!"

We discussed our decision to move, over the winter, and we decided to put our house up for sale first—eliminating the "subject to sale of our house in Smithers," clause in our offers. We put it up for sale in the middle of March. The listing hadn't even been advertised when our realtor in Smithers found a buyer. They bought it sight unseen, but they wanted us to move out in two weeks. We could not do that, so negotiated moving out in three weeks. They agreed. I had prayed, "Lord, please, if it is your will for us to move to Courtney, then please, in Jesus' name, cause our house to sell quickly. Thank you, Lord, in Jesus' name, amen." I felt in my heart that it was God's will that we sell and move.

Our plan was to live with Margaret-Anne and George until we found our own place. They had a large house outside of Courtney, so there was plenty of room for us all. I thought it was mighty kind of them to offer. Things went like clockwork. Mitch was a truck driver, so he could easily drive the U-Haul, and Jeff would accompany him. We organized a huge garage sale that was very well attended, and some friends and neighbours helped us with packing. Our realtor had a few more houses to show us, and felt confident that we would find something suitable, housing-wise.

It was an exciting endeavour because I was totally depending on the Lord. "Please, Lord, guide us and direct us as to where to go and what to do, Father God. I don't have a clue. I am just stepping out in faith because I feel in my heart that we are within your will, in Jesus' name, amen," I prayed. I prayed for everything.

"Lord, please help me to get along with Marg and George, Lord, you know how I am with people. I like being on my own, not beholden to anybody. Help me to accept this new life, in Jesus' name, amen," I prayed. I knew I could not adjust to living on the Island with so many people about if God would not help me. I felt totally dependent on Him, and I do believe that is the way He likes it.

Once we settled into Margaret-Anne and George's home, the realtor came over. She had a few houses that she wanted to show us, so we made plans to meet, and go and look at them. We had sold our house in Smithers for exactly what we asked for it, and the money was in the bank, making it easier for us to make an offer on a home if we found one.

When we arrived at the first house, my heart made a quick turn in my chest. *Oh Lord, this is a beautiful house, Father God!* If only we could afford to buy it. I stood there staring at it from the outside, mesmerized for a few minutes. I couldn't move. It looked like a castle. I liked the way the neighbourhood looked, and I liked the fact that it had a lovely 180-degree view of the surrounding mountains and a farmer's field that could be seen readily out the window. It was expensive, though.

"It has been on the market for 70 days," the realtor said "unusual, because most houses sell right away."

Perhaps God is saving this house for us? But can we afford it? I didn't think so, so we continued looking. We found a house that we liked in Campbell River that I wanted to make an offer on.

Bruce said, "If we are going to make an offer, I would like to make an offer on that first house that we saw."

"What? Okay, darling. I liked that house too, so if that is what you want to do, let us just do it," I said. We did, and the offer was accepted by the seller.

"What? Praise the Lord! Halleluiah!" I hollered. I could not believe it! I just could not believe it! God had saved this very house for us! Our God is an awesome God! Funny that. I have often felt I am a woman of great faith. However, when God answers a prayer or gives me a gift, I can't believe it. How dumb is that? We moved in on May 15, 2018.

* * *

THE FOLLOWING OCTOBER, JEFF and Jessy drove down to spend Thanksgiving with me. Bruce was in Nova Scotia visiting his brothers. I was looking forward to their visit, and I was trying to figure out how we could join the family dinner that always took place on Thanksgiving. I assumed we would be welcome, because Dad had not seen Jeff since the previous March, and he had never met Jessy, and Jeff and Jessy had been together for four years.

I talked to Melody. There was apparently already the usual group of people that would attend. There was no room for Jeff, Jessy, or myself. "Well, Gudrun usually does most of the cooking, and her Japanese students will be coming, they always do, it is a tradition," Melody told me.

"I could ask Gudrun," she said.

My dad phoned me. "I don't want you to come, I don't want to see Jeff or Jessy, I am not up to it," he told me.

I was devastated! What would I say to Jeff—he was so looking forward to it. I felt angry, rejected. *Not once have me and my family been invited to attend a family dinner since Dad and Vicky had moved to Victoria,* I thought. *I gave them all the benefit of the doubt because I thought they hadn't bothered because we lived so far away. Now I'm only three hours away, and I've been told not to come.*

Well, not much I can do about it. We'll have to figure out something else to do to minimize the sting of rejection, I realized. I told Jeff, as inoffensively as I could manage.

"Let's go to Horne Lakes and do some caving," he said. "I saw a sign on the way here, and it is not that far away. I've always wanted to do that," he said.

So, I made a phone call, made arrangements, and the three of us went exploring the local caves. We had a lovely visit, and Jeff and Jessy even had a story to tell when they returned home.

I had also had made plane reservations for Cordell, Jade, and David to come and spend Christmas with Bruce and I. We had not spent Christmas with them since 2007. Jade was sixteen, and David was eleven. I, again, had assumed that Thanksgiving was just a one- time incident, and thought that Dad would be happy to see both Jade and David as they were his DNA great-grandchildren, after all.

About a week before Cordell and the kids were to arrive, I got another phone call from Dad. He told me he didn't want to see his great-grand-children, or Cordell.

He doesn't even want to see his own DNA great-grandchildren. How can he be that way? I asked myself. Then I remembered the last time and only time that David and I were at Dad's house. He had said, "I don't want you, I don't need you. All I need is Bethany, and this little guy. [referring to Bethany's baby]."

I finally realized that he had truly had found a new family, and his old family was defunct. One day during our visit, Cordell was sitting on the couch with Jade, and he was telling me about his new girlfriend and her children, and how impressed he was with them, and hoped that the relationship would blossom.

Jade stood up angrily and said, "You are my dad! You are not anyone else's dad. You are my dad, and don't you even think about marrying someone else!"

I was stunned at her outburst, but I also realized that she said what I had been feeling all of these years. I think she was well aware of the feeling of rejection and the hurt that can come when a father leaves his children to become a part of a new family. She had seen it in my life, but I had not been aware of how perceptive she was.

"How am I supposed to deal with this, Lord?" I prayed.

"Honour your father and mother," He answered me. "That is what it says in the Bible."

I know that, Lord, but I don't know if I can do that, I thought. I was reminded of Philippians 4:13, which says, "I can do all things through Christ which strenghteneth me." I had always known that I can't be held responsible for what others think and do. I can only be responsible for my own thoughts and actions. I had to do what God wanted me to do. Honouring your father and mother was one of the Ten Commandments. I would bury my hurt inside and continue to share the gospel of salvation with Dad whenever the opportunity was given to me.

I was thankful that at least I had a heavenly Father who loved me and cared for me so much that He sent His own son—His DNA son to die on the cross for my sins. Wow! He adopted me into His family when I gave my heart to Jesus on July 2, 1984! What a revelation!! "Yes, Lord, I will honour my father, just like you commanded me to do," I prayed.

CHAPTER 32

MY DEAR OLD DAD deteriorated rapidly between Christmas 2018 and the day he died, which was June 29, 2019. His cancer was rapidly spreading, and he was in constant pain. He knew he was "going down," as he frequently told me, and I watched him deteriorate to the point where he began to lose his independence—his greatest fear.

I continued to try to convince him that he needed to be born again. Sometimes I wondered if he had asked Jesus into his heart. He had never said anything to me, and I remembered others who had asked Jesus into their hearts, and they could not stop talking about it. I gave him my old Bible with its worn and thin pages. Many passages were highlighted, and there were hundreds of comments in the margins. I thought that if he read it, his heart would be opened to understanding.

However, when I asked him, he said, "No I don't have time to read that thing."

I left it with him, praying that he would even just open it.

My dad had discussed medical assistance in dying with Melody, his health representative. It was legal in Canada. He had always said that if he didn't want to live any more, he would park his car in his garage, turn the motor on, and kill himself by carbon monoxide poisoning. Several times he had asked me if I could get hold of some street drugs such as fentanyl, so he could deliberately overdose and die. The opioid crisis hitting British Columbia and killing many gave him that idea. I was unable to help him, for the drug scene in British Columbia was far beyond my reach. I didn't think I would have, even if I could have. He asked others, in both his new family and his old family. None were willing to help him.

He chose medical assistance in dying, and Melody made the arrangements for him. It was what he had always wanted as long as any of us had known him. He picked the time, and date, June 29, 2019, at 12:00 p.m. Louise and I were in Victoria. We arranged to meet Melody and Bethany in Dad's room. Louise and I arrived first, and when he woke up a bit, we got him sitting in a chair comfortably, just in time for Melody and Bethany to arrive. Bethany got down on her knees in front of Dad and started to kiss his hands. That is when I realized how much she loved and worshipped him.

He perked up and wanted to sit on his bed, so Melody helped him. Dad started to sing silly songs. He always loved singing silly songs, and Bethany, then Melody joined in, while Louise and I sat there observing. He tired quickly, so we settled him into bed again.

He had previously stated, "I don't want to see Vicky, and I don't even want to talk to her." I wasn't sure how serious he was, and I don't think Bethany or Melody were either.

A couple of minutes later Vicky called, and when I answered the phone, she was crying, "Can I please come down and see your dad, Loraine? I promise I won't talk. I just want to sit there and hold his hand. He has such soft hands, I just want to hold them," she begged.

I asked Dad.

He said, "No, No, No!"

I told Vicky, and she started to sob. "I just want to sit. I promise I won't say a word!" it was the most pathetic plea I had ever heard in my life. Bethany heard, and started to leave the room to get her grandma.

Melody said, "He doesn't want to see her."

Bethany said, "Well if I bring her down, he might be glad!"

"No!" my dad hollered as loud as he could. "I don't want to see her!"

Bethany backed down, and I was crying." Poor Vicky," I thought to myself. "How devastating that must be to her." My heart went out to her.

I realized how much Dad's new family all loved him then, and it touched my heart in a strange way. I wasn't jealous, or angry. I thought, *My dad will die happy, with those he loves beside him. That is important to him.*

The doctor arrived to do the deed, and Louise and I left and went for a walk. We knew that when we returned he would be dead. We sat on a bench under a tree, and my cell phone went off, and Leona, my life-long friend, sent me a text. "I believe God wanted me to send this to you." It was a song called "Even If" by Mercy Me, a popular Christian music group.

I listened, held my cellphone up high, and I knew Dad's spirit was gone. I started to sob.

Louise said to me, "Your heart is breaking, isn't it?"

"No," I said.

The song "Even If" talks about winning and losing, and that we should retain our hope in Christ, even if God chooses not to move the mountains that we ask him to move. I felt in my heart that I had lost the battle with, and for my dad. I had spent my Christian life sharing the gospel of salvation with my dad. I had prayed over and over that he wouldn't die until he had asked Jesus into his heart.

Even in the week prior to his death, he denied the existence of Jesus. I felt that it was the greatest rejection in the world. That is why I was so broken. I knew I had done everything I could, but God, when he created each and every one of us, gave us our own mind, and gave us the ability to choose salvation freely, or not.

As far as I know, my dad chose not to accept God's most precious gift.

The end

CPSIA information can be obtained
at www.ICGtesting.com
Printed in the USA
LVHW031212120322
713134LV00003B/375